Banner of the Arahants

The History of the Theravāda Order of Buddhist Monks and Nuns

Bhikkhu Khantipālo

Buddhist Publication Society

Kandy • Sri Lanka

Buddhist Publication Society
P.O. Box 61
54, Sangharaja Mawatha
Kandy, Sri Lanka
E-mail: bps@bps.lk
web site: http://www.bps.lk

First Edition: 1979
Newly typeset Edition: 2008

National Library of Sri Lanka-Cataloguing in Publication Data

Khantipalo, Bhikku
Banner of the Arahants/Bhikkhu Khantipalo.-Kandy:
Buddhist Publication Society Inc., 2008.-p.260; 21cm

ISBN 978-955-24-0311-8 Price:Rs.

i. 294.384 DDC 22 ii. Title
1. Laws and Decisions

ISBN 978-955-24-0311-8

Typeset at the BPS in URW Palladio Pali

Printed by:
Ajith Printers
85/4, Old Kesbewa Road, Gangodawila, Nugegoda. Tel: 2517269

Contents

INTRODUCTION

This book covers in outline, but with many interesting stories and examples, the history and development of the Sangha, the Buddhist Order of monks and nuns from their beginnings in the Buddha's time to the present day. Much of the information contained in this book is scattered widely in many different works or is the result of the author's own experience as a Buddhist monk for the last twenty years in India, Sri Lanka, and Thailand. The chapter on the Sangha as found now in the principal Buddhist countries of Southeast and South Asia contains information until now not available elsewhere, while that on bhikkhunīs, the Buddhist nuns, is unique in its coverage. New translations of some of the inspiring verses of the enlightened disciples of the Buddha are found in these pages and the author shows how this living tradition of enlightened Teachers comes down to the present day.

This is a book about Buddhist monks and nuns, their history, organisation and lives. When people travel to Southeast Asia and see the numerous monasteries in cities and countryside, with so many monks living in them, sometimes they wonder, what do they do, what is their role in society, what is their aim? Besides the monks in orange, brown, or yellow robes there are the nuns, also very numerous in Burma and Thailand. What is their place in the Buddha's teachings? This book will attempt to answer these questions, though in brief, for to do so in detail would require many more than these pages.

To answer such questions satisfactorily we must go back to the beginnings of the Buddhist Order, the Buddha himself. He was the first bhikkhu or Buddhist monk. But why was he called the Buddha, Awakened or Enlightened? As a short answer to this question an outline of the Buddha's experience of Enlightenment is given in the first chapter. In the second, the history of the Buddhist Order begins with the Buddha's first five disciples. Chapter three, upon the rules, which Buddhist monks must keep, is a little technical and could be omitted upon a first reading of the book. However, the rules are an integral and important part of the life of both monks and nuns since without some discipline no spiritual path can be followed successfully. Chapters four and five provide the history of the spread of Buddhism and the position of Buddhist monks now in the countries of Southeast Asia. The next chapter gives details of the life of Buddhist monks in both town and country. The seventh chapter is all about the formation of the original Order of Buddhist nuns called bhikkhunīs, how it became extinct, with a possibility for its resurrection and then something about the nuns now found in Thailand and Burma. The last chapter, on Westerners in the Sangha, is about the increasing numbers of Westerners, both men and women, who get ordination and live and train with their teachers in Thailand and Sri Lanka.

Having said what this book contains one should say too what it does not. It is not an introduction to the Buddha's teachings although some of them are referred to in the course of the book. Also it does not contain much about the Buddha and his life. So the first two treasures, the objects held most sacred by Buddhists: the Buddha and the Dhamma (Teaching or Law) are only mentioned where this is necessary and then not in detail; while the third treasure, the Sangha (Order or Community), is given in seven out of eight chapters. This is the reverse of most books on Buddhism, which give the most space to the Buddha and the Dhamma and little to the Sangha.

Before closing this introduction something should be said about the book's title. The word Arahant, one who is Enlightened after hearing and practising the teachings of a Buddha, will be defined in more detail in Chapter Two. Most Arahants have been monks or nuns and the robes, which they wear, are their "banner." They are an army of peace, happiness, and security bringing with them these qualities out of compassion for the sufferings of the world. So when Buddhists see a bhikkhu in patched robes of orange or brown, they are reminded of the Arahants. The Banner of the Arahants

(*Arahantaketu* in Pali language) is a sign of a person striving towards the Purity, Wisdom, and Compassion of Enlightenment.

I should like to acknowledge permission to quote freely from the issues of the Pali Text Society and the Buddhist Publication Society. Dr. I. B. Horner, President of the Pali Text Society has most kindly answered several queries. Venerable Nyanaponika Mahāthera has offered valuable suggestions for which I am most grateful. Translations where there is no acknowledgement are by the author.

Messrs Bruno Cassirer of Oxford has kindly permitted me to quote from *Buddhist Texts through the Ages* about the history of bhikkhunīs in China (Ch. VII).

Thanks to an excellent typist, Lynne Jackson, this book has reached completion quickly.

Bhikkhu Khantipālo
Wat Buddharangsee,
Stanmore, Sydney, Australia.

Proclaiming indeed my deep Dhamma-voice,
And drumming upon my good Dhamma-drum,
While winding the conch of the Dhamma-way well,
Fare ye for the weal of gods and for men!

And raising my standard of victory high,
And hauling aloft my fair Dhamma-flag,
And flourishing then my bright Dhamma-spear,
Fare ye in the worlds together with gods!

The Path to the Deathless well proffered by me,
But thorny the track to the tortures of hell,
So foully defiled is the Evil One's face—
Say this to the world together with gods!

Now since my arising in this very sphere—
And since the appearance of Dhamma as well—
And since have arisen my Dhamma-born sons—
Illumine the world by faring therein!

In caves, in the rocks and far in the woods,
Tree root, the place lonely—there, self-controlled
Is founded my dwelling and sure Dhamma-path—
Teach these in the world for gods and for men!

Praise of the Peak of Peaks
(*Samantakūṭa-vaṇṇanā*)
Verses 498–500, 502–503.

Banner of the Arahants

Chapter I

The Buddha: Unsurpassed Perfect Enlightenment

Siddhattha—Life as a Prince and Renunciation—with meditation teachers—Practice of severe austerities—his meditation before Enlightenment—the Three Knowledges—inspired verses after Enlightenment—who to teach? The five ascetics—Añña Kondañña, the first Arahant.

In spite of his father's endeavours, Prince Siddhattha, heir to the throne of the Sakyan kingdom, saw old age, disease and death and a religious wanderer in yellow robes who was calm and peaceful. When he had seen these first three things, which had been withheld from him until then, he was shocked by the sight and realised that he too would suffer them. But he was inspired by the fourth and understood that this was the way to go beyond the troubles, and sufferings of existence. Even though his beautiful wife, Yasodharā presented him with a son who was called Rāhula, he was no longer attracted to worldly life. His mind became set upon renunciation of the sense pleasures and uprooting the desires which underlay them.

So at night he left behind his luxurious life and going off with a single retainer, reached the Sakyan frontiers. There he dismounted from his horse, took off his princely ornaments and cut off his hair and beard with his sword. Then he changed into yellowish-brown patched robes and transformed himself into a bhikkhu or wandering monk. The horse and valuables he told his retainer to take back with the news that he had renounced pleasures and gone forth from home to homelessness.

At first he went to various meditation teachers but he was not satisfied with their teachings, when he became aware that they could not show him the way out of all suffering. Their attainments, which he equalled, were like temporary halts on a long journey: but they were not its end. They led only to birth in some heaven where life, however long, was nevertheless impermanent. So he decided to find his own way by practicing bodily mortification. This he practised for six years in every conceivable way, going to extremes, which even other ascetics would be fearful to try. Finally, on the verge of life and death, he perceived the futility of bodily torment and remembered from boyhood a meditation experience of great peace and joy. Thinking that this might be the way, he gave up depriving his body, and took food again to restore his strength. Thus, in his life, he had known two extremes: one of luxury and pleasure, when a prince; the other of fearful austerity. Both, he advised his first bhikkhu disciples, should be avoided.[1]

Having restored his strength, he sat down to meditate under a great Pipal tree, later known as the Bodhi (Enlightenment) Tree. His mind passed quickly into four states of deep meditation called *jhāna*. In these, the mind is perfectly one-pointed and there is no disturbance or distraction. No words, no thoughts and no pictures, only steady and brilliant mindfulness. Some mental application and inspection is present at first, along with physical rapture and mental bliss. But these factors disappear in the process of refinement until, in the fourth jhāna, only equanimity, mindfulness and great purity are left. On the bases of these profound meditation states certain knowledge arose in his mind.

These knowledges which, when they appear to a meditator, are quite different from things which are learnt or thought about, were described by him in various ways. It is as though a person standing at various points on a track, which is roughly circular, should describe different views of the same landscape. In the same way, the Buddha described his Bodhi or

1. See Appendix I, Discourse on "Setting in Motion the Wheel of Dhamma."

awakening experience. Some parts of this experience would have been of little or no use to others in their training, so these facts he did not teach. What he did teach was about *dukkha* or suffering, how it arises and how to get beyond it. One of the most frequent views into this "landscape of Enlightenment" is the Three Knowledges: of past lives, of kamma and its results, and of the destruction of the mental pollutions.

The wisdom of knowing his own past lives, hundreds of thousands of them, an infinite number of them, having no beginning—all in detail with his names and occupations, the human, super-human and sub-human ones— showed him the futility of searching for sense-pleasures again and again. He saw as well that the wheel of birth and death kept in motion by desires for pleasure and existence would go on spinning for ever producing more and more of existence bound up with unsatisfactory conditions. Contemplating this stream of lives he passed the first watch of the night under the Bodhi Tree.

The wisdom pertaining to kamma[2] and its results means that he surveyed with the divine interior eye all sorts of beings, human and otherwise and saw how their past kammas gave rise to present results and how their present kammas will fruit in future results—wholesome kammas, developing one's mind and leading to the happiness of others, fruit for their doer as happiness of body and mind—while unwholesome kammas, which lead to deterioration in one's own mind and suffering for others, result in mental and physical suffering for the doer of them. The second watch of the night passed contemplating this wisdom.

In the last watch he saw how the pollution, the deepest layer of defilement and distortion, arise and pass away conditionally. With craving and ignorance present, the whole mass of sufferings, gross and subtle, physical and mental—all that is called *dukkha*—come into existence; but when they are abandoned then this burden of *dukkha*, which weighs down all beings and causes them to drag on through myriad lives, is cut

2. Meaning, "intentional action." This word, in Sanskrit spelt "*karma*" never means fate in a Buddhist context.

off and can never arise again. This is called the knowledge of the destruction of the pollutions: desires and pleasures, existence and ignorance, so that craving connected with these things is extinct.

When he penetrated to this profound truth, the arising and passing away conditionally of all experience and thus of all *dukkha*, he was the Buddha, Enlightened, Awakened. *Dukkha* he had known thoroughly in all its most subtle forms and he discerned the causes for it's arising—principally—craving. Then he experienced its cessation when the roots of craving had been abandoned, this cessation of *dukkha* also called Nibbāna, the Bliss Supreme. And he investigated and developed the Way leading to the cessation of *dukkha*, which is called the Noble Eightfold Path. This Path is divided into three parts:

of wisdom—Right View and Right Thought;

of moral conduct—Right Speech, Right Action and Right Livelihood;

of mind development—Right Effort, Right Mindfulness and Right Collectedness. It has been described many times in detail.[3]

We are told that, while experiencing the bliss supreme of Enlightenment, the following two verses occurred to the Buddha:

> Through many births in the wandering-on
> I ran seeking but finding not
> the maker of this house—
> dukkha is birth again, again.
>
> O house maker, you are seen!
> You shall not make a house again;
> all your beams are broken up,
> rafters of the ridge destroyed:
> the mind gone to the Unconditioned,
> to craving's destruction it has come.

(Dhp 153–154)

---

3. See, *The Word of the Buddha* Nyanatiloka Mahāthera (BPS, Kandy). *The Eightfold Path and Its Factors Explained* by Ledi Sayādaw; Wheel, (BPS); *The Buddha's Ancient Path* by Piyadassi Thera (BPS).

Now that he had come to the end of craving and desire, a thing so difficult to do, and after reviewing his freedom from the round of birth and death, he concluded that no one in the world would understand this teaching. Men are blinded by their desires, he thought, and his mind inclined towards not teaching the Dhamma. Then, with the divine eye, he saw that there were a few beings "with little dust in their eyes" and who would understand. First he thought of the two teachers he had gone to and then left dissatisfied but both had died and been reborn in the planes of the formless deities having immense life spans. They would not be able to understand about "arising and passing away." Then he considered the whereabouts of the five ascetics who had served him while he practised severe bodily austerities. The knowledge came to him that they were near Benares, in the Deer-sanctuary at Isipatana; so he walked there by slow stages. Thus, he began the life of a travelling bhikkhu, the hard life that he was to lead out of compassion for suffering beings for the next forty-five years.

When the Buddha taught these five ascetics he addressed them as "bhikkhus." This is the word now used only for Buddhist monks but at that time applied to all religious wanderers. Literally, it means "one who begs" (though bhikkhus are not allowed to beg from people, they accept silently whatever is given. See Chapter VI). At the end of the Buddha's first discourse[4], Koṇḍañña[5] the leader of those bhikkhus, penetrated to the truth of the Dhamma. Knowing that he had experienced a moment of Enlightenment—Stream-winning as it is called, the Buddha was inspired to say, "Koṇḍañña truly knows indeed, Koṇḍañña truly knows!" Thus he came to be known as Aññā-Koṇḍañña—*Koṇḍañña who knows as it really is.*

Koṇḍañña, bowing his head down to the Buddha's feet, then asked to become a bhikkhu, the first Buddhist monk to follow the Buddha. It is at this point that our account really begins.

---

4. See Appendix I, Setting in Motion the Wheel of Dhamma.
5. Pronounce *Kondanya, Anya Kondanya.*

Chapter II

The Beginnings of the Sangha

Stream-winning and Arahantship—four more Arahant bhikkhus—Buddhas and Arahants—meanings of Sangha—Arahants and attachment—the Holy Life—Going forth—Story of Yasa—Exhortation to the 60 Arahants—1st, 2nd and 3rd methods of ordination (acceptance)—the 30 bhikkhus—the three Kassapa brothers—the pair of Foremost Disciples—the lives and verses of some Arahants.

Venerable Aññā-Koṇḍañña had only to hear one discourse of the Buddha to gain Stream-winning, the first glimpse of Nibbāna and of Enlightenment. But he did not become Arahant or perfectly enlightened immediately and before this could happen, the Buddha had to teach a second profound discourse (on the Mark of Non-self[6]). Before he did this he instructed the four other ascetics, Vappa, Bhaddiya, Mahānāma and Assaji until they too attained the Stream. When all five were Stream-winners, then, the Buddha taught about non-self—how we wrongly identify mind and body as "self" or "soul" —and how such identification should be avoided —by the giving up all attachment to the concept "I am"—and as a result of this, all five won Arahantship. At the conclusion of this discourse those four ascetics also asked to become bhikkhus.

What distinguishes a Buddha from an Arahant? Both are enlightened, free from pollution and defilement, both have penetrated the Four Noble Truths, but one who does so first, "the discoverer of the undiscovered Way" is a Buddha. He is like a man who in utter darkness lights a great fire so that many can see. Indeed, he is called the "Kinsman of the Sun" for this

6. For a translation see *Three Cardinal Discourses of the Buddha;* Wheel No. 17, Buddhist Publication Society, Kandy, Sri Lanka.

reason. Those who hear and practise his teaching, having enough wisdom to realise its light, spread his teachings further.

The word Arahant, literally "one who is worthy" (to accept homage, almsfood, etc.) is also used of the Buddha, who was the first. With those five bhikkhus as well it is said, "Then there were six Arahants in the world."

One or two bhikkhus do not constitute a Sangha, for which there has to be a quorum of at least four. So the Sangha came into existence when those four Arahants requested to become bhikkhus.

"Saṅgha" can have two meanings: any order of bhikkhus four or more in number is a *bhikkhusaṅgha*; and the community of all people who have seen Nibbāna, whether they have had only a glimpse—and so become Noble Ones such as Stream-winners, Once-returners or Non-returners—or whether they are Arahants able to enjoy the bliss of Nibbāna whenever they wish—all are the *Ariyasaṅgha* or Noble Sangha. Lay people may well become Stream-winners, Once-returners and Non-returners; but if a layperson becomes an Arahant it is necessary for him or her to become a monk or nun[7]. Lay life is bound-up with craving but an Arahant has none, and an arahant can best continue his life in the Sangha where craving is not a necessary adjunct to life. Why is this?

Let us take the case of those first five bhikkhus. To what indeed could they have been attached even before they became Arahants? They had lived in the forest and meditated at the foot of trees. They maintained their bodies on food collected on alms round when they walked silently and householders placed cooked food in their earthenware bowls. These ascetics covered their bodies with rags picked up from rubbish heaps. These they washed, sewed together and then dyed a brownish orange with earthen-colours. When they were sick, they made-up simple medicines from roots and bark, fruits and herbs.

---

7. It is incorrect to use the word *saṅgha* for a group of lay Buddhists who do not constitute a Sangha in either of the accepted senses defined above.

One of the commonest (to relieve fevers) is still used in India: myrobalan fruits pickled in fermented urine. As far as possessions went, there was not much to be attached to! These four, clothing, food, shelter and medicine, were the basic requirements for a human being but in lay life they became elaborated and extended by craving into hundreds of thousands of things, all of which are thought to be "necessary" for happiness.

Those first six Arahants, who lived with just the bare necessities, were supremely happy for they were without attachment to worldly things and to any idea of "self." They had no attachment to mind and body, which they saw were processes continuing, while life lasted, until the complete attainment of Nibbāna, which followed at the break-up of the body.

The purpose of this life, as stated by the Buddha himself was to discover in oneself the end of *dukkha*, which is the end of craving. In the beginning, no directions were necessary while the Sangha was composed of Arahants and other Noble Ones who caused no harm, either to others or to themselves. They led the holy life and so needed no rules or regulations. It is said in a commentary that no serious offence against the holy life was committed by anyone in the Sangha for the first twenty years. Those not yet enlightened, however, still have biases towards greed, aversion, delusion and fear in their minds, and are in need of some rules to guide them. To this end, the bhikkhus' way of life later became regulated by the Buddha.

The "Holy Life," what does this mean? This word in Pali (the language spoken by the Buddha) is *brahmacariya*. *Brahma* here has the sense of "purity" or "excellence" and *cariya* can only be rendered reasonably well by an archaic English word "faring," meaning both going and practising. This means the practice is made with effort, which is excellent and strives towards further excellence or purity. Therefore it means going against the current of passions and defilements—all kinds of greed, lust, and attachment, all sorts of anger, hatred and violence, rooting out even the defilements connected with delusion: dullness, sloth, boredom, distraction, worry, depression, uncertainty, pride and fear. So the *brahmacariya*, the way of pure practice also implies chastity, as sexual relations always have an element of lust in them.

When one is able to leave behind sex, one is able to go beyond the many requirements for the household life. All that goes along with sexual relations with another, the money needed for a family and its very many needs, all can be dispensed with by the bhikkhu.

Some people will say, "Oh, this is just escape! It's running away from responsibilities! Escaping from the real world!" But it is not the good bhikkhu who "escapes"; it is people pursuing their numerous sense-pleasures who try to do so. Whenever an unpleasant defilement arises, say boredom, they escape by turning towards some attractive object of the senses. But bhikkhus cannot escape in this way because they do not (or should not) have the possibilities for escape. They cannot evade defilements, the causes of *dukkha* in their own minds, in this way, so they have the splendid opportunity instead to be mindful of the arising and passing away of these defilements. When one is mindful and cultivates insight like this, it is called the beginning of seeing the world as it really is. Confused minds, lacking mindfulness, never understand this world; they are too attached to it. Thus the bhikkhu's life is lived free from family responsibilities and all the worries, which are a usual accompaniment, so that he can deal with his mind.

Sometimes one hears the expression used of a bhikkhu that: "He renounced the world." This is not a Buddhist way of describing the renunciation of household life. One cannot "renounce the world" because even if one goes from the middle of a crowded city to stay in a cave far up some mountain slope, remote from humanity, "the world" goes with such a person. Memories and thoughts do not get left behind! Furthermore, the Buddha calls this mind and body "the world" and mind-body continue, changing endlessly according to kamma and other causes, until Arahantship is reached and then lived out, when there is an end. The Buddha used the expression, "Going forth from home to homelessness," to describe the person who ceased to be a householder and took upon himself the training of a bhikkhu.

Ordination as a bhikkhu will be outlined below. This procedure of ordination is called "ordination of the body," that is, hair and beard are shaved off, and the new bhikkhu from that time on wears the yellow robes. These are the outward marks of his renunciation of those pleasures, which are enjoyed by the householder. Then, by this practice he has to cultivate inner renunciation—the attitude of turning away from any matters in which greed and craving are involved. This is known as "ordination of the heart", for the heart or mind usually only follows slowly what has been accomplished quickly in the ordination procedure. Of course, there are some people who in the lay state can practise so well that their power of renunciation is very strong and they do not need the "ordination of the body." But even so, in Buddhist countries many people who are like this become ordained so that their practice is unimpeded by the troubles of lay life.

So the reason for doing this, often repeated in the Suttas (or Discourses of the Buddha) runs like this, "Lord, as I understand the Dhamma given by the Exalted One, it is not possible while living in a household to lead the holy life as utterly perfect and pure as a polished shell. Lord, I wish to shave off my hair and beard, put on the yellow robe and go forth from the home life into homelessness." This is what one young man, Raṭṭhapāla[8], said to the Buddha. Sometimes the household life is said to be "crowded and dusty" (with the dust of passion) "while life gone forth is wide open" as the Buddha proclaims he felt at the time of his own Going-forth. The same reasons apply today to those who go forth, not for reasons of tradition, but because they want time to practise the whole of the Buddha's Dhamma.

Perhaps some people will say that Going-forth to find the way beyond *dukkha* is selfish, an aim which brings little fruit.

8. See the Discourse about him and by him in Appendix I.

But the Buddha did not see it like this. Once a young Brahmin came to visit him and stated that his Brahminical sacrifices were of great fruit to many people whereas the Going-forth benefited only one person. The Buddha replied with his own case: that after Going-forth and by great efforts reaching Enlightenment, he then was able to teach the way to innumerable people some of whom benefited to the utmost extent by becoming Arahants. (See, Saṅgārava Sutta, AN 3:60).

One who goes forth must spend some time, usually a number of years, with Teachers who guide his learning and practice. But when this period of training ends, then possessed of learning and good practice, perhaps with penetration of the Dhamma too, he can teach and help others on the way beyond *dukkha*. It is like a medical student who must spend some years at study and practice before he can perform delicate operations on the body. After he is qualified and experienced as a doctor he will be able to remove bodily *dukkha* from his patients. The well-trained bhikkhu, likewise, can help remove mental *dukkha* from those who seek his advice.

Many of the first bhikkhus in the Sangha did not have to spend much time at practice before penetration of the Dhamma. As with the first five bhikkhus, so it was with the next one, a rich young man called Yasa.[9] He became disenchanted with his pleasure-filled life and one night after seeing his dancing girls and musicians strewn around the floor sleeping and looking like so many corpses, he wandered out of his palace. As he wandered he exclaimed of his life, "It is fearful, it is oppressive!" (That such a young man should speak these words shows his spiritual eminence). The Buddha heard him and calling to him, said, "This is not fearful, this is not oppressive. Come, Yasa, sit down. I shall teach you Dhamma." When Yasa heard this he rejoiced and after listening to a gradual Dhamma talk: on giving, moral conduct, the heavens, the dangers, vanity and defilement of sensual pleasures, the

---

9. Most of the quotations in this chapter are from *The Life of the Buddha* translated from the Pali by Ven. Ñāṇamoli Thera, BPS, Kandy, Sri Lanka.

advantages of renunciation, then on the Teaching peculiar to the Buddhas—the Four Noble Truths, he attained with a spotless mind to the Eye of Dhamma, "Whatever has the nature to arise, all that has the nature to cease." He became a Stream-winner at this time.

As Yasa's mother and father worried about his absence, his father sent out search parties and he went to look for him. When the father came to the Buddha he too listened to Dhamma and became a Stream-winner but while the sermon was being given and Yasa was listening to it, he attained Arahantship. So when the father knew that Yasa had become an Arahant and consequently could not return to a life of pleasurable indulgence, he praised his son, and invited the Buddha and Yasa as his attendant-bhikkhu to his house for the meal that day. Yasa's father became the first lay disciple to go for Refuge to the Buddha—the Enlightened One, the Dhamma—the Path to Enlightenment, and the Sangha—the Community of those who have attained Enlightenment by following that Path.

When Yasa also asked to be accepted as a bhikkhu, the Buddha answered, "Come bhikkhu, well-expounded is Dhamma. Live the holy life for the complete ending of *dukkha*." Then, Yasa became the seventh of the Arahants.

At the offering of food in Yasa's former house, his mother and former wife both listened to Dhamma and became Stream-winners. They were the first laywomen to go for Refuge to the Three Treasures: The Buddha, Dhamma and Sangha.

Now Yasa was a well-known young man; so when four of his friends: Vimala, Subāhu, Puṇṇaji, Gavampati, all of them sons of leading merchant families in Benares, heard that he had become a bhikkhu they said amongst themselves that it must be an extraordinary Teaching which would cause Yasa to leave home. They went to see him and he took them to the Buddha asking him to teach them. After they had listened to his gradual Dhamma-talk they also became Stream-winners, and asked to become bhikkhus and then, after being instructed from time to time by the Buddha, also attained Arahantship. So there were eleven Arahants in the world.

Yasa had more friends and acquaintances in the countryside, also from the merchant class. Fifty young men from these families got together and went to visit venerable Yasa. They attained Arahantship in exactly the same way as his four friends mentioned above. The only difference is that we are not told their names either here or anywhere else in Buddhist scriptures. Their names were forgotten in the course of time and it may be that they passed away during their subsequent wanderings in remote parts of India.

The Buddha spoke to those bhikkhus the words so often quoted in connection with spreading the Dhamma: "Bhikkhus, I am free from all shackles whether human or divine. You are free from all shackles whether human or divine. Go now and wander for the welfare and happiness of many, out of compassion for the world, for the benefit, welfare and happiness of gods and men. Teach Dhamma that is good in the beginning, good in the middle and good in the end, both in the spirit and the letter. Explain the holy life that is utterly perfect and pure. There are beings with little dust in their eyes that will be lost through not hearing Dhamma. But some will understand Dhamma. I shall go to Uruvelā, to Senānigama, to teach Dhamma." We should note that these inspiring words were spoken to Arahants, not to ordinary men still with passions.

Then we must picture those bhikkhus, who were truly great men, after paying homage to the Buddha's feet, taking their robes and bowls and setting-off one in this direction and two or three in that. A thin small ripple of yellowish robes spreading out over the countryside from the Deer Park outside Benares. Though few in number how great was the movement that they started! When people asked them questions what profundity and directness there was in their answers! Those words spoken by them were born out of pure, compassionate hearts, desireless, hateless and brilliant with penetrating wisdom. With emissaries like this the Dhamma was sure to spread.

From amongst the people who heard Dhamma from these Arahants a number wished to take up Dhamma-practice full-time, unobstructed by worldly activities. They requested those venerable ones to accept them as their disciples. But the Arahants told them that they must go with them and receive the words of acceptance from the Buddha himself. Then those Arahants would bring their pupils all the way back to the Deer Park even though the way was rough and travelling difficult.

The Buddha, after considering this matter, then allowed the bhikkhus to give the going-forth and acceptance to those who asked for it. Hair and beard had to be shaved-off, the applicant clothed in the yellow-dyed lower robe like a sarong, with the upper robe over the left shoulder, leaving the right one bare. He must then pay homage three times to his Teacher's feet after which, kneeling down with his hands held palms together, be should say: "To the Buddha I go for Refuge, to the Dhamma I go for Refuge, to the Sangha I go for refuge. For the second time to the Buddha ... Dhamma ... Sangha I go for Refuge. For the third time to the Buddha ... Dhamma ... Sangha I go for Refuge."

This is the second stage in the development of the Going-forth and Acceptance as bhikkhus. The first, the words spoken by the Buddha for instance to Yasa (see above), was called the "Come-bhikkhu-acceptance." The revised method is known as "Acceptance by Going to the Three Refuges." The procedure for becoming a bhikkhu changes once more to the form used today. It was found that the second method of Acceptance did not deal with a number of matters which arose so that some undesirable people with wrong motives and the wrong intentions became bhikkhus. To rectify this, the Buddha, when such cases came to his attention, laid down matters which should be clear before Acceptance, (such as possession of one's own bowl and robes), as well as other matters which qualify or disqualify a person from bhikkhu-hood. (For an outline of the procedure see Appendix II).

The third method, as finally laid down by the Buddha, incorporates the second stage, which now becomes the way of Going-forth to become a sāmaṇera or novice. It is followed by a procedure in which the Sangha of not less than five bhikkhus gathers first to hear the motion chanted that so-and-so requests

Acceptance and then listens in silence to three announcements of this fact. So long as the text for this formal act of the Sangha is completely and perfectly recited and so long as no bhikkhu in that Sangha speaks, the motion is "carried"—by silence. If any objections are raised then the act has no validity.

Finally in this chapter the Buddha's acceptance of a further thirty bhikkhus, the conversion of the Kassapa brothers, the arrival of his foremost pair of disciples, and some stories of individual Arahant bhikkhus, should be mentioned. When he was on his way to the area around Gayā where the three brothers Kassapa and their disciples lived, he stayed for a while in a wood. A party of thirty young men came from the town to that place to enjoy the coolness of the forest, most with their wives and servants. One of them was unmarried and had brought along a prostitute as his companion but she ran off with his valuables while they were enjoying themselves. Everyone searched for her but instead of finding her they came across the Buddha seated in another part of the wood. When they asked him if he had seen a woman, he said, "Young men, what have you to do with a woman?" They told him what had happened and he said, "What do you think about this, then; which is better for you—that you should seek a woman or that you should seek yourselves?" They replied that it was better to seek for themselves so the Buddha invited them to sit down and listen to Dhamma. After paying homage to him and listening to a gradual discourse on Dhamma, they all became Stream-winners and then asked to become bhikkhus. The Buddha accepted them with the "Come-bhikkhu" formula.

We are not told what happened to this group of thirty. It seems that they did not accompany the Buddha on his journey to Gayā as he had, apparently, no company when he was with the Kassapa brothers.

The Buddha, meanwhile, first went on to seek the eldest of the brothers, Uruvelā Kassapa. He was the teacher of five hundred ascetics who had coiled or matted hair, and practised various ceremonies such as fire-worship and austerities such as baptising themselves in the icy river during the winter to wash away their sins. As he was teacher of such a large number his fame spread far and wide so that he received abundant offerings. He could not be taught by the usual methods of instruction for he had become proud of his reputation, so the Buddha employed various special means to impress him. Sometimes these means are wrongly called "miracles" but there is nothing miraculous about them. Although they are certainly out of the ordinary they also become possible by cause and effect; they are not powers granted from above. As Gotama the Buddha had penetrated all the darkness of the mind with the brilliance of his Enlightenment, such "super-knowledges," as they are called, became possible for him. However, he rarely used them and then only when the usual methods of teaching would not work.

In this case, to break Uruvelā Kassapa's pride he had to accomplish many strange things and though the ascetic was impressed by them, thinking, "The Samaṇa Gotama is very powerful," yet he also thought, "But he is not an Arahant like me." Uruvelā Kassapa really thought that he had got to the highest attainment and so could learn nothing further. Finally, the Buddha seeing that the ascetic would not be moved to declare himself a pupil once again, said to Uruvelā Kassapa, "You are neither an Arahant nor on the way to becoming one. There is nothing you do by which you might become an Arahant or enter into the way of becoming one." These words shocked Kassapa into awareness of his own imperfection so that he and all his disciples became bhikkhus. Similarly, his brothers and their disciples amounting to another five hundred ascetics also asked for Going-forth and Acceptance.

To them all, a thousand or more bhikkhus, the Buddha addressed the Discourse on Fire, his third recorded discourse: "Bhikkhus, All is burning. What is the All? Eye is burning, sight objects are burning, eye-consciousness is burning, eye contact is burning… Burning with what? Burning with the fire of lust, the fire of aversion, the fire of delusion…." All of them attained Arahantship at the conclusion of the discourse. Again, of all this vast concourse we know only the names of their leaders, the three Kassapas, of Uruvelā, of the River, and of Gayā. Some of the other Arahants from this assembly may be among those relatively unknown enlightened elders whose verses are included in the collection known as Verses of the Elder Monks (Theragāthā—see end of this chapter).

Even though the Buddha had now so many enlightened bhikkhus, some of them famous either in lay society or in the religious life, he did not proclaim any of them as his foremost disciples. This he did only a little later when the venerable Sāriputta and Moggallāna came to join him. They had been friends from their youth and as young men became disillusioned with the amusements and pleasures of the world. Having made a pact to tell each other about the Deathless State (Nibbāna), should either of them win to it, they journeyed all over India discussing with Teachers and meditating with them. But they could not find a Teacher who knew the way. Eventually Venerable Sāriputta saw the Arahant Assaji, one of the first five bhikkhus and sure from his composure that he had won to the Way, approached and asked him questions. The venerable Assaji modestly said that he could not expound Dhamma in detail but would do so in brief. He said:

> The Tathāgata has told the cause
> of dhammas causally arisen
> and of their cessation too—
> thus proclaims the Great Samaṇa.

So bright and quick was venerable Sāriputta's wisdom in comprehending conditionality that with the first half of this verse he became a Stream-winner. (When we hear it, or see it, the profundity in the verse has to be explained to us, demonstrating how dull our minds are). After honouring his Teacher, venerable Sāriputta went to inform his friend, who after hearing the same verse from him also attained to the Fruit of Stream-winning. Then both of them proceeded to honour the Buddha's feet and be acclaimed by him as his foremost pair of bhikkhu disciples. Both attained Arahantship soon after, venerable Moggallāna after a week and venerable Sāriputta when a fortnight had gone by.[10]

The Sangha had grown to great numbers and in a very short time. With the Dhamma perfectly expounded by the Buddha all who wore the bhikkhu's robes were then Noble Ones, attained to the insights of Stream-winning, Once-returning, Non-returning or won to the Enlightenment or the Arahant. Difficult situations did not arise with such Noble Ones nor were evil actions done by them; so the Sangha needed little regulation as yet.

As a fitting conclusion for this chapter let us look at some brief accounts of the lives of a few bhikkhus who became Arahants. There is a collection of their verses[11] in which they describe how they lived prior to ordination, how they came to ordain and their Enlightenment experience afterwards. Out of the two hundred and fifty nine theras (here meaning Arahant monks) just sixteen have been chosen here to show the range of different sorts of people and their experiences. A similar selection of enlightened bhikkhunīs' poems will be given in Chapter VII.

First comes Vīra, who was a son of a minister to King Pasenadi. His name means "hero" and fittingly he became a great athlete and a warrior. When he married and a son was born to him he saw the troubles in the round of birth-and-death and so went forth to homelessness and making great effort attained Arahantship. Then his former wife tried to lure him back to her in various ways and venerable Vīra said, "This woman, desiring to seduce me, is like one wishing to shake Mount Sumeru with the wing of a gnat!" And he showed her the futility of her actions by reciting this verse:

---

10. For a detailed account, see *The Life of Sāriputta*, Wheel No. 90/92, BPS.

11. The Elder Monks' Verses have been twice translated in the P.T.S. Translations Series (see, *Psalms of the Brethren/Sisters*; and *Elders' Verses I & II*). The translations appearing here, while they have been newly made by the writer, drawn on the previous renderings in some places. The writer readily acknowledges his debt to the translators of both volumes.

Who was hard to tame is by the Taming tamed,
a hero, contented, from all doubts released,
victor over all, completely rid of fear,
Vīra stands firm and quenched[12] perfectly. (Th 8)[13]

The woman hearing him was deeply moved and thought, "My husband has won to this—what good is domestic life to me?" She went forth as a bhikkhunī and soon attained Arahantship.

In the case of Sundara-samudda it was not a wife who tried to lure him back to lay life and its pleasures but a prostitute engaged for this purpose by his grieving parents. He came of a wealthy merchant family and his parents feared that the wealth of the family would be lost if their son continued in the bhikkhu life. They promised that woman the hand of their son in marriage if she could prevail upon him to disrobe. Accordingly she invited him upon alms round to receive alms food from her at the house door on the first day, later inviting him to sit within the house and finally persuading him to take his food alone with her upon the house's topmost floor. Then she tried to seduce him. The thera perceiving her efforts and their effects upon himself, resolved to make a supreme effort and sitting there won to concentration, insight and Arahantship. Concerning this it is said:

Adorned she was, well-dressed
crowned with a garland, decked with gems,
her feet made red with lack
and sandals on—a prostitute
stood before me and sandals doffed,
holding her hands in reverence,
she spoke to me softly, sweetly
and with an opening compliment:

---

12. Quenched—put out the fires of lust, aversion, delusion and attained to the cool peace of Nibbāna, to Arahantship.

13. Numbers refer to verses in the text of the Verses of Elder Monks (Theragāthā).

"Young you are for the going-forth!
Stay within my Teachings[14] here,
enjoy the pleasures of mankind
and I indeed shall give you wealth.
This I promise you in truth
(or if you doubt my words)
I'll bring you fire and swear!"[15]

And when I saw that prostitute
beseeching me, hands reverent,
adorned as she was, well dressed too,
just like a death's snare laid,
thorough application of mind arose,
the danger was revealed and then
weary with the world was evenness established.

Then my mind was free!
See the Dhamma's normality!
Possessed is the triple knowledge,[16]
done is the Buddha's Sāsana. (Th 459–465)

Isidinna was another merchant's son born in Western India but eventually heard the Buddha give a Dhamma talk and then became a Stream-winner. While he was still living as a householder a deity who had compassion for him roused him with these words:

I have seen laymen learned in Dhamma,
"Pleasures are transient," so often they say
but passionately they are attached to
caring for children, jewellery, wife.

---

14. Teachings is a translation of the religious term *sāsana,* left untranslated in the last line. Literally it means instructions but covers all aspects of Buddhism which is called the Buddhassana in Buddhist lands.

15. Swear an oath on fire or go through an ordeal by fire to prove veracity.

16. Triple knowledge described as the Enlightenment experience in Chapter I.

They know not the Dhamma as it really is
though often they say "O transient pleasures"
they're lacking the power to cut their desire
and therefore attached to children, wife and wealth.

(Th 187–188).

When Isidinna heard this, he was deeply moved and going forth, not long after won Arahantship. And when he confessed his penetrative knowledge, he repeated these verses.

Satimattiya also spoke about laymen though in this case, about their faith. He came of a brahmin family and as a young man entered the Sangha and lived in the forest. His practice won for him Arahantship after which he lived instructing bhikkhus and teaching lay people especially the Three Refuges and the Five Precepts. One family in particular had faith in him and his Dhamma-teachings and in that house there was a beautiful daughter who served him very respectfully with food. A hallucination resembling him appeared to her and the family and it seemed as though he took hold of her hand. She knew that is was not him but the others lost faith in him. The next day when he called to receive alms food he perceived their changed manner and investigating with his mind, knew what had happened. Then he explained to them what had really occurred and the householder begged his pardon, but the thera to show his non-attachment spoke these verses:

Formerly with faith in me
you have it now no more,
what is yours is yours alone,
no bad conduct here I've done.
Faith changes and is shakeable,
this indeed I've seen.

Folk respect, then disrespect
but why should a wise man waste?
A sage's food, little by little,
is cooked in various families—
I'll go around for my little alms,
my legs are strong enough! (Th 246–248)

Also a Brahmin, Mahānāma, heard the Buddha teaching Dhamma and gaining faith, entered the Sangha. After receiving a meditation object from the Buddha he retired to the seclusion of Mount Nesādaka. But he was not able to stop evil thoughts and desires arising and exclaimed "What use is life to me with this corrupted mind?" Disgusted with himself he climbed up to a steep place and prepared to throw himself down, first uttering this verse:

> By this mountain found inferior[17],
> to ruin come on Mount Nesādaka,
> far-famous with its many peaks,
> all covered with woods of sālā. (Th 115)

While he was exhorting himself with this verse the thera won insight and Arahantship so that this verse became his declaration of penetrative knowledge.

Sappadāsa, too, tried to kill himself out of despair because of his wandering mind. He was born as the son of King Suddhodana's ceremonial priest and therefore of brahmin stock. When the Buddha returned to his own people to teach them, Sappadāsa obtained confidence and went forth. He was overpowered by defilements of mind, however, and so could not win one-pointedness of mind. Finally he became so distressed that he got to the point of committing suicide but, then, insight arose and Arahantship was attained. Declaring his perfect knowledge he said:

> Five and twenty years since I went forth
> and not so much as a finger-snap
> of peaceful mind have I obtained
> Never getting one-pointedness of mind
>
> since afflicted by sense-desires,
> lamenting and with arms outstretched
> I went away from my dwelling-place.
> Shall I, shall I take a knife—

---

17. Found inferior and to ruin come attempt to convey the meaning of one difficult Pali verb.

what use is life to me?
Giving up training, such as I,
how am I to die?

Taking then my razor
I sat upon my couch
with the blade placed on my throat
to cut my own artery;
thorough application of mind arose in me,
the danger was revealed and then
weary with the world was evenness established.

Then my mind was free!
See the Dhamma's normality!
Possessed is the triple knowledge,
done is the Buddha's Sāsana. (Th 405–410)

The Buddha taught that one is not a brahmin by birth but by deeds, a teaching mirrored in the story of Sunīta. He was born in a family of outcastes whose traditional work was to throw away the garlands and flowers used in peoples' homes, festivals and worship. One night as the Buddha sat in meditation of the Net of Great Compassion, Sunīta came to his knowledge and he saw the requirements for Arahantship in his heart, shining like a lamp within a jar. When dawn came the Buddha took his bowl and followed by the bhikkhus set out on alms-round, until he came to the place where Sunīta was working. He was sweeping up rubbish into heaps, putting it into baskets which he then took away on a carrying-pole. (Now according to caste laws, outcastes such as Sunīta must not come into contact with or approach those of the higher castes). Sunīta, seeing that the Buddha was filled with joy and finding no place to hide in on that road, placed his pole in a corner of a wall and stood as if stuck to the wall honouring the Buddha with his hands together. When the Buddha came near he said to Sunīta, "What is this wretched way of life to you? Can you bear to go forth?" And Sunīta, experiencing the rapture of one who has been sprinkled with the Deathless, said: "If even such as I, Exalted One, may in this life go forth, why should I not do so? May the Exalted One, having compassion on me, let me go forth!" And the Buddha said, "Come, bhikkhu!" and that was his Acceptance.

After hearing the Buddha's instructions, he won attainments in due order until Arahantship—and Sakka and Brahma with their heavenly retinues came to pay him homage. Many bhikkhus hearing of his attainment, came to ask him questions—"From what family did you go forth?" "Why did you go forth?" "How did you penetrate the four Noble Truths?" Sunīta told them the whole matter in these words:

> Humble the clan in which I was born,
> poor and having little food,
> lowly the work I had to do—
> I threw away the flowers.
>
> I was despised by men,
> disregarded, reviled by them,
> so making my mind humble,
> respectful was I to many folk.
>
> Then I saw the All-Enlightened One
> revered and leading the Bhikkhu Saṅgha,
> the Great Hero as he was entering
> the chief city of the Magadhese.[18]
>
> Laying down my carrying-pole
> I approached to honour him,
> out of compassion just for me
> the Best-among-men stood still.
>
> Having honoured the Teacher's feet,
> then standing near at hand
> I requested the going-forth
> from the best-of-beings-all.
>
> Then the Teacher compassionate,
> compassionate with all the world,
> spoke these words to me, "Come bhikkhu"
> and that was my Acceptance.

---

18. Rājagaha (modern Rājgir).

Afterwards I lived alone
in the forest, diligent
I did the Teacher's bidding
as the Conqueror exhorted me.

And in the first watch of the night
I recollected my former lives;
then in the night's middle watch
the Eye Divine was purified;
and in the last Watch of the night
I tore asunder the mass of gloom.

Then as the day was dawning
and the great sun arising,
hither came Indra and Brahma too,
their hands together revering me—
'Homage to you, nobly born of men!

To you homage, highest among men!
Now your pollutions are destroyed,
worthy of gifts you are, noble sir."

Then the Teacher seeing me
revered by the deva-hosts
assembled there, revealed a smile
and spoke about this matter:

"By effort, by the Holy Life,
by self-restraint and taming,
by this one is a holy one,
this is the highest holiness."[19] (Th 620–631)

Sumaṅgala was also a poor man who earned a sparse living in the fields with a sickle, plough and mattock. One day when King Pasenadi had given a great offering to the Buddha and the Bhikkhu Saṅgha, he saw this and thought, "These Sakyan samaṇas live in sheltered lodgings and have fine robes—what if I were to go forth too?" When he had gone forth, he took a

---

19. The words translated "Holy Life," "holy one," and "holiness" are *brahmacariya, brahma* and *brāhmaṇa.*

meditation exercise to the forest but he could not stand the solitude and thought to return to his village. But as he went along he saw peasants in the fields working hard with soiled clothes, covered with dust and seared by hot winds and it occurred to him how much misery they had in their lives. So roused to great exertion by this he attained Arahantship and to celebrate his emancipation from suffering he uttered this verse:

> Free from three crooked things, free indeed!
> Free from my sickle, plough and mattock!
> Even though they are here, ever here,
> Enough of them for me, enough of them!
> Meditate, Sumaṅgala, meditate, Sumaṅgala!
> Live diligently, O Sumaṅgala. (Th 43)

Kappaṭakura was even worse off since, born of a poor family, as a boy the only way he could support himself was to go round clad in rags and begging for rice—hence his nickname "Rags-and-rice" (Kappaṭa-kura). Later, he lived by cutting and selling grass. One day engaged in cutting grass in the forest, he saw a thera and sitting down near him, heard the Dhamma. Then he thought "What is this wretched way of life to me?" and so entered the Sangha, putting his ragged cloth aside. Whenever discontent with the bhikkhu-life assailed him he would go and look at his rags, put them on and then lead a layman's life again. He left the Sangha in this way, seven times and bhikkhus told the Buddha about him. One day, as he was a bhikkhu again, he sat nodding on the outside of the assembled bhikkhus while the Buddha was giving a Dhamma-talk. The Buddha admonished him with these verses (quoting Kappaṭakura's thoughts about his rags):

> "(Compared) with this painful and too heavy (robe),
> this is the rag of Kappaṭakura"; (who though having)
> Dhamma
> in measure full (likened to) a vessel containing
> Deathlessness,
> (yet) no step he takes to accumulate concentrations.[20]

Do not nod off, Kappaṭa!
Do not make me cuff (the Dhamma) into your ear!
Nothing indeed, Kappaṭa,
have you learnt, nodding off in the Sangha's midst.

(Th 199–200)

This strong exhortation of the Buddha pierced, as it were, even to his bones and he thus managed to establish insight and soon attain Arahantship. Then he repeated these verses which had been his goad as his declaration of perfect knowledge.

In accordance with his past kamma, Dasaka was reborn in Sāvatthī as the child of a slave of Anāthapiṇḍika would find a corner on the outskirts of the assembly and sit there snoring. To stir him the Buddha one day spoke this verse:

A dullard drowsy with much gluttony,
engrossed in sleep, who wallows as he lies,
like a great porker stuffed with fatting food,
comes ever and again unto the womb.[21] (Th 17)

Aroused by this exhortation the thera shortly afterwards won Arahantship.

Now we come to the verses of two boys, both called Sopāka, meaning "of low caste" and both born poorly. The first of these boys lost his father when young and was brought up by his uncle, who, instigated by his own son attempted to have Sopāka killed by taking him to the charnel-ground at night and there tying him to a corpse, thinking, "The jackals will kill him." But when the jackals came young Sopāka cried out for help and the Buddha at that time sitting in meditation saw his plight and that his heart contained the conditions for

---

20. Bracketed words are partly explanations supplied by the Commentary and partly guesswork The text seems rather corrupt—meaningless if translated literally. There is as little of metre in the Pali of the first verse as in my rendering.

21. Translation by Ven. Ñāṇamoli Thera, in *The Guide* (Pali Text Society, London). This is also verse 325 of the Dhammapada (*The Path of Truth*, Mahamakut Press, Bangkok).

Arahantship. So he projected a vision of himself and spoke to Sopāka words of comfort, and the boy burst his bonds and went to where the Buddha stayed, already a Stream-winner. The Buddha later taught this boy's mother the Dhamma so that she won the fruit of Stream-winning while Sopāka, concealed from her, became an Arahant. Then, when the Buddha wished to give him the Acceptance[22] he asked him what later became called "The Boy's Questions." All the ten questions, beginning with "What is the one?" (A. All beings are sustained by food), were answered accurately by Sopāka, so this was his Acceptance. Sopāka Thera told of his Acceptance in this way:

> Seeing the Best-among-men
> pace up and down in the terrace's shade
> I approached him there
> and homage paid to the Chief-of-men.
>
> Arranging my robe right shoulder bare
> I placed my hands together then
> and followed after the Stainless One,
> He who is Chief among beings all.
>
> Then He-who-knows, skilled questioner,
> questions asked of me
> and I, fearless and unafraid,
> replied to the Teacher then.
>
> When the questions had been answered,
> the Tathāgata commended me
> and turning to the Bhikkhu Saṅgha
> spoke about this matter:
>
> "For the Anganese and the Magadhese
> it's gain for them indeed,
> for them (whose gift of) robe and bowl,
> lodgings and medicine,
> reverence and conduct helpful,
> this one enjoys—it's gain indeed!

---

22. This is an exceptional case since Sopāka was nowhere near twenty years old.

From this day onward, Sopāka,
come and see me when you wish
and let our discourse, Sopāka,
be the Acceptance for you."

At the age of seven from my birth
the Acceptance I received,
now my last body bearing.
Ah! the Dhamma's normality! (Th 480–486)

The second boy Sopāka's mother had great difficulties at his birth and fell into a coma. Relatives, thinking her dead, carried her with Sopāka still unborn, to the charnel-ground and began to cremate "the body" and having lit the pyre, went away. Rain put out the fire and Sopāka was born, though the mother died. The watchman of that place adopted the boy who, when seven years old, came to the notice of the Buddha seated in meditation. Realizing that this boy could win Arahantship, the Buddha went there and Sopāka rejoicing, saluted him. After obtaining the consent of the father, Sopāka became a member of the Sangha, the Buddha giving him the meditation-subject of loving-kindness (*mettā*). And after winning Arahantship through this method, Sopāka encouraged all the other bhikkhus and sāmaṇeras to practise in the same way—making no difference between those who are friendly, indifferent or hostile—for all alike; their love should be one and the same nature, including all states of existence, all beings in all ages:

As she would be good
to her only son,
so one should be good
to all beings everywhere. (Th 33)

Brahmadatta was another bhikkhu who showed the power of his loving-kindness, though in his case, in the face of difficulties. He was a prince, son of the King of Kosala and saw the greatness of the Buddha when the Jeta Grove was presented. Having faith, he entered the Sangha and in due course attained Arahantship. One day on alms-round, a brahmin abused him but the thera continued in silence. Again the brahmin reviled him and people commented on the thera's silence. At this, Brahmadatta taught them Dhamma:

> How can anger arise for the angerless,
> tamed and living evenly,
> freed by perfect knowledge,
> tranquil, one who's 'Thus'?[23]
>
> For he is worse when vilified
> who then reviles the angry man,
> but he who pays not back in kind
> wins a battle hard to win.
>
> For the benefit of both he lives—
> himself and the other one,
> knowing the other's anger
> mindful he is and calm.
>
> He is indeed healer of both,
> himself and the other one,
> yet people who know not Dhamma
> think he is a fool.

That brahmin, hearing these words, asked both for forgiveness and for the Going-forth and practising the development of loving-kindness was taught in this way by Brahmadatta Thera:

> If anger should arise in you
> reflect on the Simile of the Saw,[24]
> if craving for flavours should arise
> remember the Son's flesh Simile.[25]
>
> If your mind runs craving
> pleasures and existences
> bind it quickly with mindfulness
> as a beast found eating corn.[26] (Th 441–446)

---

23. "Thus"—seeing things as they really are.
24. Simile of the Saw, see MN 21
25. Simile of the Son's Flesh, see SN 12:63 (and Wheel No. 105–106, BPS)

Out of loving-kindness and compassion, Passika helped his unbelieving kinsfolk. He came of a brahmin family and after gaining confidence in the Buddha, entered the Sangha. While he was practising he fell sick and his relatives attended upon him and healed him. Greatly moved by the illness to the dangers in life, he increased his efforts and so won Arahantship. Afterwards, he established his kinsmen in the Refuges and Precepts so that when they died, rebirth took place in the heavenly realms. And when the Buddha asked him about his relatives, Passika Thera replied:

> Though only I from unbelieving kin
> had wisdom as well as confidence,
> firm in Dhamma and possessed of virtue
> this was for my relatives' good.
>
> I rebuked my kinsmen,
> from compassion urged them on
> and relatives for love of me
> served the bhikkhus well.
>
> They, in due time, died,
> gaining the joy of the Thirty-three,[27]
> my mother and brothers rejoice
> realizing their varied desires. (Th 240–242).

Another bhikkhu who was ill was Vakkali, born in a brahmin family and proficient in the three Vedas with their ritual. He one day saw the Buddha and so great was his attraction that he left home for the homeless life, so that he could see more of his person. He followed the Buddha everywhere and never took his eyes off him until one day laid low by illness he could not see him any more. When bhikkhus saw that he was depressed, he explained to them that he could not see the Buddha and they arranged for the Buddha to visit him. The Teacher said to him "What is there in seeing this vile body. He who sees Dhamma sees me—he truly sees me".[28]

---

26. Simile of the Cow Eating Corn, see SN 35:246.
27. The thirty-three—a name for one of the sensual realm heavens.

Vakkali no longer gazed, but his attachment was still strong, so the Buddha sent him away at the end of the rains-retreat. Vakkali dwelt on the Vulture Peak near Rājagaha gradually maturing his insight but suffered from insufficiency of food, so one day the Buddha, visited him and said:

Brought low by colic as you are,
dwelling in the forest grove
where it is rough, with little food,
how, bhikkhu, will you fare?

Vakkali: With abundant bliss and rapture
suffusing this body,
even enduring what is rough
I shall dwell in the forest grove.

Developing bases of mindfulness,
the faculties and powers too,
the factors for Enlightenment,
I shall dwell in the forest grove.

Having seen my fellow-monks
resolutely making effort,
ever-strong in energy,
living together harmoniously,
I shall dwell in the forest grove.

Recollecting the Enlightened One,
Chief of the tamed with mind composed,
always diligent day and night,
I shall dwell in the forest grove. (Th 350–354)

With these words the thera aroused insight and attained Arahantship.

And now, by way of a lighter interlude, here is Usabha who was born among the Buddha's own people, the Sakyans and

---

28. The Buddha is unique among Indian teachers in not agreeing to the common worshipful attitude among devotees (*bhaktas*) of blind faith. He wanted people not merely to follow but to practice and understand thoroughly. This is shock treatment for a *bhakta*!

when the Buddha visited his kinsfolk out of compassion for them, Usabha saw the Buddha's power and wisdom and having confidence, entered the Sangha. But all his days after this were passed in company with others while all his nights went in sleep and he neglected all practice of Dhamma. One day, confused in mind and negligent, he dropped off to sleep and dreamt that he had shaved his head and beard, put on a purple cloak and then seated on an elephant, entered the town for almsfood! Seeing the people there he dismounted for shame and awoke then thinking, "Why, it was a dream! Confused and unmindful I saw myself in sleep!" Roused by this incident he established insight and in due course won Arahantship. And as he had made the dream his road, so he celebrated it when declaring his perfect knowledge:

> Putting on my shoulder
> a robe the colour of mango-shoots,
> seated on an elephant's neck
> I entered the village for alms,
> (ashamed) I dropped from the elephant
> and profoundly moved (awoke).
> At first on fire, then at peace
> attained to pollutions' end.[29] (Th 197–198).

29. Destruction of the pollutions (*āsava*): the pollution of sense-desires, the pollution of existence, the pollution of unknowing, and sometimes added: the pollution of views. See the *Buddhist Dictionary*, Nyanatiloka Mahāthera, BPS, Kandy, for definitions.

Chapter III

The Sangha and the Development of Vinaya

Rāhula ordained as first novice—Why are there rules?—Meaning of Vinaya—How Vinaya began—Contents of the Pātimokkha—allowances and prohibitions—few things, few troubles—Legal procedures in the Sangha—Ten Reasons for Vinaya.

When the Buddha returned to Kapilavatthu, the Sakyans' principal city, at the entreaty of his father, King Suddhodana, the Buddha's son, Rāhula was ordained as the first novice or *sāmaṇera*.[30]

It happened in this way. The Buddha and the bhikkhus accompanying him having received no invitations to the Sakyans' houses, walked for alms food. It caused a great stir in the town that the Buddha— formerly the Crown Prince there—should do such a thing. When the king heard about it he too was disturbed and ran into the streets to stop the Buddha, saying that he was disgracing his lineage. The Buddha replied that in his lineage people always went on alms round, a statement which the king contested saying that no Sakyan prince had ever done so. But by his own lineage the Buddha meant the lineage of the Buddhas from past times. When the Buddha spoke some verses about this, the king attained to the Noble Path and Fruit of Stream entry, and, immediately perceiving his own lack of courtesy, invited the Buddha and all the Bhikkhu Saṅgha to a meal in the palace.

At the end of the meal when the Buddha was about to depart, the Buddha's former wife, Princess Yasodharā, said to

30. For a full account see the essay, "The Life of Rāhula" in *The Novices Training* (*Sāmaṇerasikkha*), Mahamakut Press, B.E. 2509 (1966).

Rāhula, "That is your father, Rāhula. Go and ask for your inheritance." So prince Rāhula went to the Blessed One and stood before him, (saying), "Your shadow is pleasant, monk." Then the Blessed One got up from his seat and went away. Prince Rāhula followed behind the Blessed One, saying, "Give me my inheritance, monk; give me my inheritance, monk!" Then the Blessed One told venerable Sāriputta, "Then, Sāriputta, give him the Going-forth." The Commentary elaborates and says that the Buddha considered the worldly inheritance of power and riches as leading only to more sufferings and so gave him his inheritance in the Dhamma. The Buddha saw that Rāhula had all the potential necessary to attain Arahantship.

At this time Rāhula was only seven years old. (Six years had been spent by the Buddha before Enlightenment in seeking the Way while one more year had passed since then). Venerable Sāriputta therefore enquired how he should do this and the Buddha told him to use the second style of Acceptance—Going-for-Refuge, which was described in the previous chapter. So Rāhula became the first sāmaṇera, literally meaning "a little Samaṇa," Samaṇa being a word used for all who cultivate peacefulness in mind, speech, and body.

But King Suddhodana was not happy. When Prince Siddhattha left home he had lost his son and heir to the throne. Just prior to Rāhula's going-forth, Prince Nanda, the Buddha's cousin, a youth about to be married, had become a bhikkhu. "Rāhula is too much," as the King said. He requested the Buddha not to allow the going-forth of children without their parents' permission—and the Buddha laid down a ruling that this was not to be done in future and to do so would be an offence of wrong-doing.

This brings us to a discussion of the rules, which govern the life of a bhikkhu.[31] First, for what reason are there rules? It was characteristic of the Buddha that he never laid down rules

31. For a complete treatment of this subject see *The Pātimokkha; The Entrance to the Vinaya,* Vols. 1, 2. Mahamakut Press; also *The Buddhist Monk's Discipline.* Wheel No. 130/131, BPS.

unless he had to do so. In the example above, it was so that parents should not grieve and possibly take action against bhikkhus who made novices of their children, but very often the need for rules also arose through the unsuitable actions of some bhikkhus, and later of some Bhikkhunīs too.

What actions are unsuitable for those who lead the Holy Life? As this life is for ending, for destroying all the defilements, which spring up from the three Roots of Evil—greed, aversion and delusion, actions of body and speech, which are born of them, will certainly be obstructive and unsuitable. Rules are only for checking body and speech actions, not to restrain the mind, which should be trained by meditation. So the Buddha when faced with a situation where some bhikkhu had failed to be restrained in actions of body and speech, first upbraided the guilty bhikkhu and then convened an assembly of bhikkhus in which he laid down a rule of training. No doubt he thought, "If they do such things while I am alive, what will they do when I am no longer here?" But before such incidents actually arose the Buddha had not laid down any rule at all, even though such a thing as theft, for instance, was sure to occur sooner or later.

Rules, after all, are needed even by the weakest members of any society. Those who are strong in moral principles just naturally keep to good conduct. So it was in the Sangha, and most of the rules laid down were because of a bhikkhu's greed, aversion, or delusion, which made him act in a way, which disturbed other people, his fellow-bhikkhus, or householders.

Those who were training themselves diligently and applying the Dhamma all the time were unlikely to do anything which was unsuitable to the bhikkhu life. While of course, the Noble Ones and the Arahants in particular hardly ever fell into an offence. If they did so it was in matters, which never involved a moral lapse, only small things which had been overlooked. Venerable Sāriputta for instance, one day was leaving the monastery to go into town and one side of his sarong or under-robe had slipped down. A young sāmaṇera noticed this and very respectfully informed him, at which venerable Sāriputta rearranged it and thanked the sāmaṇera, with true humility called him "Teacher.'[32]

Sometimes an Arahant was involved in a more serious affair, which the Buddha did not approve of and made the subject for a ruling. There was the very spectacular case of Venerable Piṇḍolabhāradvāja who exhibited his mighty powers to many people.[33] The Buddha heard the noise of the vast multitude that had seen him levitate and fly, and enquired about it. When he was told how the venerable Arahant had brought down a precious sandalwood bowl from on top of a pole, he censured him strongly saying that he had done it just as a woman who exhibits her private parts for money. In this case no doubt venerable Piṇḍolabhāradvāja intended to use his powers just to win over the rich merchant who was offering the bowl to anyone who could show him the marvel of levitation. In other words, his intention was to use his powers to teach Dhamma, but the Buddha did not approve of this method. Though the Buddha possessed in full all sorts of powers, he rarely used them, esteeming the gradual method of leading people to discover Dhamma step by step as more wonderful.

To return now to the rules, all the varied material-rules, prohibitions and allowances and the formal acts of the Sangha, together with accounts of the events, which had given rise to them, are included in the Basket of Vinaya or Discipline.[34] Although Vinaya has been translated by the word Discipline, English cannot convey the full flavour of the word, for it means literally that by which one is led out. Led out of what? Led out of *dukkha*, of all the sufferings experienced in the round of birth and death. So Vinaya extricates the person who practises it from making evil kammas by speech and body and so continuing in the wandering-on; while on the other hand purifying exterior actions so that the interior ones, the

32. See *The Life of Sāriputta*, Wheel No. 90/92, BPS.

33. See the account in *The Book of Discipline* Vol. 5 p. 150–151; or the more embroidered version in the Dhammapada commentary, *Buddhist Legends*, Vol. 3. pp. 35–38. P.T.S.

34. See the complete translation in *The Book of the Discipline*, Vols 1–6, P.T.S.

workings of the mind, can be purified through the meditations of calm and insight. But without Vinaya none of the higher steps in the training will be successful. This applies not only to bhikkhus but to lay people as well. Their Vinaya basically is the Five Precepts, though a wider application of these is seen in the discourse of the Buddha to the young man called Sigāla, a sutta that is also called The Householder's Vinaya."[35]

The rules of the Vinaya arose gradually in the course of the forty-five years of the Buddha's teaching. A commentary tells us that no serious challenge to the Holy Life arose for the first twenty years after the Buddha's Enlightenment. During this time and later until the time of the Buddha's Final Nibbāna, these rulings were remembered and put in some kind of order by bhikkhus who specialised in memorising Vinaya. They are known as Vinayadharas—literally, "those who hold (or preserve) the Vinaya" and it is due to their diligence that we have the Vinaya today. Among the group of "discipline-holders" the venerable Arahant Upāli Thera was the most distinguished. Even during the Buddha's lifetime he was an authority on Vinaya and after the Final Nibbāna he led the First Council in the codification of what we now call the "Basket of Discipline."

This contains a vast amount of material though it is not all rules, fortunately for bhikkhus! Its present arrangement, the work of the First Council (See Ch. IV), probably differs from the way that it was preserved while the Buddha was alive. Then its beginning may have been the long passage describing how the Buddha attained Enlightenment and the events which followed up to the arrival of the two foremost disciples. After this the Vinaya describes how situations arose showing the need for new bhikkhus to have Teachers and the Buddha makes rules about this. However, this long section is not now the opening of the Vinaya, as it stands at the beginning of the Great Chapter, the Vinaya's second half. The opening section of the Vinaya now relates how venerable Sāriputta requested

35. See translation in *Everyman's Ethics,* Wheel 14, BPS.

the Buddha to lay down the fundamental code of rules called the Pātimokkha. The Buddha declined to do so until it became necessary, in accordance with the principle of not making rules unless they were needed. Sometime after this, such a need arose when venerable Sudinna Kalandakaputta defiled the Holy Life when he was lured into having sexual intercourse with his former wife. This was the first time that a ruling upon a serious matter of Vinaya had to be made by the Buddha.

As we have the books of the Vinaya now, the first two present their material, the fundamental rules in the sequence of the Pātimokkha, of bhikkhus and bhikkhunīs respectively. The Pātimokkha is the code of 227[36] rules (for bhikkhus) recited every fortnight when bhikkhus have a chance to confess infractions and then, purified, listen to their recitation. But in the Vinaya these bare rules are supplemented with their origins in this or that incident, further events, which may modify the rule, analysis as to when one has or has not fallen into an offence, a word-by-word commentary, and finally excusable circumstances which do not count as infractions. All this accounts for the bulky nature of the first two Vinaya books.

The second two books, the Great Chapter and the Lesser Chapter may just be mentioned here. After their beginning, from which much material for the first two chapters of this book has been taken, they deal with many different subjects, each one introduced by long and interesting stories. There are the numerous allowances and prohibitions that the Buddha had to make, as well as the legal procedures established by him for the Sangha. Finally, there are two chapters on the first two Buddhist Councils, one of which was held just after the Buddha's Final Nibbāna and the second, one hundred years later (see Ch. IV).

The classification of rules in the Pātimokkha may be reviewed briefly so that readers understand what sort of actions are unsuitable for the Holy Life. But not all of the offences against these rules are of the same order. There are some, like the offence of wrong doing mentioned above, which

36. In fact, 220 are training rules, while the last 7 are legal procedures for settling monastic disputes, etc. (BPS ed.)

are minor matters in the sense that they can be cleared away by simple confession with another bhikkhu. (Though only "minor" offences, good bhikkhus are careful not to commit them, wherever possible). On the other hand, some defeat the doer of them, in the sense that he has defeated his own purpose—to practice the Holy Life for purification and Enlightenment. After doing any of the following four things, a bhikkhu is called "incurable," loses his state and must disrobe: intentional sexual intercourse of any sort, theft of an object having some value, murder of a human being which includes aiding abortion or praising suicide to someone who then takes his own life, and last, boasting of or hinting at superhuman attainments which one does not have, whether they are deep states of meditation or degrees of insight and Enlightenment.

If a bhikkhu does these things knowingly, he is no longer in communion with other bhikkhus and not regarded as a bhikkhu by them. Even if he continues to wear the yellow robes he is not a bhikkhu. And so serious are these offences that if he continues to pose as a bhikkhu, even though he makes great efforts to progress in Dhamma, he will not be able to realise anything. Moreover, a pseudo-bhikkhu who deceives the lay people supporting him in this way is likely to get a very long and painful rebirth. An honest man disrobes himself without any force being necessary, though, in some Buddhist countries today a defeated bhikkhu who refuses to disrobe can be compelled to do so by secular law. When a bhikkhu has been defeated he can never again, in that life, become a bhikkhu again. This shows the wisdom of the Buddha who allowed bhikkhus who were no longer happy in the Holy Life, to disrobe when they wished to do so. This allowance accounts for the fact that there have been very few defeated bhikkhus.

The next class of very serious offences which are "curable" after the prescribed penance, number thirteen. When it is said that they are "curable" this does not mean that the penance having been properly performed by the guilty bhikkhu, will wipe away the results of the bad kamma, which has been made. It only means that such a bhikkhu is pure again and can continue in his training without the burden of a guilty conscience. Of the thirteen offences, five are concerned with relations just short of sexual intercourse—such as deliberate emission of semen, touching women lustfully and with intention, speaking lewd words to them, or praising intercourse as the highest way of making merit. Also included here are making arrangements for men to meet women (or vice versa), for marriage or for casual intercourse. A bhikkhu thus can never "marry" a couple in the way that priests do in Western religion. This is not his job—though bhikkhus are usually invited before a wedding to chant auspicious stanzas. Buddhist weddings are therefore performed by any competent friend of the family who knows the tradition.

Other serious matters included under this heading are establishing a monastic residence on land which has not been appointed by competent senior bhikkhus and which has no proper surrounding area, or the building itself is too large. A bhikkhu, if building for himself, is allowed to construct a hut about thirteen feet long by seven foot six inches wide—inside measurements.

Trying to oust from the Holy Life another bhikkhu who is innocent by accusing him of one of the four Defeats is the subject of two offences here. Attempting to cause a schism in the Sangha, and being followers of one who attempts to do this, are two more offences. Last but one is the case of a bhikkhu who is difficult to admonish, who adopts the attitude "Well, I shan't say anything to you about your deeds, so don't you say anything to me!" And last comes the bhikkhu who is a "corrupter of families," that is, he gives gifts here and there intending to make himself popular so that he will receive plenty of offerings, he is also guilty of an offence entailing "initial and subsequent meeting of the Sangha."

A bhikkhu who falls into any of these offences must first confess them to his Teacher who then informs the Sangha of some special procedure to be enacted. When the bhikkhus have met, the guilty bhikkhu must inform them of the nature of his offence and then ask for the six-night penance. If he has concealed his offence he must first undergo a period of probation equal in length of time to the concealment, then carry out the six-night penance. In any case, during the entire period he loses all his seniority and must be seated as the youngest bhikkhu, also he cannot take part in official Sangha acts such as ordination, nor can he teach the Dhamma. All visiting bhikkhus have to be informed by him of his offence. At the successful conclusion of this penance, he has to request rehabilitation to his former status in the presence of not less than twenty bhikkhus.

Next in seriousness are a number of wrong actions which have no specific number as they are scattered here and there in the Books of Discipline. These are the grave offences, such things as appearing naked in public (unless forced to do so when robes have been stolen), drinking blood and deliberately stimulating the sexual organs. Such offences are not included in the bhikkhu's code of discipline—the Pātimokkha—because they are often, though not always, a lesser degree of some more serious offence which is in that code.

But the next group, the thirty offences of expiation with forfeiture, are in the Pātimokkha. They mostly concern requisites—robes, or funds for buying them, rugs, bowls, medicines, and so on, which a bhikkhu can keep only within a certain number of days or of which he can possess only a certain quantity. There are also important rules about bhikkhus not receiving money, handling it, nor trafficking with it in any way. A good bhikkhu tries to be free from the taint of money, which promises to buy "happiness" for him. This protects him from the latent greed in his own mind. Articles which he possesses in excess, or over time or should not be possessed at all, have to be forfeited to another bhikkhu, who, for example, in the case of money intended for the Sangha arranges for its disposal. The guilty bhikkhu confesses his offence and promises that in future he will be restrained. This method of purification applies also to the class of grave offences mentioned above and to all the remaining groups of offences to be outlined below.

Among the minor offences, though some matters here are serious enough, are the ninety-two offences of expiation. This is a class dealing with a very wide range of topics from matters of importance at all times such as not being respectful (to other Teacher-bhikkhus or to the Way of training), round to subjects which now have little relevance, such as not having a needle-case made of bone, ivory or horn. There is also a whole section of ten rules limiting the dealings of bhikkhus with the bhikkhunīs. This has little significance now as bhikkhunīs have disappeared in Theravāda lands (see Ch. VII), though some of the rules could still apply with the present upāsikās or nuns.

An important principle is illustrated here concerning of time and place. The Buddha spoke of certain rules, which have application only at certain, times or places. For instance, a rule here makes bathing more frequently than once a fortnight an offence of expiation, though one is encouraged by the number of exceptions to note that usually bhikkhus will have bathed more frequently! But this rule applies only in "the Middle Country" or the eastern Gangetic valley where the Buddha mostly taught; even there it may have applied only in times of drought. The Buddha was sometimes accompanied by a thousand or more bhikkhus and bhikkhunīs and if all of them bathed from a village's wells the water would have been finished very quickly! At special times he allowed, for sick bhikkhus, what was usually unallowable, such as making a fire for warming the body. The variety of matters covered by the rules in this section is so great that interested readers should consult the Pātimokkha or the Book of the Discipline for details.

Four minor rules of a slightly different sort follow the expiations and then comes the group of seventy-five ways of training. These brief rules are mostly about good manners and polished conduct regarding the wearing of robes and bearing of the body, collecting alms food and eating it, occasions suitable for speaking Dhamma, and places for passing urine and excrement. If they are broken they are only offences of wrong-doing, but Teachers stress their importance since they cover everyday matters. They would not be so important for those coming from refined and well disciplined families but many bhikkhus, then as now, have come from the country and need these Trainings. They apply not only to bhikkhus but also to sāmaṇeras who usually learn them by heart.

Many of the allowances and prohibitions are in the second part of the Vinaya, the Great and Lesser Chapters. The Buddha found it necessary to lay them down as the Sangha expanded and gained more supporters. This brought more possibilities of using a variety of articles. To take an example: bhikkhus were offered honey by a rich merchant. At first they declined to accept this offering as honey had not then been allowed by the Buddha. Then he made it allowable and the bhikkhus accepted it. Or a prohibition: the turbulent group of six bhikkhus began wearing all manner of decorated and expensive sandals, which the Buddha had to prohibit as unsuitable for those leading the homeless life. Showy, decorated, and expensive things generally are unsuitable for bhikkhus who should use plain and ordinary things. Prohibitions, such as these, are often backed up by the phrase, "and whoever shall use them falls into an offence of wrong-doing."

Common things of no great value are suitable for bhikkhu-life, but if a bhikkhu has great valuables he becomes liable to the same troubles as householders who have to guard their wealth and possessions from envy and theft by others. He should reflect, "All that is mine, dear and delightful, will change and vanish" and so not become attached to many or valuable possessions. Here are eight "blessings" enjoyed by bhikkhus as related to a king in the power of the passions, by a Pacceka-Buddha (a Buddha who is unable to teach in detail):

> Now as blessing for a bhikkhu,
> one who is homeless, with no wealth:
> no stores or pots or pans has he,
> only he seeks what others leave
> and so keeps going righteously.
>
> Second blessing for a bhikkhu,
> one who is homeless, with no wealth:
> he uses alms food blamelessly
> and no one's there who hinders him.

Third, as blessing for a bhikkhu,
one who is homeless, with no wealth:
at peace his alms food he enjoys
and no one's there who hinders him.

Fourth, as blessing for a bhikkhu,
one who is homeless, with no wealth:
he wanders free throughout the realm
to which he has no tie.

Fifth, as blessing for a bhikkhu,
one who is homeless, with no wealth:
that if the town should burn right down
nothing of his is burnt.

Sixth, as blessing for a bhikkhu,
one who is homeless, with no wealth:
that if the realm should be despoiled
nothing of his is carried off.

Seventh blessing for a bhikkhu,
one who is homeless, with no wealth:
though robbers should control the road
and highwaymen abound,
yet having taken his bowl and robe
the holy one in safety goes.

Eighth, as blessing for a bhikkhu,
one who is homeless, with no wealth:
whatever direction he proceeds,
he goes with equanimity. (J 529)

Now we can consider some of the legal procedures, which are methods for dealing with four sorts of occurrences in the Sangha. These are: contentions, accusations, faults and duties. Regarding the first of these—two bhikkhus might have different understandings of Dhamma and Vinaya and so begin to dispute with each other. The Sangha has the duty then to examine them both and then pronounce judgement on who is right and who is wrong.

In the second case, sometimes a bhikkhu accuses another of committing some undeclared offence, which accusation may or may not be true. The Sangha must meet to decide what is true and what is false.

When a bhikkhu has an offence against one of the training-rules, then he should take the appropriate steps to purify himself, by confession to the Sangha or to an individual bhikkhu. The Sangha has to meet here only if the offence is serious, one of those in the group of thirteen causing initial and subsequent meeting of the Sangha.

Lastly, there are duties to be done, such as the bhikkhus who are invited to accept an applicant as a new bhikkhu, or those who participate in establishing a new boundary for an ordination (acceptance) temple. These duties should be thoroughly carried out for it is the responsibility of bhikkhus to see that the Sangha's business is properly done.

In all these cases the Sangha, which is present for those matters, has to act in harmony. Decisions are not taken by a person in authority (say an abbot) and then handed down for obedient submission by juniors. The Buddha himself came from a people, the Sakyas, who though they had a form of monarchy, were among the democratic and republican tribes. In those states there was a Sabhā or legislative assembly in which all the leading citizens had a voice. We may assume that the raja was the most prominent among the citizens and leader of this assembly. With this background the Buddha would be unlikely to institute an authoritarian system of government in the Sangha. So when he came to lay down the legal procedures for the Sangha, he did so with a group (Sangha) making decisions on the basis of the rulings that he had given.

A Sangha in this sense means the group of bhikkhus who have gathered, or been invited, to attend to one of the above legal procedures, the number of them depending on the function they are to perform. Thus, if they gather to recite the Pātimokkha on the Uposatha days four bhikkhus at least are needed for a quorum. But five are necessary in an acceptance ceremony for a new bhikkhu in "outlying countries" which means everywhere except the Gangetic Valley. In the Middle

Country there, ten bhikkhus are needed for this same function. A group of not less than twenty bhikkhus are a Sangha for an offending bhikkhu who asks for rehabilitation after having done his penance, as mentioned above.

In each case there will be competent and learned senior bhikkhus (or theras) who ensure that the procedures are fully carried out so that they cannot be challenged by other bhikkhus. A procedure, which is not thoroughly accomplished, is not fit to stand; it carries no weight. For instance, if a man under twenty goes through the ordination procedure correctly in the presence of a sufficient number of bhikkhus he is, nevertheless, not a bhikkhu since he is less than the required age. Similarly if words or sentences are omitted in these procedures they have no validity. Hence the care with which all the functions of a Sangha are carried out.

Their form depends on the pattern laid down by the Buddha but broadly speaking they consist either of a motion put to the Sangha, by one or more bhikkhus, followed by three announcements, or a motion followed by one announcement. The more important Sangha functions are of the first type and those of lesser weight, the second. At the end of the motion and before the conclusion of the announcements any bhikkhu in that Sangha who wishes to object has the chance to do so. If there is an objection—and this is very uncommon, then that legal act is broken and must be performed again to become valid. The motion is carried by silence, for example; at the end of the Acceptance of a new bhikkhu, these words are chanted:

> "If Acceptance is agreeable to the venerable ones of (name) with venerable (Preceptor's name) as preceptor, let them be silent. He to whom it is not agreeable should speak. The Acceptance has been given by the Sangha to (name) with venerable (Preceptor's name) as preceptor. It is agreeable to the Sangha, therefore it is silent. Thus do I remember it."

As a conclusion for this chapter, here is a short discourse of the Buddha explaining the advantages of the Vinaya. (Bracketed words are my explanations).

Thus have I heard. At one time the Exalted One was staying near Sāvatthī at the Jeta Grove, Anāthapiṇḍika's monastery. Then venerable Upāli approached the Exalted One, bowed down to him and then sat down nearby. Sitting there he asked the Exalted One, "Lord, what are the reasons why the rule of training was laid down for the disciples of the Tathāgata and the Pātimokkha appointed?"

For ten reasons, Upāli, the rule of training was laid down and the Pātimokkha appointed:

For the good establishment of the Sangha. *(Without Vinaya the Sangha could not last long).*

For the comfort of the Sangha. *(So that bhikkhus may have few obstacles and live peacefully).*

For the riddance of obstinate men. *(Who would cause trouble in the Sangha).*

For the happy abiding of well-behaved bhikkhus. *(Pure precepts make for happiness here and now).*

For guarding against troubles (*āsava*) in this present life. *(Since much trouble is avoided by one with good moral conduct).*

For guarding against troubles liable to arise in a future life. *(They may not arise for the well-practised person).*

For pleasing those not yet pleased. *(People who do not yet know Dhamma are pleased by a bhikkhu's good conduct).*

For the increase of those who are pleased. *(Those who know Dhamma already are pleased to see it practised).*

For the establishment of True Dhamma. *(The Dhamma lasts long when Vinaya is well practised by bhikkhus).*

For the benefit of Vinaya. *(So that Vinaya, the leading out, can benefit many beings out of dukkha, towards Nibbāna).*

These, Upāli, are the ten reasons why the rule of training was laid down and the Pātimokkha appointed for the disciples of the Tathāgata.

Thus spoke the Lord. Delighted, venerable Upāli rejoiced in the Exalted One's words.

(AN 10:31).

CHAPTER IV

THE SANGHA AND THE SPREAD OF BUDDHISM

Wandering bhikkhus and the rains—Residence—support of bhikkhus—merchants and kings—bhikkhus never "missionaries"—qualities for spreading Dhamma—the learned and the meditative—Reciters—lost discourses—reasons for the First Council—its work—the Baskets of Vinaya and Sutta analysed—the Abhidhamma—the minor rules—Pūraṇa and the variant traditions—Second Council and lax Vinaya—Schism created by the Great Assembly—their wrong views and corruption of their texts—Emperor Asoka and the Third Council—the attitude of one successful bhikkhu who spread Dhamma.

In the Buddha's time most bhikkhus wandered. For most of the year they travelled by themselves or in larger or smaller groups around a Teacher-monk (*Ācariya*). They might stop in a place they found suitable for their practice for a few months or intermittently even for years. In some cases people might invite them to stay and guarantee their alms food and other simple needs. These people would have huts and a meeting-hall erected, these small buildings being the beginnings of Buddhist monasteries. There are many stories in the Dhammapada Commentary[37], which picture such wandering bhikkhus and their friendly reception by villagers who were not always Buddhists.

During the rains, the monsoon from July to October, the Buddha laid down a rule that bhikkhus were to stay in one place and this period is now called the rains-residence. It is observed

37. See *Buddhist Legends* Vol. I p. 146f, and *Minor Readings and Illustrator"* p. 267f.

by all bhikkhus (sāmaṇeras as well) as a time for the intensification of meditation practice, or for greater efforts to study. Generally bhikkhus gather round well-known Teachers to be instructed and exhorted by them for these three lunar months. Lay people also have the chance to learn Dhamma at this time, perhaps becoming Buddhists if they had not already Gone for Refuge to the Triple Gem, while at the end of the rains some or all of the bhikkhus would move on.

Wandering is one way in which Dhamma was spread throughout India and beyond by bhikkhus. They do not have many possessions, unlike householders who must have a lot of things, so they can come and go easily. The Buddha compared the bhikkhu to a swan, a bird that is plain and unadorned but capable of flying very far and strongly. The layperson is compared to the peacock, beautiful but burdened by its beauty and therefore slow and unable to fly long distances. It is for this reason that Dhamma was spread far and wide mostly by bhikkhus. It is very rare to read of a layman or woman propagating the Dhamma in distant lands for usually they would have their families to look after. Of course, there have always been learned lay Buddhists, and those who have been able to practise meditation deeply, but they have rarely travelled far. Their influence was usually limited to their own towns or villages where they would be foremost among the supporters of the local Teacher-monks and leaders of the lay Buddhist community.

But the bhikkhus did not have the burden of family and possessions. They could come and go freely after their first five years. (After the Acceptance-ceremony a bhikkhu had to stay with a Teacher-monk for at least five years.) There were Teachers to go and learn with, holy shrines to revere, invitations of lay people to accept, new monasteries to establish—many reasons for travel. So the Dhamma spread in these ways. It was never a methodical effort at "conversion" because it is not the aim of Buddhism to convert everyone. Such an idea was not considered possible by the Buddha for he recognised that people have many and various opinions. Their views will never be one, however hard organisations, religious or political, try to coerce them into it.

Dhamma is for those who want to understand, who want to know why there is suffering (*dukkha*) in this world and all worlds and what can be done about it. For the Buddha's teaching was simply and directly just this, "*Dukkha* and its Cessation. If one is really interested in its cessation, or at least in lessening it, then the teachings of the Buddha based on the subtle cause-effect relations in the mind, will be very appealing. Belief and dogmas are not at all important—clear understanding is what is needed without a clutter of views and opinions. The Dhamma then "spreads" to those who are ready to investigate themselves fearlessly. It is like one candle held against another, the light of one causes light to come into existence on the other. Dhamma is present in the heart of every person but is more or less obscured by the defiling passions of greed, aversion and the views which arise upon them.

A bhikkhu should have no money. This means that if he travels in the present time it will be either on foot or with tickets bought by supporters. In the Buddha's time his travel had to be on foot and even down to the last century and the beginning of this one, in Thailand for instance, this was the case.

This meant that he had to be able to rely upon his bowl as the way of obtaining alms food. He could, of course, accept invitations from householders when they wanted to make merit but mostly he would maintain his body on the offerings which lay people were happy to make him. This method worked well enough in India. (Even today it is still possible for a bhikkhu to get alms food there). But it is not a method which would succeed very well once bhikkhus get out of the sphere of Indian culture. Among people who had no traditions of supporting wandering religious, a bhikkhu's alms bowl was likely to be as clean on his return from the alms round as when he set out! And there are other factors, which will affect the bhikkhu. Alms rounds are possible in reasonably warm climates but it would become rather difficult in England say, in midwinter! When you consider that a bhikkhu should go on alms round barefoot and with no covering on his head, it becomes obvious that in some seasons or weathers bhikkhus could not get their support in this way. Yet they have no money, nor can they cultivate their own food, nor cut or pick any vegetable or fruit, nor cook their own food, for the Buddha in the Vinaya has intentionally made them completely dependent upon lay supporters. (Sāmaṇeras or novices cannot possess money but they can do all the other things mentioned. Hence a bhikkhu may travel with a sāmaṇera who can help with food, or with a layman who can aid him with both money and food).

So a bhikkhu who ventures outside the Indian sub-continent needs some other arrangements for support. Unlike missionaries of other religions, he could not take along a fund of money to set himself up in a new place until he had gained supporters there. And, if he was going to travel into Central Asia, or to the lands of South-east Asia he would have to have an invitation.

Invitations in the early times of Buddhism came frequently from merchants. They usually travelled in great caravans, even of hundreds of carts or pack-animals or in fleets of ships, some of their journeys lasting longer than a year. If a merchant had faith in the Buddha's teachings, before he set out on his long and often perilous journey, he would go to his Teacher-monk and make offerings to all the bhikkhus in that monastery and no doubt request their blessings upon his venture. He would be happy too if he could find a monastery or two along his route where he could pay his respects to the Triple Gem—the Buddha, Dhamma, Sangha—and set out again, his confidence renewed.

It was likely, however, that he would reach towns so far distant that nobody there had ever heard of the Buddha, let alone have a Buddhist monastery. So, on his long homeward journey, he would not be able to hear the wise words of a good Teacher nor the sound of all the bhikkhus chanting the Buddha's discourses. And perhaps, while slowly making his way back, he would decide, along with other like-minded friends, to invite a Teacher monk and some bhikkhus to accompany them on their next journey and to establish them in a monastery which they would build and finance. When this was done, at first, support would come only from the fund provided by such merchants and administered by some local trading partners, but soon some of the people of that place would become interested and want to know what the bhikkhus taught. And so the Dhamma spread …

Sometimes too, invitations came from kings, for bhikkhus were bearers of the high Buddhist culture. Small outlying states and even great empires through their kings and nobles received the blessings of this culture founded upon the Buddha's teachings. Even where bhikkhus did not go at the invitation of the king, it was often the king and his court that became firm Buddhists before other people, as in Sri Lanka. This is because the Dhamma can be understood—at least intellectually best by those whose minds are developed through education.

Bhikkhus were never missionaries—nor are they now, in the sense that this word is used in Western religion. Wherever they have gone, either they would get support anyway as we have seen, or they have gone by invitation. An invitation means that one is welcome, that support is guaranteed and that the Dhamma will be listened to respectfully and probably practised well too. So a bhikkhu does not impose anything. He harms no one—as the Buddha says in the Dhammapada:

> As the bee to a flower goes
> and having gotten its nourishment
> harms neither colour nor scent,
> so in a village should the *muni* fare. (Dhp 49)

A *muni* is a wise man, one who is silent, as a bhikkhu is, when collecting alms food—no one comes to grief through the gentle conduct of the bhikkhu.

Bhikkhus who take the Dhamma with them to far countries are called Emissaries of Dhamma, in Pali language *dhammadūta*. The Buddha said that a bhikkhu is fit to be a

Dhammadūta when he has eight qualities:

1. He is one who has listened (to much Dhamma-Vinaya),
2. and leads others to listen (he is able to teach them),
3. he is learned (having reflected upon what he has heard),
4. and remembers (what he has learned),
5. he is one who understands (the letter and spirit of Dhamma-Vinaya),
8. and leads others to understand,
7. he is skilled in what is beneficial and not beneficial (for the practice of Dhamma),
8. and he does not make trouble (between bhikkhus or lay people). (AN 8:16)

Among the qualities listed above, a Dhammadūta bhikkhu should be one who has great learning, which in the Buddha-time did not mean from books as there were no religious books then and the art of writing was used only for business transactions and possibly for secular poetry. Such a bhikkhu learnt by heart from his Teacher a certain section of the Buddha's discourses.

We have a picture of such three young bhikkhus in venerable Soṇakuṭikaṇṇa who spent a night, at the Buddha's invitation, in the Buddha's *kuṭi* (hut). When they had meditated most of the night and the dawn gladdened the sky, the Buddha asked him to recite some Dhamma. He recited all the sixteen Octets[38], intoning them. When he had finished, the Blessed One approved, saying: Good, good, bhikkhu. You have learnt the sixteen Octets well; you know them and remember them well. You have a fine voice, incisive and without faults, which makes the meaning clear.'" (Ud 5.6)

Even before the First Council the discourses of the Buddha were classified for easy memorisation, but it seems that their general order was not as we have them now. The first method of classification was probably the Teacher's Ninefold

38. The Aṭṭhaka-Vagga (Chapter on the Eights) in Suttanipāta. See *Group of Discourses,* K.R. Norman, P.T.S. This passage is from *The Life of the Buddha,* translated by Ven. Ñāṇamoli, BPS.

Instruction, a list of different types of discourses often mentioned by the Buddha: Prose-discourse, Song, Exegesis, Verse, Inspired Utterance, Saying, Birth-story, Wonderful event, Question and Answer.

Young bhikkhus, then, would learn part of the Buddha-word by heart, usually specialising in one particular section so that they became experts on Dhamma (or Vinaya). This kind of bhikkhu had to recite some part of his learning every day in order to keep it fresh in his mind. And because chanting out loud during the day or night would disturb those bhikkhus who were developing their minds through meditation, senior bhikkhus, like venerable Dabba Mallaputta, who were in charge of allotting lodgings to newly arrived bhikkhus, were careful to segregate the different types of bhikkhus. "He allocated lodgings in the same place to bhikkhus who knew the Suttas, saying, "They will be able to chant over the Suttas to one another." He allocated lodgings in the same place to bhikkhus versed in the Vinaya rules, saying, "They will decide upon the Vinaya with one another." He allocated lodgings in the same place to the Dhamma-preaching bhikkhus, saying, "They will discuss the Dhamma with one another." He allocated lodgings in the same place to meditative bhikkhus, saying, "They will not disturb one another." He allocated lodgings in the same place to the bhikkhus who lived indulging in low talk and playing about, saying, "These revered ones will live according to their pleasure." (A nice touch, this last sentence!) (Basket of Discipline, Bhikkhu–Vibhaṅga, Saṅghādisesa VIII)

It seems that even from the time when the Buddha was still alive that some rivalry existed between the scholars and the meditators. Here is a discourse given by venerable Mahā-Cunda, a famous Arahant disciple.[39] (Words in brackets are commentarial.)

"Thus have I heard. Once the venerable Mahā-Cunda

39. Translated by venerable Nyanaponika Mahāthera in *Aṅguttara Nikāya, An Anthology, Part II*, Wheel 208–211, BPS.

lived at Sahajāti among the Ceti people and there he addressed the bhikkhus, saying:

"Venerable Sirs, there are bhikkhus who are keen on Dhamma (the preachers and those with an intellectual approach) and they disparage those bhikkhus who are meditators, saying, 'Look at those bhikkhus! They think, We are meditators, we are meditators! And so they meditate and meditate, meditating up and down, to and fro! What then do they meditate and why do they meditate?' Thereby neither these bhikkhus keen on Dhamma will be pleased nor the meditators. (By acting in that way) their life will not be conducive to the welfare and happiness of the people nor to the benefit of the multitude; it will not be for the welfare and happiness of gods and men.

Then, venerable sirs, there are meditative bhikkhus who disparage the bhikkhus who are keen on Dhamma, saying: 'Look at those bhikkhus! They think, We are Dhamma-experts, we are Dhamma-experts! And therefore they are conceited, puffed up and vain; they are talkative and voluble. They are devoid of mindfulness and thoughtful awareness, and they lack concentration; their thoughts wander and their senses are uncontrolled. What then makes them Dhamma-experts, why and how are they Dhamma-experts?' Thereby neither these meditating bhikkhus will be pleased nor those keen on Dhamma. By acting in that way ... it will not be for the welfare and happiness of gods and men.

There are Dhamma-experts who praise only bhikkhus who are also Dhamma-experts, but not those who are meditators ... And there are meditators who praise only those bhikkhus who are also meditators, but not those who are Dhamma experts. Acting thus ... it will not be for the welfare and happiness of gods and men.

Therefore, venerable sirs, you should train yourselves thus: 'Though we ourselves are Dhamma-experts we shall also praise those bhikkhus who meditate.' And why? Rare in the world are such outstanding men who have personal experience of the Deathless Element (Nibbāna).

And (the other bhikkhus too) should train themselves

thus: 'Though we ourselves are meditators we shall also praise those bhikkhus who are Dhamma experts.' And why? Rare in the world are such outstanding men who can by their wisdom clearly understand a difficult subject." (AN 6:46)

We shall have more to say about these two classes of Bhikkhus in Chapter V, and their ways of life in Chapter VI.

Bhikkhus who learnt the Buddha's discourses (or Vinaya) by heart were called *bhāṇakas* or reciters. They would usually be present when the Buddha spoke, committing his words to memory while he was speaking. If there were no reciter-bhikkhus present then the foremost among them, venerable Ānanda who was also the Buddha's attendant, would request the Buddha to repeat his teaching so that it could be preserved. The Buddha made the memorising of his discourses easier (though this may have been a general feature of teaching in the age before books), by repetition of key phrases and the harmonious grouping of words.

It may be partly for this reason that the Buddha often spoke in verse. The idea of a religious teacher speaking verse instead of prose is not familiar now in the West (though many of the Old Testament Prophets did so). But this is not strange because in his youth as a prince his education would have included poetics, the ability to compose extemporaneous verse being valued highly. No doubt there were other reasons too for speaking in verse: it could be more forceful than prose even acting as a shock or it could inspire deep faith. Besides this, much teaching could be compressed into a short discourse. A large number of such verse discourses have been preserved, the most important collection of which is the Suttanipāta (The Book of Discourses) in the Minor Collection.

To return now to the reciter-bhikkhus who later that day would meet and chant that teaching together so that variations due to individual memories could not obscure the Buddha's words. That discourse would then be added to one of the nine sections mentioned above. In this way the great collections of what are now called the Basket of Discipline and the Basket of Discourses in the Pali Canon, were built up through the forty-five years of the Buddha's teaching.

Some material has certainly been lost, or perhaps it would be more accurate to say that it was never recorded. We hear of discourses delivered by the Buddha, which have not come down to us. For instance, after the first discourse when venerable Aññā-Kondañña was already a bhikkhu and a Stream-winner, the text of the Vinaya relates, "Then the Blessed One taught and instructed the rest of the bhikkhus with talk on Dhamma." But we do not know what that talk consisted of, though it was probably an amplification of the headings in the First Discourse. Again, in the case of the venerable Yasa's mother and former wife, we read, "He gave them progressive instruction, that is to say, talk on giving, on virtue, on the heavens; he explained the dangers, the vanity and the defilement in sensual pleasures, and the advantages of renunciation. When he saw that the minds of Yasa's mother and former wife were ready, receptive, free of hindrance, eager and trustful, he expounded to them the teaching peculiar to the Buddhas: *Dukkha,* its causal arising, its cessation, the path to its cessation. (Vinaya Piṭaka Mahāvagga Ch. I) Although there are many discourses extant upon subjects like giving and the rest, we do not know the precise content of this talk which resulted in the two ladies becoming Stream-winners.

However, the reciter-bhikkhus were marvellously diligent for it is due to them that we have today the Discipline (Vinaya), and the Discourses (Sutta), which were divided, in the First Council, into the five Collections (*nikāya*).

This brings us to the time after the Buddha had passed away or as Buddhists say, after the Great Parinibbāna. Many bhikkhus were no doubt concerned that the Dhamma-Vinaya should last long. Some time before this, after the Jain teacher Nigaṇṭha Nātaputta (or Mahāvīra) had died, his disciples quarrelled over his teaching and different parties formed. It was to prevent this that venerable Sāriputta spoke, in the Buddha's presence, the Recital Discourse (Saṅgīti Sutta) in which important teachings are classified in groups from one to ten.

Already, just after the Parinibbāna, the bhikkhu Subhadda who had gone forth in his old age, said to the other bhikkhus:

"Enough friends, do not sorrow, do not lament. We are well rid of the Great Samaṇa (an epithet of the Buddha). We have been frustrated by his saying, "This is allowed to you; this is not allowed to you." But now we shall do as we like and we shall not do as we do not like." This was cause enough for venerable Mahā-Kassapa to say at a meeting of the Sangha: "Now friends, let us rehearse the Dhamma-Vinaya. Already wrong teachings and wrong discipline have been courted and right teachings and right discipline have been flouted. And already upholders of wrong teachings and wrong discipline are strong while upholders of right teachings and right discipline are weak." So it was agreed that a Sangha of five hundred Arahants should stay in Rājagaha for that rains-residence and systematically recite the Buddha's teachings.

The leader of the Sangha in this great assembly was venerable Mahā-Kassapa, possibly the most senior of the Buddha's disciples still alive, while the authority for the Vinaya, was venerable Upāli and that for Dhamma, venerable Ānanda. The account as we have it says that venerable Mahā-Kassapa asked questions about the rules of the Pātimokkha in the order we now have them and then about the Suttas, beginning with the Collection of Long Discourses, in the order we have them now. If nothing has been omitted from the account of this Council (which is very brief), then it must be surmised that the Vinaya was put in its final order during the days of the Buddha—likewise the Suttas were ordered into the five Collections then. This seems unlikely. As the account of the first Council suggests that this classification was complete it may rather be a retrospective view of what happened, perhaps added at the time of the Second Council, one hundred years later. Of course, this is surmise.

It is more probable that at this great assembly, the rules, allowances, prohibitions, and legal procedures were collected and the Vinaya codified. The old word-by-word Commentary would have been added, or at least received the approval of all the venerable Arahants and those portions of the Analysis (Vibhaṅga) which systematically clarify when a bhikkhu has committed an offence and when he has not, would probably have been settled and "incorporated" into the Vinaya. These parts may not be even as old as this but certainly they did not come from the mouth of the Buddha.

In the case of the Discourses, it is likely that they were previously arranged as the Teacher's Ninefold Instruction. This may not have proved a convenient classification and certainly would not have been as systematic as that of the Five Collections. The re-sorting of this great mass of material into these Collections may then have been the main work of this Council. It will certainly have been necessary as some of the Discourses were known only to a very few bhikkhus and lay people. Without any use of writing, this was a stupendous achievement.

The reciter-bhikkhus would not only have to chant the Discourses known to them at the Council, but then to re-order them in their memories in the sequence decided upon. It is difficult for us to imagine how this could have been accomplished. Perhaps the summaries of the different collections were written down at this time as a check and guide to their order. Some of the small books in the Minor Collection could well be the material memorised by particular groups of bhikkhus—such books as the Suttanipāta, Udāna and Itivuttaka. The Dhammapada[40], a collection of 423 verses spoken by the Buddha, might be the personal compilation of a great Arahant, which has been incorporated as it stands.

Here is a chart showing the classification of the Basket of Discipline and the Basket of Discourses as we have them now:

---

40. The most translated book of Buddhist scriptures. See *The Dhammapada*, translated by Acharya Buddharakkhitha, B.P.S.

VINAYA (DISCIPLINE) Vinaya-Piṭaka[a] – *Basket of Discipline*				
1. *Analysis of Bhikkhu's Rules (Bhikkhu-Vibhaṅga)*	2. *Analysis of Bhikkhunī's Rules (Bhikkhunī-Vibhaṅga)*	3. *The Great Chapter (Mahāvagga)*	4. *The Lesser Chapter (Cullavagga)*	5. *The Appendix (Parivāra)*
Divided into rules, their origins and analysis.		Divided into sections on different subjects, including one on Nuns (bhikkhunīs).		A summary and classification. The earliest parts may have been added at this council, or at the second one.

a. For a detailed account see *An Analysis of the Pali Canon*, by Russell Webb, Wheel 217/220, BPS.

DHAMMA (DOCTRINE) Sutta-Piṭaka[b] – *Basket of Discourses*				
Collection of Long Discourses (Dīgha-Nikāya)	**Collection of Middle-length Discourses** (Majjhima-Nikāya)	**Collection of Connected Discourses** (Saṃyutta-Nikāya)	**Collection of Numerical Discourses** (Aṅguttara-Nikāya)	**Minor Collection** (Khuddaka Nikāya)
34 Discourses	152 Discourses	Traditionally 7762 discourses divided into 56 related groups (Saṃyuttas) of subjects.	Traditionally 9557 discourses divided into 11 books (Nipātas) of The Ones, The Twos... The Elevens.	Divided into: 1. Minor Readings (Khuddaka Pāṭha) 2. Path of Truth (Dhammapada) 3. Inspired Utterances (Udāna) 4. Sayings (Itivuttaka) 5. Book of Discourses (Sutta Nipāta) 6. Stories of Heavenly Mansions (Vimānavatthu) 7. Stories of Ghosts (Petavatthu) 8. Verses of the Elder Monks (Theragāthā) 9. Verses of the Elder Nuns (Therīgāthā) 10. Birth Stories (Jātaka) 11. Analytic Explanation (Niddesa) 12. The Path of Discrimination (Paṭisambhidāmagga) 13. Legends (Apadāna) 14. Lineage of the Buddhas (Buddhavaṃsa) 15. The Basket of Good Conduct (Cariyāpiṭaka)
Translated as *Dialogues of the Buddha*, 3 Vols. and *Long Discourses of the Buddha* , 1 Vol.	Translated as *Middle Length Sayings*, 3 Vols, and *Middle Length Discourses*, 1 Vol.	Translated as *Kindred Sayings*, 5 Vols.	Translated as *Gradual Sayings*, 5 Vols, and *Connected Discourses of the Buddha*, 2 vols.	

b. All available from the Pali Text Society, except volumes marked with double asterisk.

According to the traditional Commentaries to the Buddha-word, which were written down in Pali about the year one thousand of the Buddhist Era, though of much earlier origin, another collection called Abhidhamma, a philosophical and psychological treatment of Dhamma, was also classified at this Council. But though this is claimed by the Commentaries, the record of the Council in the Vinaya mentions only the Dhamma and the Vinaya as having been the subject of deliberation. Even the seven Abhidhamma books themselves make no mention of their origin, only the Commentaries inform us that the Buddha had spoken them. This is a controversial matter and cannot now be decided one way or the other. It has become a tradition to speak of the Tipiṭaka, the Three Baskets including the Abhidhamma as the third part of the Buddha-word. It is these Three Baskets which are often called the Pali Canon in the West.

When the business of recitation and classification had been concluded, venerable Ānanda said that the Buddha before his Parinibbāna had allowed the abolishment of the minor and lesser rules. But he had not been mindful enough to ask which these rules were. Then the assembly expressed various opinions on this matter at which venerable Mahā-Kassapa spoke these words: Let the Sangha hear me, friend; there are certain of our training rules that involve laymen, by which laymen know what is allowed to bhikkhus who are sons of the Sakyans and what is not. If we abolish these minor and lesser rules, there will be those who say, The Training Rule proclaimed by the Samaṇa Gotama to his disciples existed only for the period ending with his cremation: they kept his training rules as long as he was present; but now that he has finally attained Nibbāna they have given up keeping his training rules. If it seems proper to the Sangha, let not what is undeclared be declared, and let not what is declared be abolished; let the Sangha proceed according to the training rules as they have been declared.[41] This motion was

41. In this last sentence venerable Mahā-Kassapa is quoting the Buddha, see Appendix 1, "Seven conditions for the non-decline of bhikkhus." (Vinaya Pit. Cv. Kh II).

accepted by the Council and is still the ruling in Theravāda countries, being the reason why the Sangha in those lands has changed least in its form and still preserves the original teachings and practices of the Buddha.

Due to the wisdom of the Arahants in that Council and to the diligence of successive generations of bhikkhus the Dhamma has been transmitted to us today. But for their great efforts there would be no teachings of the Buddha remaining, for who could have or who would have preserved them? Only the Sangha had the freedom and time to pass on this great body of teaching. Out of gratitude to them many passages and lines in Buddhist devotion are respectfully chanted, such I revere that Noble group who are perfectly purified.

Only five hundred Arahants attended the Council but there were at that time tens of thousands of bhikkhus, some of them also with great followings. We have a picture of one of these Teacher-monks in a little incident recorded at the end of the account of this Council. Venerable Purāṇa came to the Council-elders when they had finished. He was asked, "Friend Purāṇa, the Dhamma-Vinaya has been rehearsed by the elders. Do you support that rehearsal?" His rather cryptic reply was, "Friends, the Dhamma-Vinaya has been well rehearsed by the elders. I, however, shall remember it as I heard it from the Blessed One's own lips."

Here is the beginning of the many slightly differing Buddhist traditions which were later found in India. The Buddha had already allowed bhikkhus to learn his teaching in their own dialects,[42] a fact which could easily make for varying traditions in course of time; no doubt with the slow communications of those days, with the Sangha spread far and wide, this tendency would be increased. But variation in the texts (the original meaning of the word Pāli) established by that First Council would be more difficult since large numbers of Teacher-monks, some of them Noble Ones, knew them by heart.

---

42. See *Concept and Reality*, Bhikkhu Ñāṇananda, BPS, pp. 41–45.

There follows a period of one hundred years about which we have very little information. We have to picture bhikkhus steadily spreading out from the Middle Country into the surrounding areas. Already in the days of the Buddha we find venerable Mahā-Kaccāna in North central India, in the area where the famous stupas of Sāñchī are found. But he had difficulty to assemble ten bhikkhus there for an Acceptance ceremony and only managed it after three years. There is also the story of venerable Puṇṇa, who went on the long journey to Sunāparanta and who was such a successful Dhammadūta, which will be told at the end of this chapter. The Buddha himself taught as far West as the country of the Kurus which was around New Delhi, while he had at least one pupil, Bāhiya Dāruciriya, who heard about him as far away as Bombay. So even in the Buddha's time bhikkhus were travelling far afield.

The Second Council was held one hundred years after the first. It is known as the "Council of the Seven Hundred" since that number of Arahants participated. The reason for calling the Council was the wrong Vinaya practices of the Vajji bhikkhus of Vesālī. They had started to practise Vinaya in ways which would be comfortable for themselves and the stricter bhikkhus saw that this could easily lead the Sangha into decline. What things did they do? The most important things are as follows. They ate after noon. The Buddha laid down that the bhikkhu's food must be finished by midday. So long as the shadow cast by the sun was not past the meridian by more than two finger-breadths. A bhikkhu can eat more than once in the period from dawn to that time but he must have finished his food, when the shadow cast by the sun is shortest. Without such a rule and with the strength of attachment that people often have to food, some bhikkhus would have taken afternoon tea, dinner and supper too! So this lengthening of the mealtime was a danger—and showed lack of restraint and contentment.

The Vajjian bhikkhus said that in large monasteries it was allowable for different groups of bhikkhus to do the Uposatha ceremony—which is confession of offences followed by the recitation of the 227 rules of the Pātimokkha—separately and in different places. This ceremony, which is held on each Full Moon and New Moon day, the Buddha said must be attended by all the bhikkhus in a monastery. To do as the Vajjians did, would only encourage the formation of parties and sectarian differences.

The Vajjians also allowed official acts of the Sangha to be carried out in the absence of some bhikkhus who resided within the boundary of the monastery, expecting that they would agree afterwards. This is also a dangerous practice probably leading to contentions. The Buddha had laid down that bhikkhus who could not be present, for instance, at the Uposatha or an Acceptance-ceremony, could send their consent by way of another bhikkhu.

Again, the Vajjian bhikkhus stated that one could do things, proper or improper, taking one's Teacher as one's example. The Buddha never agreed to "blindly following a guru"—which is typically an Indian trait; he told people to question even his own actions to see whether the influence of greed, aversion and delusion could be seen in them. One's Teacher should be followed therefore when he practises according to Dhamma, but if he does things contrary to Dhamma then, respectfully, he could be advised what he should better do. The last of such Vajjian bhikkhus' practices was to a similar position with regards sense-pleasures as a lay person. He will be able, apparently, "to buy happiness." By making it an offence for a bhikkhu to possess or handle money, the Buddha pointed to the real source of happiness, a mind purified through meditation: not one scattered through indulgence in sensual pleasures. These are some of the Vajjians' ten wrong practices.

The Council met and condemned them all, showing that they were offences under various headings in the Vinaya. Also, the Dhamma and Vinaya were rehearsed again and a few late discourses, given by different bhikkhus after the Great Parinibbāna, must have been added on this occasion. Possibly small books in the Minor Collection like the Lineage of the

Buddhas (*Buddhavaṃsa*) and the Collection of Ways of Practice (*Cariyāpiṭaka*) were also added at this time. And two non-canonical works[43] which are manuals to guide one in composing commentaries perhaps come from this period. These books contain quotations of the Buddha-word which cannot now be traced in the Pāli Canon. Here, it seems, some discourses have been lost but where and how we shall probably never know.

A great assembly of bhikkhus must have been attracted to the town of Vesālī by the presence of so many Arahants in solemn assembly. Among them the decisions of these enlightened senior bhikkhus did not go unchallenged. We read in the Chronicles of Sri Lanka that the Vajjian bhikkhus and their supporters, out of their conceit, did not accept the decisions of the Arahants and decided to hold their own meeting, the Great Assembly, calling themselves the Great Assemblists (Mahāsaṅghikas). By doing so they became guilty of causing the first great schism in the Sangha. To cause schism is not only to burden oneself with a serious offence (see under the thirteen offences entailing initial and subsequent meeting of the Sangha, in Chapter III) but also is among the heaviest kinds of evil kamma that can be made.[44] The immediate result of splitting the Sangha is to be born without fail in one's next life in hell.

And in an effort to besmirch the purity of the Arahants and the original tradition they represented, the rebel party's account of the Proceedings (not in Pāli) omitted all mention of their deficiencies in Vinaya but discussed instead some supposed deficiencies in the Arahants!

The Chronicle of the Island (of Sri Lanka, the *Dīpavaṃsa*) says this about them: "The bhikkhus of the Great Assembly

---

43. For these works, all P.T.S. publications, see *Chronicle of the Buddhas* and *Basket of Conduct*, 1975; *The Guide* (*Nettippakaraṇa*), 1962; *Piṭaka-disclosure* (*Peṭakopadesa*), 1964.

44. Five kinds of kamma with immediate fruit: Killing one's mother, killing one's father, killing an Arahant, wounding a Buddha, causing schism in the Sangha.

made a reversed teaching. They broke up the original collection (of the Buddha-word) and made another collection. They put the Sutta collected in one place elsewhere. They broke up the sense and the doctrine in the Five Collections."

Scholars considering the evidence found in early Mahāsaṅghika texts are now aware that it is from the party of the Great Assembly (Mahāsaṅghika) that Mahāyāna, the Great Vehicle, grew up. This matter however, belongs to the history of Buddhist thought, so we must leave it here. It remains only to say that the schismatics, (as so often seen in other religions), were themselves rent by even more schisms until Buddhist authors could talk of the eighteen schools of the disciples (*sāvaka*).

The doctrinal differences in many cases were not very great as can be seen from the Book of Discussions (Kathāvatthu)[45] in the Theravāda Abhidhamma. It is unlikely that these many minor points, or the minor variants in discipline among the different schools will have made much impact upon lay people. Most of these matters will have been of interest only to the more scholastic bhikkhus. One suspects that many bhikkhus with more practical interests will have taken little or no part in these polemics, the sort of wrangling of which the Buddha had never approved. He had condemned the holding of views and opinions which are only another extension of the ego, but this is exactly what many later generations of Indian Buddhists did. Much of it is politely called Buddhist Philosophy these days. This only made for weakness when the Dhamma was eventually confronted with the new strength of the brahmins and, later, the violence of marauding Muslims.

When one hears of Buddhist sects, such sectarianism was confined to bhikkhus and lay people generally being supporters of any good Teacher-bhikkhu, whatever his sect. And even amongst these bhikkhus, in spite of the differences, there was undoubtedly much contact and friendship between them for, whatever their orientation, Buddhists rarely lost

---

45. Translated as *Points of Controversy*, P. T.S. London.

sight of the Buddha's teaching on the importance of loving-kindness.

The bhikkhus in groups headed by the original teaching, later called Theravāda, the Doctrine of the Elders, continued to spread the Dhamma from the time of the Second until the Third Council.

This took place in the reign of the great Buddhist Emperor Asoka (reigned 325–288 B.C.). By this time it seems that differences in the Sangha were irreconcilable, for the Third Council consisted of bhikkhus only from Theravāda. The position was that the Theravāda Sangha had become famous for its purity of teaching and practice and, therefore, had many wealthy patrons. The monasteries they erected were splendid in construction and the comforts which bhikkhus could enjoy, still without breaking the Vinaya, were ample. With good robes, food, shelter and medicine provided by devoted followers, it is not surprising that some wrong sorts of people were attracted and many became bhikkhus. Once they were in robes some of them began to display and propagate their wrong views so that eventually there was once again such disharmony in the Sangha that it was no longer possible to hold the Uposatha ceremony.

This went on for several years until venerable Moggaliputta Tissa, an Arahant, came to the notice of the Emperor Asoka. He asked the venerable Arahant what should be done about the discord and was told that if a meeting of the Sangha was held then a purification of its members could be instituted. He told the Emperor to enquire from each bhikkhu what philosophical method the Buddha had practised and upheld. Any who stated that he was an eternalist (believing in an eternal soul) or an annihilationist (declaring that death is followed by nothing) or other such positions, were to be politely but firmly handed a pair of white cloths with the invitation to disrobe themselves. Only those bhikkhus who said that the Buddha was an analyst, a proclaimer of an analytical way (*vibhajjavādi*), were to continue as bhikkhus. We do not know how this sorting out of the bhikkhus was organized but the Great Chronicle (of Sri Lanka, the *Mahāvaṃsa*) tells us that large numbers of bhikkhus were disrobed. Presumably this refers only to people masquerading as Theravāda bhikkhus, but maybe this purification of the Sangha also affected some of the other schools which would also have agreed that the Buddha was a Vibhajjavādin.

When the Sangha was again in harmony, the Uposatha ceremony was held and the Dhamma-Vinaya rehearsed as it had been in the two previous councils. In this council certainly the Abhidhamma piṭaka was completed since venerable Moggaliputta Tissa added to it the Kathāvatthu or Book of Discussions already mentioned.

Emperor Asoka was not yet satisfied that he had done as much as he could do to support the Buddha-Dhamma, so he requested that a number of groups of bhikkhus be sent in different directions both inside and outside his frontiers. He would see that they had adequate support and protection while they should teach Dhamma to all the peoples in his empire and to the various nations on his frontiers and beyond. The Emperor states in his edicts engraved on stone that such parties proceeded to the furthest points of the Mauryan state and beyond to Sri Lanka in the south, to the Golden Land in the east (perhaps Burma or peninsular Thailand), to the Indo-Greek kingdoms on his northwest frontier and also to the Hellenized lands of the far west—Syria, Egypt, North Africa, Epirus and Macedonia. Regarding this latter expedition, the first Buddhist mission to the West, we do not know how it fared so far away from India though Christian writers have recorded the presence in Alexandria (Egypt) of bhikkhus before the Christianization programme that followed Constantine.

The group sent to Sri Lanka was very successful, for the mission was headed by the Emperor's son, the Arahant Mahinda who was able to teach and lead to the Three Refuges the Sinhalese monarch Devānampiyatissa. Thereafter, Sri Lanka was the island of Dhamma (Dhammadīpa) and the fortress in which the original teachings of the Buddha were preserved under the name Theravāda or Doctrine of the Elders. This was forgotten in large parts of India where speculation, metaphysics and logic combined with a taste for mystical experiences which were not properly understood, provided the basis for all sorts of Buddhist schools. As time went on these departed further and further from the Buddha's genuine teachings.

We are not sure what happened to the group sent to the Golden Land or exactly where it was they went to. No Buddhist remains from the period of the Emperor Asoka have yet been found in either Burma or Thailand (as far as the writer is aware), but this does not mean that they do not exist: The Buddhist custom of continually rebuilding monasteries and temples on same site means that the later buildings would obscure the former, so Asokan remains may yet be found. In Burma of course, the revered Shwe Dagon pagoda in Rangoon is held to go back even beyond Asokan days—to the Buddha-time—when the merchants Tapussa and Bhallika, the first people to give food to the Buddha after his Enlightenment and the first Buddhists, received from him some hair from his head which they enshrined in their own country. This history, like that of the Buddha's three visits to Sri Lanka, still needs to be confirmed.

However, the general result of the Emperor's efforts to stimulate Dhammadūta work cannot be doubted. His royal support must have been of great value and given many the chance to hear Dhamma who otherwise would not have known of it. But it goes too far to state, as some authors have done, that it was due to the Emperor that Buddhism began to spread, as though it had not been spread before by bhikkhus! The Dhamma would have spread anyway due to its universal appeal: it did not have to wait for an emperor before it could spread! But the fact that so powerful a king advocated the Dhamma would have lent it prestige in the eyes of other kings and princes.

We have mentioned already some examples of Dhammadūta work from the days of the Buddha. Here, as a conclusion to this chapter, is the story of one bhikkhu from the Buddha-time:

"Thus have I heard: At one time the Exalted One was staying near Sāvatthī at the Jeta Grove, Anāthapiṇḍika's monastery. Then venerable Puṇṇa, emerging from solitary meditation towards evening, approached the Lord, bowed down to him and sat down nearby. Sitting there, he spoke thus to the Lord: "It would be good, revered sir, if the Lord would exhort me briefly so that having heard Dhamma from the Lord, I might live alone, remote, diligent, ardent and aspiring."

"Puṇṇa, there are forms cognizable by the eye, sounds cognizable by the ear, smells cognizable by the nose, tastes cognizable by the tongue, touches cognizable by the body, mental factors cognizable by the mind, all of which are agreeable, pleasant, enticing, connected with sense-pleasures, alluring. If a bhikkhu delights in them, welcomes them and persists in clinging to them, then because of this, attachment arises in him. From the arising of attachment, there is the arising of dukkha, thus I declare, Puṇṇa. But if a bhikkhu does not delight in them, does not welcome them, does not persist in clinging to them, then, because of this, attachment ceases in him. From the cessation of attachment, there is the cessation of dukkha, thus I declare, Puṇṇa.

And in what district will you stay now that you have been briefly exhorted by me?"

"There is a district called Sunāparanta—I shall stay there, Lord".

"The people of Sunāparanta are fierce and rough, Puṇṇa. If they revile and abuse you, how will it be for you there?"

"If they revile and abuse me, revered sir, it will be like this for me there—(I shall think) "Good indeed are the people of Sunāparanta, very good are the Sunāparanta people, in that they do not give me blows with their hands." In this case, Lord, it will be like this for me, like this, Welfarer."

"But if they do give you blows with their hands, how will it be with you there?"

"If they give me blows with their hands, ... (I shall think),

'Good indeed are the people of Sunāparanta in that they do not give me blows with clods of earth.'"

"But if they do give you blows with clods of earth, ...? "

"If they give me blows with clods of earth, ... I shall think, 'Good indeed are the people of Sunāparanta in that they do not strike me with a stick.'"

"But if they do strike you with a stick, ...?"

"If they strike me with a stick, ... I shall think, 'Good indeed are the people of Sunāparanta in that they do not stab me with a dagger,'"

"But if they do stab you with a dagger, …?"

"If they stab me with a dagger, ... I shall think, 'Good indeed are the people of Sunāparanta in that they do not deprive me of life with a sharp dagger.'"

"But if they do deprive you of life with a sharp dagger, …?"

"If they stab me with a sharp dagger and deprive me of life, … I shall think, 'There are disciples of the Lord who when tormented by and disgusted with the body (as when severely diseased) look around for a weapon (to take their own lives). I have come upon this dagger without looking round for it.' In this case, Lord, it will be like this for me, like this, Welfarer."

"Good, Puṇṇa, it is good! You will be able to live in the Sunāparanta district since you have much calm and tranquillity. 'Now you should do whatever you think is proper to do.'"

Then venerable Puṇṇa, gladdened by and rejoicing in the Exalted One's words, rising from his seat; bowed down to the Lord, circumambulated him keeping him on the right, set in order his lodging and taking his bowl and robes, set off on his journey to Sunāparanta. Journeying by stages, he gradually approached Sunāparanta. While he was there, venerable Puṇṇa stayed in that district among the people and during the rains he brought into (the Dhamma) about five hundred laymen and five hundred lay-women. During the rains, also, he realized the Three Knowledges. After a time, venerable Puṇṇa attained Final Nibbāna.

When this had happened, many bhikkhus approached the Lord; bowed down and sat down nearby. Sitting there they spoke this to the Lord: "Revered Sir, that young man of excellent family who was briefly exhorted by the Lord, has died. What is his bourn, what is his future state?"

"Puṇṇa was wise, bhikkhus. He followed the Dhamma according to Dhamma. He did not harass me with (senseless) queries on Dhamma. Puṇṇa has attained Final Nibbāna."

Thus spoke the Lord. Delighted, those bhikkhus rejoiced in the Exalted One's words."

(MN 45: The Exhortation to Puṇṇa)

Chapter V

The Sangha Now in Buddhist Countries

Brief history of Theravāda—anonymity of Great Teachers—specialisation of bhikkhus—"the works of books" and practice—popular Buddhism—ordination for custom or merit—rains-bhikkhus—disrobing—ritualism—why do people go to vihāras?—why go to see bhikkhus?—why bhikkhus go to the houses of laypeople—wrong livelihood—the government of the Sangha—divisions in the Sangha—in Sri Lanka, Burma, Thailand and other countries—buildings in a town vihāra—in a forest vihāra—some popular devotional verses.

Theravāda Buddhism gradually dwindled in northern India with the onslaught of anti-Buddhist activities by many brahmins intent on upholding the views and rituals of their religion. Other Buddhist schools also displaced the original tradition perhaps because they believed in sugaring the slightly bitter pill of the Four Noble Truths with sweet confections of bhaktic devotion, or else serving up complicated dishes of the Bodhisatta's path through aeons of striving. Had the Sāsana remained entire with numerous Arahants to adorn it, like jewels in a golden crown, there is no way that it could have declined.

In South India, Theravāda remained strong for many hundreds of years[46] aided by its firm establishment in Sri Lanka. From these two bases bhikkhus were invited to go to the Golden Land to reform the Buddhism, which had taken root there. This was not always Theravāda and the purity and good conduct of the bhikkhus from Sri Lanka caused people to love them so that various sects, corrupting the Buddha-word, dwindled away. Theravāda spread through Burma due to the

46. See, *Buddhism in South India*, Wheel 124–125, BPS.

influence of those bhikkhus and across into the Siamese kingdoms of Sukhotai and Ayudhya. Sinhalese-style Buddhism also spread up the Isthmus of Kra from Nakorn Sri Dhammaraj where there is still a great stupa in Sinhalese form. From Siam it reached Cambodia at the time when the Khmer Empire was going into decline and so replaced the costly cults of imperially sponsored Mahāyāna with a popularly based teaching. Theravāda in Laos, or the various princely states which now compose Laos, also originated in Siam but its spread was late, about 400 years ago. Thais, even those now within China, turned to Theravāda Buddhism which continues its spread in a small way within the borders of the present Buddhist states wherever there are hill-tribes or other ethnic minorities.

In brief this is the history of Theravāda Buddhism from the time of the Emperor Asoka down to the present. To some extent also, this was the history of the Sangha though in some periods and some countries our knowledge is meagre. We have the names of a few prominent bhikkhu-scholars and their Pali compositions but little or nothing of their lives. As to the other side of Theravāda, that is, the Teachers of meditation and how and where they taught: usually we do not even have their names. The latter wrote books only rarely and so their fame was limited to their own days, to the times of their disciples and then gradually forgotten.

This of course, was in the great tradition of anonymity established by the Buddha himself. He did not instruct his Arahant disciples to record his own life, the early events of which he seldom mentioned, let alone write an account of it himself. The Arahants in the Buddha-time and later also did not set down their own biographies. If we know anything about them it is because their own disciples, or the disciples of their disciples, thought it worthwhile to record the few events remaining in their minds. No doubt those who are Enlightened and so have no longer any view of self or soul find it uninteresting to record events from their own lives. It is for this reason that in the Buddhist countries of South and South-east

Asia, few names are known of the great spiritual masters of even two or three hundred years ago. This anonymity has also been rendered more absolute by the steady turn of the wheel of change, including such factors as tropical climates and insects and, of course, war.

So now we come to the present time. We should examine one important question: Is the purpose of becoming a bhikkhu now the same as it was in the Buddha's days? We have seen in Chapter IV that, even then, there was specialisation in the Sangha. Some made strong renunciation efforts in the forests by themselves or with a Teacher or a few companions. They aimed at and often attained the end of the Holy Life. They were Arahants of whom it was often said, "Birth is exhausted, the Holy Life has been lived out, what was to be done is done, there is no more of this to come." They numbered thousands and thousands in the days of the Buddha but the numbers of bhikkhus who were not Arahants and whose aim was not directly Arahantship, was greater yet. Their aims were various, some of them approved for bhikkhus and some not.

Among those whose aims accorded with the Dhamma were the reciter-bhikkhus, though sometimes too they would take up meditation practice when their learning was complete and they had passed it on to others. These reciters were the ancestors of the bhikkhus engaged in scriptural study who are so numerous in Buddhist countries now. The pattern of development went something like this: In the Commentaries, the Sāsana, the Buddha's whole range of teachings, his instructions or religion, was divided into the Dhamma of thorough learning (*pariyatti*), the Dhamma of practice (*paṭipatti*) and the Dhamma of penetration (*paṭivedha*). These three are logically parts of a whole process. One goes to a Teacher and learns thoroughly, which means both learning by heart and reflection upon his teachings. Then one begins to practise according to those instructions, with the words and thoughts being turned to the Dhamma and then disappearing in meditation, until finally the Truth of Dhamma is penetrated in this very mind and body. For example, a Teacher would give a talk on impermanence, which his disciples would remember, more or less, according to their memories. Then they practised meditation in which change in mind and body is seen to be continuous. Finally some of them were liberated by persistent meditation from the view I am and the notions of permanence, which trail along with it; they then flowed along with impermanence knowing it all the time, without any fear. These three stages are one explanation of why the Buddha's teachings are said to be "good in the beginning, good in the middle and good at the end."

Some bhikkhus quite early on must have found learning more to their liking than intensive practice, which still means that they could be good bhikkhus imbued with loving kindness and keeping strictly to the Vinaya. Other bhikkhus, however, found a meditation Teacher quickly after their Acceptance, and practised under his guidance caring little or nothing for the study of texts. In the Commentaries these two types have crystallised as "the work of books" and "the work of insight" and are regarded there, as down to the present day in Buddhist countries, as quite distinct. They are even attributed in the Commentaries to the days of the Buddha, a strange anachronism since there were then no books to study!

Thorough learning of oral texts eventually developed into "the work of books" because of the Sangha's decision at the Fourth Council (in Ceylon, about 85 BC)[47] to write down the Three Baskets, the Vinaya, Sutta and Abhidhamma, on palm leaves rather than rely solely on continuing the oral repetition of them. When they had been written down then other works explaining them could also be written and thus began the production of Commentaries, sub-commentaries and works of all kinds, which continue to be produced in the Pali language down to our own days.

---

47. The Fifth Council was held in Burma in the reign of King Mindon-min, C.E. 1871, when the text of the Tipiṭaka was inscribed upon 729 marble slabs to be seen in Mandalay. The Sixth Great Council was international and held in Burma to mark the 2500th year of the Buddhist Era (1956).

Another cause for the increased importance of books was that in moving the centre of Theravāda from the Gangetic valley to Sri Lanka, the language of Pali had to be used. In its home it was the people's language, perhaps a lingua franca over a wide area, but it was not intelligible without Pali study to people in Sri Lanka. So Pali became a "dead" language, a unique one since it has only the Buddha's words enshrined in it, with the advantage over a living tongue of not changing in words or concepts, so that the exact meaning of the Buddha can be ascertained by anyone who learns Pali well.

Also, during the early centuries of Buddhism in Sri Lanka, the Sinhalese bhikkhus decided that study was more important than meditation practice (an attitude which persists down to the present in Sri Lanka[48]). This attitude is stressed in some places in the Pali Commentaries but runs counter to the Buddha's own teachings: He did not arrive at Enlightenment by studying texts; only by practice, especially of meditation, did he reach the final attainment. In the Suttas, no encouragement is given to study divorced from practice. To give an example, we have the Buddha's words in Dhammapada, (verses 19–20 quoted below) spoken about two bhikkhus, one of whom became a scholar and famous teacher of texts with many pupils. The other got a subject of meditation and retired to the forest, after strenuous efforts attaining Arahantship. They met after a number of years and the teacher of texts, proud of his learning, decided to tax the Arahant with his lack of scriptural knowledge. The Buddha seeing how much harm the scholar would bring on himself by doing so went and questioned both of them on Dhamma. The scholar could explain only according to the texts and only some way but the Arahant could clarify subtle points of Dhamma dealing with attainment. These were the Buddha's words on that occasion:

48. See, *The Heritage of the Bhikkhu*, Walpola Rāhula, pp. 26–27.

Though often reciting sacred texts
the heedless man's no practicer,
as cowherd counting others' kine—
in Samaṇaship he has no share.

Though little reciting sacred texts
according to Dhamma he practises,
rid of delusion, lust and hate,
in wisdom perfect, a heart well-freed,
one who clings not here or hereafter—
in Samaṇaship he has a share.

Even though those bhikkhus in the Fourth Council, most of whom are likely to have been from among the reciters, laid more stress on learning, the tradition of practice continued. Doubtless the Teachers of meditation, who may have been Noble Ones, even Arahants, smiled to themselves, but it should also be remembered that, Even if there would be a hundred or a thousand bhikkhus arousing themselves to insight, if there would be no study of the doctrine, then there could be no realisation of the Noble Path[49]. The practising bhikkhus were little esteemed by those who wrote the books in Sri Lanka, but wise lay disciples will have looked at it differently.

The help that lay people can get from a scholar and from one on the path to Enlightenment by practice, is different. The first gives the Buddha's words and the commentarial explanations and perhaps some illustrations of his own but the meditation Teacher though he rarely quotes the Buddha and hardly ever the Commentaries yet offers advice from his own experiences. There is no question at all as to who keeps the Buddhasāsana alive: it is those who have realised its truth through practice and penetration. Great Enlightened Teachers of the present day emphasise that one should come back to study after one has done this, when the Buddha's words will have such profundity, as they could not have to the unenlightened, and be such a great

---

49. Ibid, pp. 26–27 quoting Aṅguttara Commentary.

help to formulating Dhamma and teaching it. The venerable Ānanda when asked why the Buddha's teachings would decline,[50] replied that it was when people no longer practised the four foundations of mindfulness.[51] And these are the key to successful meditation.

Fortunately, there are still a good number of bhikkhus who engage in effort, mindfulness and meditation, in all Buddhist countries, especially Burma and Thailand. Certainly the proportion of bhikkhus engaging in practice is much smaller now than was the case in the Buddha-time, while those who study are numerous.

Another factor which has affected this change, is the popularisation of Buddhism. In Thailand, over 90% of the people are Buddhists. But this does not mean, as some idealists imagine, that they all practise meditation every day (and how different things would be then!). For many people Buddhism is a vital part of their lives but it consists of their own Buddhist cultural mixture: This will be composed of Buddhist festivals, occasions of making merit in their own homes and at the monasteries having their sons ordained as novices or bhikkhus, and consulting bhikkhus they know well on how to protect themselves against various dangers, also enquiring about what is likely to happen through astrology. Among these things, only making merit (by supporting the Sangha) and ordinations go back to the Buddha's time. Other features have been added later, as people desired them.

The Sangha is composed of the people and some remain monks for life, but others stay in the Sangha for periods ranging from days to many years and then leave to become householders again whenever they wish to do so. They bring with them superstitions from lay society, which may be dispelled by their bhikkhu practice, but may not be. This situation could be illustrated by picturing the most highly

---

50. See *The Splendour of Enlightenment*, Ch. XVI, Mahamakut Press.
51. See *The Heart of Buddhist Meditation*, Ven, Nyanaponika Thera, Rider and Co., London, p. 141 (SN 47:22–23).

dedicated (always few in number) in the innermost of several concentric circles, while around them in ever increasing numbers, as one moves outwards, are the other classes of people. Where this is the case—and all human beings have the same basic characteristics—study is bound to appeal to a greater number, meditation to fewer.

Again, in Buddhist countries now, becoming a novice or a bhikkhu may be for yet other reasons, such as custom and merit making for people who have died. It is a custom in Thailand, Laos, Cambodia and Burma for a young man to become a bhikkhu for one rains residence. Sometimes it is done for less than this but occasionally the "rains bhikkhus," as they are called in Thailand, stay on in the Sangha because they find the life to their liking. This custom has both good and bad effects on the Sangha. The good effects are that Buddhist knowledge and conduct are carried back into lay society when the rains-bhikkhu disrobes. Also, there is little feeling of strangeness about the Sangha among laymen, for they have been in the Sangha themselves. On the negative side is the worldly influence brought by the rains-bhikkhus into the monasteries, a worldliness that if there are many of them, easily rubs off onto the more permanent inhabitants. Also, much time and energy must be expended on these temporary monks, which could otherwise go into deeper learning or into more practice.

It is a custom to make merit for a dead relative or for some other loved and respected person (such as the king) by becoming a bhikkhu for a few weeks or months and dedicating all one's good kammas or merits to the dead person. One might indeed help them provided that something good is practised but this custom too can be debased when the ordination alone, just dressing as a bhikkhu, is considered to be sufficient.

All this has changed considerably the attitude to disrobing, that is, to reverting to lay status. In the Buddha's days most bhikkhus ordained for life and could live happily all their days in robes because they practised the work of insight-meditation.

(Even now, in Sri Lanka it is common for bhikkhus to remain all their lives in the Sangha but as most of them are engaged in study the result is not always so happy). Lay life was called by the Buddha the low state and often he spoke strongly about not reverting to the low state. Certainly he allowed disrobing by bhikkhus knowing that some would find the Holy Life impossible after some time but he exhorted those like venerable Nanda[52] who thought of doing so to practise more intensively instead. In most Theravāda countries now, excluding Sri Lanka, disrobing carries no blame, indeed in Thailand the young man who has been a rains-bhikkhu and returned to his home is still called, in the countryside, *dit*, an abbreviation for *paṇḍita,* a wise man.

With the increased emphasis on study went a corresponding increase of ritual. This grew up in the Buddha's teachings, in its purest forms the most unritualistic of paths, firstly due to the more devotee-type of bhikkhus and second, to the pressure exerted by lay people who wanted ceremonies to mark the principal events of life: birth, marriage and death. Indeed, something had to be provided, for if Buddhist ways of doing things were not available then the laity could turn, in India, to the brahmins and elsewhere to other pre-Buddhist priests.

But bhikkhus have managed fairly successfully not to become "priests." The Dhamma, of course, supplies no basis for a Buddhist "priest," in the sense of a "mediator between God and man." As no Creator exists, no mediator priest is necessary. We have seen already that bhikkhus cannot marry people, nor can they guarantee them passage to a good future life. That depends on the kammas made by people while alive and in the last moment of consciousness at death. But bhikkhus are invited at such occasions and requested to chant traditional verses and discourses of the Buddha which are thought to promote harmonious vibrations and to set up a

52. For his story see, *The Life of the Buddha*, BPS, Kandy, and *Buddhist Legends*, Vol. I p. 217.

good wholesome environment. This is particularly true when the bhikkhus who do the chanting are pure-hearted and practising well.

Of course, ritual has its advantages as well as its dangers. The simple rituals of Theravāda usually have a basis in the Dhamma. For instance, people offer flowers to a figure of the Buddha and while doing so repeat, "These flowers, bright and beautiful, fragrant and good-smelling, handsome and well-formed, soon indeed discoloured, ill-smelling and ugly they become. This very body, beautiful, fragrant and well-formed, soon indeed discoloured, ill-smelling and ugly it becomes." If mindfulness is not strong while doing this or the act becomes mechanical then its value is lost, but when done with awareness and concentration, it is a short contemplation of impermanence. Repeated many times with devotion in the course of a life it could lead to the attainment of insight. The dangers have been spoken of already and can be seen easily by critical eyes. It is such dangers of ritualism which are the frequent target of Westerners in the East. But it is unfortunate that such criticism is often made without considering the state of mind from which it has sprung—and this is nearly always unwholesome.

We have already touched on some of the relationships, which exist between bhikkhus and laypeople. Some other features should be considered here as well. For instance, what do people go to a temple monastery for? The temple building, to be described below, will be visited more or less frequently to make offerings of flowers, incense and lights, followed by the triple prostration and perhaps chanting in Pali well-known verses or passages recollecting the virtues of the Triple Gem.[53] Such a visit to the temple is often a personal or family devotion with just one person or a small group participating. The reason for the visit could be the birth of a child, some fortunate business circumstances, or the death anniversary of a beloved relative. Buddhist temples and shrines are usually open and

53. See Ch. VI and *Pali Chanting with Translations,* Mahamakut Press.

anyone may make his devotions at any time. On the other hand, the occasion for such visits could be on the Uposatha days when many people go to the temple, undertake the Eight Precepts and probably spend a whole day and night there in the practice of Dhamma.[54] People may go to the temple, which is in the monastery grounds, but they may not meet any of the bhikkhus who are resident there.

If they go to see bhikkhus, what is the purpose of their visit? Usually they take with them a small gift, perhaps some incense, or candles and flowers to give to the bhikkhu they will visit. They may also take with them, if it is during the morning when bhikkhus eat, cooked food for one particular bhikkhu or for distribution to many. Even in the afternoon or evening food may be taken to the monastery as an offering though it is not accepted by the bhikkhus then, but put aside for the next day when a lay attendant will prepare it. Lay people may request bhikkhus to chant at the time of their visit or upon some future occasion, such as an invitation to their houses. This is made for all sorts of anniversaries or celebrations, in fact any time is a good time to help support the Sangha and so make good kamma, or merit. These invitations will include either a breakfast or a forenoon meal and the number of bhikkhus invited may vary from one to several dozen.

When they are visiting the monastery lay people may also ask questions about Dhamma, or about how to apply the Dhamma to the problems and difficulties they have to face in life. They may also request a formal sermon to be delivered on an anniversary either in the temple or in their homes. Again, they may go to an abbot with money donations for repair work or new construction in his or other monasteries. He will not accept the donation directly but have a layman, called a steward (*veyyavaccakāra*), look after it and give a receipt for it. To some bhikkhus who are known to have healing abilities, laypeople may take those who are afflicted mentally or physically and ask him to use his powers and sometimes

54. See, *Lay Buddhist Practice*, Wheel 206–207, BPS.

knowledge of herbs, too, to cure them. At other times, when in danger or sorrow, people may go to ask the blessing of a bhikkhu which he will give in a number of ways, from a sprinkling with water to the gift of small Buddha-images or sections of Buddhist scripture, to hang round the neck.

As a contrast, with this there are the most devoted lay people who will go to a monastery and under the guidance of the meditation Teacher there, stay as long as they can do meditation all the day and much of the night. They would retire, of course, to those monasteries which specialise in meditation practice, very often far away in the forest, on a mountain or clustered round a group of caves.

These are just some of the many reasons why lay people go to temples and monasteries.

When we consider the reverse, why bhikkhus go to the houses of laypeople, some points have been mentioned above. The commonest reason is the bhikkhu's alms round which may be early in the morning as in Thailand and Burma or later as in Sri Lanka.[55] The bhikkhu is silent, walking barefoot silently, never asking for anything and passing by quietly the houses and shops where nothing is given. When he is offered food, he opens his bowl silently and when the donor has finished giving, in silence he goes on his way to collect just enough to keep the body going. On the alms round, to be seen every morning throughout Buddhist countries, bhikkhus do not usually enter peoples' houses as the food is given at the doorstep.

At the time of a previously arranged invitation to a home, however, bhikkhus enter and are seated in due order on seats which have been prepared for them. As honoured guests they are offered something to drink—tea or fruit juices and then the family may request the Three Refuges and the Five Precepts, which they will repeat after the senior-most bhikkhu. After this follows the auspicious chanting, varied according to the

55. See, *The Blessings of Piṇḍapāta, (The Almsround)*, Wheel No. 73 and the accounts in Ch. IV.

occasion. A meal may be offered when this has finished and afterwards a short sermon and then some verses called anumodanā—rejoicing with the merits of the donors, are chanted. Gifts of necessities may be offered to the bhikkhus before these last verses, or money for their support, may be placed in the hands of their attendant and the bhikkhus informed of this.

In Buddhist countries now, indeed since the days of the Buddha, there are bhikkhus who engage themselves in ways which the Buddha did not approve. They should be mentioned here so that readers, if they go to, or have been, in Buddhist lands, may not be surprised. The commonest among offenders are those bhikkhus who do little or nothing except wear their robes and eat two meals a day. Another Buddhist tradition has called them "rice bags and clothe-hangers," an apt name indeed. When the number of bhikkhus who do little except chat pleasantly with relatives or friends becomes great, then Buddhism is sure to be in trouble. Among the graver departures from the Buddha's intentions are those bhikkhus who become famous as possessors of real or supposed powers which they exploit— as the Thai expression puts it, "they want it loud"—that is, their own reputations. They dispense holy water, Buddha-amulets and the like and, while they may lighten the burdens of others to some extent, they certainly make their own karmic burdens heavier! Such bhikkhus can become quite wealthy, but not in Dhamma.

Others achieve fame through astrology—of which the Buddha sceptically said (in a previous life when a Bodhisatta) "What will the stars do!" In teaching bhikkhus he called such knowledge "low science." Some have reputations for being able to cast out demons and spirits and are known in Thailand as "ghost-doctors." To help people in this way is of course unobjectionable but it can be dangerous for those who wield power, since conceit increases easily in the unenlightened mind.

Then there are bhikkhus who have medical knowledge of herbs and different sorts of treatment such as massage. But their knowledge is not systematic and will be derived from their Teachers or from what they have gathered going through life. A greater or lesser admixture of magical elements also makes their treatments uncertain in results. The Buddha advised bhikkhus to treat other members of the Sangha and near relatives only, thus avoiding awkward situations, which could arise if a bhikkhu's prescriptions turned out ineffective, or worse, killed the patient. However, in past times, when there were no trained doctors, a bhikkhu faced with a plea for medical assistance would very likely act upon compassion rather than the Vinaya, the rules of which are to prevent him from becoming a regular doctor with an income.

Bhikkhus who become landowners or politicians also follow improper ways of livelihood. Landowning, indeed any property, cannot be held by individual bhikkhus but must belong to the Sangha. And while it is proper for the bhikkhus who shoulder the "work of books" to be concerned about the well being of laypeople, it goes too far when they ally themselves with this or that political party. In fact, such support only calls down obloquy on their heads when party-leaders do not live up to their programme or are unsuccessful in their attempts at government. Politics and parties, with all the strife that usually accompanies them, are for lay Buddhists to take an interest in. In Thailand, bhikkhus have no vote and are expected to keep out of political matters. If they wish to engage in politics, which is the layman's world, then they disrobe and become laymen. Sri Lanka, with the difficult heritage left by colonialism, has had bhikkhus who have attached themselves to various parties. In Burma, too, some bhikkhus became too interested in politics until this was discouraged by the present government.

The two approved ways of bhikkhu livelihood will form the subject of the next chapter.

It is obvious that since there are bhikkhus whose practice is not so good, some measure of government must exist in the Sangha. There are also various matters to be organised, which require some kind of administrative structure. The Buddha laid down that seniority among bhikkhus, that is, how many "rains" they have passed in the Sangha, was to be the reason for paying respects. Thus the senior-most bhikkhu would be the one whom all others revered as their leader. This works well when he is learned, a meditation master or both, but what if he is just "old in vein" while younger bhikkhus have more virtues than he has? This difficulty has been solved by the creation of "abbots" of vihāras. They are appointed and elected (in Thailand) on the basis of their merits and the preferences of both bhikkhus and leading lay people. They hold that post, "lord of the *āvāsa*, as long as they wish or until they die but though they have this position of rank and title too, still they must still pay respect to bhikkhus with no such appointments or learning as they have, but who are senior in ordination.

Thailand, Cambodia and Laos have hierarchies similar in character, with the country divided into provinces, counties and districts, each division having an abbot appointed as the Chief of the Sangha. From among the highest-ranking abbots in the capitals a council is formed and from among its members the King (in Thailand) appoints the most senior to be *saṅgharāja*, literally the Ruler of the Sangha. This council meets frequently to discuss matters of importance for the Sangha; also to take action when necessary about infractions of the Vinaya.

Sri Lanka and Burma do not have such a systematic method of Sangha government. In fact, in the three countries first mentioned, the abbot has a large measure of autonomy but this is still greater in Burma and Sri Lanka. There are no kings (*rājā*) in these countries now so there are no saṅgharājas, though this office did exist in the past. Differences in the Sangha, which have been smoothed over better in Thailand, with its Sangha administration and saṅgharājas, have caused more dissension in the other two main countries of Theravāda, making different groups in the Sangha there more prominent.

The Sangha in Theravāda countries has hardly ever been without some divisions. It is wrong to speak of sects since most laypeople take little interest in such matters which depend on interpretations of the bhikkhus' discipline or Vinaya. In Sri

Lanka, for instance, there are three main groups: the Siam Nikāya, the Amarapura Nikāya and the Rāmañña Nikāya.

The Siam Nikāya derives its lineage from Siam, before the fall of the capital of Ayudhya to the Burmese in 1767. About twenty years before this, a delegation was sent by the king of Sri Lanka to Thailand for the purpose of establishing the Sangha in Sri Lanka where no pure bhikkhus could be found, only novices living in a few of the temples. A number of Thai theras were sent by the king of Ayudhya to restore the lineage of Acceptance or ordination and to establish the Sangha soundly in both study and practice. Much credit for the success of this mission and its lasting results must go to the untiring work of the venerable Sri Saraṇaṅkara, a Sinhalese monk of great determination and devotion as well as scholarship and pure practice, who was later designated to be Saṅgharāja by the king, the last such leader of the Sangha in Sri Lanka.

The second group, the Amarapura Nikāya, evolved out of an incident relating to the caste system: A man of "low caste" who had been accepted as a bhikkhu saluted the king, who took offence and ordered that low-caste men should not be accepted into the Sangha.

This calls for a few words of explanation. To begin with, caste was not a teaching that found favour in the Buddha's eyes. He criticized brahmins and other "high" caste people frequently; for their haughty behaviour, as well as the oppression which such a system brings to those of "lower" castes. "High" and "low," according to the Buddha, are matters of conduct in mind, speech and body:

> One's not by birth an outcaste
> nor a brahmin by one's birth,
> by kamma one's an outcaste,
> by kamma one's a brahmin. (Sn 142)

Therefore, men and women from all sections of society might be accepted into their respective Sanghas provided that they were free from the obstacles to ordination (see Ch. VIII). The verses and stories which have been translated in this book of both bhikkhus and bhikkhunīs from all levels of society confirm that the Sangha was open to all. The Buddha also allowed bhikkhus to conform to a royal (or government) law provided that it was in accord with Dhamma. We shall see the application of this shortly.

Another point here is that bhikkhus, who respect Buddha-images and stupas like everyone else among men, only honour bhikkhus senior to themselves, those who have more years or rains in the Sangha, and never laypeople even though they may be kings and queens.

But that bhikkhu, aforementioned, did wrong in honouring the king while the king, perhaps out of ignorance, did wrong in ordering that low-caste men should not be accepted into the Sangha. The Siam Nikāya, however, still upholds this royal law.

Caste has no place, even in lay Buddhist society, let alone the Sangha, but still there were Buddhists in Sri Lanka, who due to their proximity to India were infected with this caste attitude. At the same time, there were men, designated as lower-caste, who desired acceptance as bhikkhus, and who were adversely affected by the above-mentioned ruling. A solution came about when a novice from this background, having been refused acceptance, in Sri Lanka, went to Burma and there became a bhikkhu. On his return in the early years of the nineteenth century, he founded the Amarapura Nikāya, which continues to admit people from all sections of society.[56]

The third group, the Rāmañña Nikāya, has some similarities with the Dhammayuttika in Thailand which is also derived from Mon or Rāmañña practice. Reform of Vinaya practice, accurate calculation of the Uposatha days (full moon and new moon when special precepts are undertaken by laypeople and

---

56. There are more than 20 subgroups in the Amarapura Nikāya. All these arose due to caste and regional differences. The earliest one is the Mahāmūla Nikāya founded by a bhikkhu belonging to the cinnamon pickers' caste who ordained in Burma. The latest (or one of the latest) is the Shwegyin Nikāya, which was brought to Sri Lanka by Sinhalese who ordained in the monasteries of the Mahāsi Sayādaw tradition in Burma. (BPS Ed.)

the bhikkhus have recitation of the Pātimokkha) and emphasis on a return to simplicity and absence of luxury, are Rāmañña principles. This group, though small in numbers, has a very considerable influence. To some extent, like the Dvāra Nikāya in Burma, this group was formerly exclusive, not eating or consorting with bhikkhus of other groups. Laypeople supporting Rāmañña temples usually did not invite or support bhikkhus from elsewhere.[57]

Each of these groups has its own administrative hierarchy with appointments and titles given to abbots in charge of the temples controlled by the respective groups in different places.

Differences in Vinaya between the three groups are only minor matters though noticeable in some respects. For example: most of the Siam Nikāya bhikkhus cover only one shoulder with their robes when among the houses while the groups derived from Burma cover both. Rāmañña bhikkhus use palm-leaf sunshades, not the Western type of umbrellas used by other bhikkhus.

The Buddha himself said that differences in Vinaya upon minor matters were not so important but differences in Dhamma would be serious: Dispute about livelihood or about the Pātimokkha, (the fundamental rules), is trifling, nanda, but should dispute arise in the Sangha about the Path or the Way (of practice), such dispute would be for the misfortune and unhappiness of many, for the harm, misfortune and suffering of gods and men.[58]

In Burma, too, only varying Vinaya practice divides the two main groups of bhikkhus. Sudhamma Nikāya, the group

---

57. Although the main body of the Rāmañña Nikāya has become fairly relaxed in terms of Vinaya standards, there is an exclusive forest group that broke away in the 1950s and which maintains very strict vinaya standards. It is called the Sri Kalyāṇa Yogasaṃsthāva and its headquarters are in Galduwa. Within the Siam Nikāya a forest group, but less strict and less exclusive, also formed. Its headquarters are in Vaturavila. For more information about these forest groups, see Michael Carrithers, *The Forest Monks of Sri Lanka*, Oxford, 1983 (BPS Ed.)

58. Trans. Ven. Ñāṇamoli Thera (MN 104).

of the good Dhamma, is by far the largest. In the time of the Burmese kings, there was a Sudhamma Council which governed the whole Sangha in Burma but gradually groups formed around one or two famous Teachers and became distinct from the Sudhamma tradition. At present, Sudhamma monasteries vary in strictness with the discipline practised and enforced by their abbots. But there are many in this tradition, particularly small monasteries, where Vinaya practice is not strict and bhikkhus from such places can be seen in the street smoking or chewing betel with their robes carelessly thrown over one shoulder. But it should be remembered that in all monastic traditions it is always laxity that is conspicuous, while well-behaved monks go unnoticed.

The other main group, Shwejyin Nikāya, the group of Shwejyin, is named after the village from which its founder, Shwejyin Sayādaw, came. He was a teacher of the queen of King Mindon, the last but one king of Burma. She persuaded the king to free this teacher from the jurisdiction of the Sudhamma Council. Shwejyin Sayādaw and those who followed him were strict in Vinaya and emphasized that bhikkhus should behave with restraint, making effort to conduct themselves well. The bhikkhus of this tradition have no dispute with their brethren in the Sudhamma group.[59]

This cannot be said of the third Nikāya, Dvāra Nikāya, a small dissident body formed in the last century. Their first Teacher, Okpo Sayādaw, was contentious by nature, though of great learning. He made much of a rewording of the usual way of paying respect to the Buddha—"by body, speech and mind kammas," teaching instead that one should say "by body, speech and mind-doors." Since "door" is *dvāra* in Pali, the group's name has been derived from this. This group is exclusive and will not eat or live with other bhikkhus. It is said to be gradually disappearing.

Formerly the Sangha in Burma was controlled by a council of theras, a kind of Sangha-government which has been

---

59. The renowned teacher Mahāsi Sayādaw was part of this tradition. (BPS Ed.)

dissolved under the present administration. Now each abbot is responsible for the discipline and practice of the bhikkhus in his temple. If he is in charge of one of the very large monasteries, a number of related temples, headed by bhikkhus trained by him, may also be his responsibility.

Thailand, formerly Siam, has only two main Nikāyas. The largest by far is called now Mahānikai or Mahānikāya, the "large group," which was the original line of ordination (acceptance) in Siam since medieval times when it was brought from Sri Lanka.

In the turmoil which followed the sack of Ayudhya, Siam's capital, until just over two hundred years ago, many bhikkhus took to wrong modes of livelihood or so defiled their robes that they were no longer bhikkhus though they continued to appear as such. The standards of both scholarship and of practice sank low, a fact that was witnessed personally by Prince Mongkut, in the days of King Rāma II.

Prince Mongkut had entered the Sangha to be a rains-bhikkhu for the usual period of three months but his father, the king, died during this time and another prince was selected to be Rāma III. Prince Mongkut decided to remain in the Sangha. He had a very intelligent and critical mind and always tried to find out what the Buddha's words meant, removing in the process the layers of commentarial explanations, ritual and superstition which clouded clear understanding. He excelled in the Pali language but spoke to people in the way that they could understand easily, thus attracting many intelligent bhikkhus and lay people as his disciples.

As he came to know more and more from his studies of the original teachings in Vinaya and Sutta, he became dissatisfied with the state of the Sangha in Siam and eventually was re-ordained by Mon bhikkhus whose conduct was correct and who were learned as well. This was the origin of the Dhammayuttikanikai or Dhammayuttika Nikāya—Dhammayut for short—meaning "the group of those who adhere to Dhamma." This group is still small in Thailand but very influential and progressive. Mahanikai has now reformed and strengthened itself, due partly to the example set by Dhammayut.

Now that we have glanced in brief over the three main Theravāda Buddhist countries, a word or two can be said upon the position elsewhere. Cambodia adopted Theravāda after the disappearance of the royal-supported northern Buddhist traditions which were plentifully mixed with Hindu elements. Now the country has the same two groups in the Sangha as Thailand though the forest bhikkhu tradition is uncommon there.

Laos is similar but Dhammayut is found mostly in the south and not recognized formally by the government.[60] Forest-dwelling bhikkhus are to be found both in central and southern areas. Many mountainous parts of the country are not Buddhist, being inhabited by animist hill tribes.

In Vietnam, both south and central, Theravāda is found in Western Cambodian-speaking districts and among Vietnamese in some of the towns. Theravāda is in a minority in this country where most temples are of northern Buddhist tradition which has come down through China. Theravāda bhikkhus with those of Mahāyāna have formed a united Buddhist body but the formal acts of both Sanghas are kept separate. It remains to be seen what will happen to Buddhism in general and the Sangha in particular in the above three countries now that they have Communist governments. Events in Cambodia (Kamboja) have not been encouraging.[61]

Bangladesh has a considerable Buddhist minority with a Sangha divided between two traditions. One is a small group

---

60. After the communist takeover of Laos in the 1970s, the Dhammayut, due to its close links with the Thai royalty and government, was abolished and merged with the Mahānikāya by the communist government of Laos. (BPS Ed.)

61. During the brutal Pol Pot regime in the 1970s, all Cambodian monks were either murdered or forcefully disrobed and put to into forced labour camps. Most Buddhist temples were destroyed. The only monks who survived the onslaught were the ones who fled abroad. Buddhism is slowly recovering in Cambodia now. (BPS Ed.)

of bhikkhus, the Mahāthera-Nikāya, the large group of senior monks or the group of the great senior monk(s), who claim to be descended from bhikkhus fleeing from Bihar at the time of the Moslem invasions. It is reported that they were corrupted in the course of time in their new home but refused the chance of re-ordination by Burmese bhikkhus. This was taken by the great majority who now form the Saṅgharāja-Nikāya, the Saṅgha-patriarch group. In fact, the latter group alone can claim to be Theravāda, although the other group has reformed itself and is hardly distinguishable now.

India, Nepal and Indonesia are countries where the Sangha did not survive though pockets of lay Buddhists struggled on. Now in all those countries Theravāda bhikkhus are found. In India many have been accepted by the bhikkhus of the Maha Bodhi Society, an organization founded by the Sinhalese teacher, Anāgārika Dhammapāla, but training facilities after ordination have not been adequate. Very few Indian bhikkhus are learned and fewer still are well practised in meditation. Very large numbers of people have become Buddhists—numbers are now into the tens of millions, so some improvement in the position of the Sangha there can be expected in future. An All-India Sangha organization has been formed. In Nepal, the position is different as a large lay Mahāyāna Buddhist population has existed since ancient times. Bhikkhus had been forced to disrobe and marry by the Hindu kings of the past resulting in a gradual decline of Buddhist scholarship and practice. Since the Second World War and after the opening of Nepal's frontiers, Nepali Buddhists have trained in Sri Lanka, Burma and Thailand and a small Sangha now exists there.

In Indonesia also, Mahāyāna has some influence through both Javanese traditions and the Chinese community. However, the majority of bhikkhus are Theravāda and friendly relations exist on the whole. Much credit for this revival must go to early Sinhalese initiative while later, Thai bhikkhus have been active.

Although divisions exist in the Theravāda Sangha at large, there is generally the minimum of sectarian feeling among bhikkhus. One or two can always be found who are ready to paint the other party as the protagonists of Māra (the Evil One) himself but they are very few. This is due to the Buddha's discourses on such subjects as the Six Conditions for Concord, a discourse which is included in the first appendix. He emphasized specially how the Sangha should remain in harmony and concord, without divisions. The present divisions have not come about through schism in the Sangha, which would imply strife indeed, but through re-ordinations or new lines of ordination or acceptance being introduced. Once groups have been established, even where there are only small points of Vinaya dividing them, it is difficult to get unity again. This was achieved in Sri Lanka by the great king Parākramabāhu I who arranged union for the three groups then existing. Other kings in Burma have done the same but it is not easy to maintain unity for long periods of time in a body like the Sangha which depends for this upon agreement of all the leading senior bhikkhus. If one should disagree and wish to practise his own interpretation of Vinaya, then others cannot stop him. Governments have helped the Sangha's unity by upholding correct Vinaya-decisions and backing up the Vinaya with secular laws.

It is common for bhikkhus of all groups to invite each other to festivals and special gatherings in their monasteries. Only formal Sangha-acts are not performed together and in other respects, particularly in Dhamma, there is complete unity.

The last topic which this chapter will outline is a survey of the buildings to be found in a Theravāda monastery. First, the word "monastery" used to translate such words as *vihāra, āvāsa* and *ārāma*, can be as misleading, just as using the word monk (or even priest') to render "*bhikkhu* into English.[62]

A monastery does not have gatehouses with closed gates; on the contrary, where it is in an urban area the whole tide of local life sweeps in and out of its open gates. The area will be walled or fenced in some way and the area enclosed may be small, perhaps an acre or less, or very large, thirty or forty acres in extent in some Bangkok *wats. Wat* is the Thai word for the whole monastery-temple complex for which we have no corresponding word in English. If we call it a temple then that suggests only a place of worship without a monastic residence. But if it is called a monastery that does not imply a public area with a temple open to all people.

The original words were *vihāra* meaning a dwelling place (for bhikkhus) or *āvāsa* having the same meaning. *ārāma* meant originally a park but has come to mean the monastery-temple built in the park. As each Buddhist country has its own words, *wat* in Thailand, *phongyi-kyaung* in Burma, or *pansala* in Sri Lanka, it is better to use the well-known term *vihāra* for all monastery-temples.

The town vihāra will be rather clearly divided into different areas sometimes by interior walls, or by lines of trees, paths and so on. One part will be the Buddha-vihāra, that is where the large Buddha images are found, either in or outside temples. The larger part of the area is called the Sangha-vihāra, the place for the bhikkhus to stay. It will consist of a number of residential buildings in wood or brick which may be large or small and house just one bhikkhu or many together. A large building with many rooms, often ornately carved or decorated, may be the kuṭi (residence) of just one bhikkhu if he is the abbot of an important vihāra. Or another large building may house many bhikkhus, each with a room and a veranda linking them. Small wooden buildings will have usually a single bhikkhu with perhaps a tiny room for a novice or lay-pupil as well. Groups of these kuṭis in various sizes may be arranged in a rectangle round a square sometimes containing trees and having in its centre a *sālā*. A *sālā* is an open-sided hall in which

62. In Christianity "monks" (from the Greek meaning "one who is alone") have a life style different from bhikkhus (from Pali. *bhik*, to beg), though as we have noted already and shall see again in the next chapter, a bhikkhu does not beg, not being allowed to ask for food. A bhikkhu is not confined to his monastery and will usually leave the monastery at least once a day for his almsround.

bhikkhus will gather for special invitations by lay people. *Sālās* may have an open area underneath which can be used as an informal kitchen by visitors, or an area for the storage of various things.

Formerly vihāras in towns, if not by the side of a river or canal, would have had wells to supply water for drinking and washing. This is still common in the country. The construction of bathrooms, even of steam baths, is described in the Vinaya though the latter are rare now. Bathrooms and lavatories these days are often constructed in blocks away from the residential buildings. These are the main structures in the Sangha-vihāra.

To return to the Buddha-vihāra, the most impressive building there will have the largest Buddha-image. It may actually be called the vihāra and is often the building open for public worship. Also, it is sometimes the place where the Sangha go to pay their respects and if so it is common to find a raised area reserved for this purpose. But this may be done in another building, as may be the formal acts of the Sangha. The large Buddha-vihāra may be the area consecrated for such acts, or there may be a separate *Sm*-building. A *sm* is a boundary for formal Sangha acts, such as ordination, and is established round certain buildings or areas and marked in a special way so that bhikkhus are aware of the boundary.

Also in the area of the Buddha-vihāra there maybe a large wooden sālā which will be the meeting place for large numbers of devotees on the Uposatha days. It may enshrine a small Buddha-image, and there is often a raised platform for bhikkhus to sit on. A more or less elaborate Dhamma-seat for the bhikkhu who expounds Dhamma is the only other item in the hall, the audience sitting on the wooden floor. Other smaller halls may accommodate overflows of the faithful on special days and provide sleeping space for pilgrim bhikkhus and visitors. Ladies will sleep in the nun's sālā where there is a section of the vihāra for nuns.

The only other important building is a special Buddhist structure called a *stupa* or *cetiya*. This is usually in the form of a spired image and situated behind the largest temple enshrining a Buddha image. When devotees revere the Buddha inside the temple they will also be paying respect to the stupa just behind the image. The earliest symbol of the Buddha to be revered was the stupa, the only way in which he was respected until the development of Buddha-images. A stupa enshrines relics of his person—objects which he has used or it may be the repository of many Buddha images, Buddhist texts, handwritten open palm-leaves, a well as gold and jewels. Buddha-relics usually do not resemble charred bone but are jewel-like crystal, found only in the ashes after the cremation of Buddhas or Arahants. But there are certain body-relics which are different, such as the Tooth-Relic enshrined in Kandy, Sri Lanka, or the Hair Relics which are contained in the beautiful Shwe Dagon Pagoda in Rangoon, Burma. Articles used by the Buddha are such things as his alms-bowl, fragments of which have been found in India. But the great majority of stupas contain the third kind of reminders of the Buddha—innumerable small Buddha-images and Buddhist texts.

Stupas may be small, perhaps only the height of a man, or any size up to 300 feet. The most massive and ancient examples are to be found in Sri Lanka at Anurādhapura, while in Burma the Shwe Dagon is pre-eminent and in Thailand, Phra Pathom Cedi at Nakorn Pathom is revered as being the first *stupa* in the country as well as the largest.

Near to the main temple and the stupa there will be a scion of the Bodhi Tree under which the wanderer Gotama became Gotama the Buddha. This may be walled round in a decorative way and set into its walls will be niches where people can offer lights, incense, and flowers. The most famous Bodhi Tree now is in Sri Lanka at Anurādhapura where, very ancient, is the southern branch of the tree under which the Buddha sat. It has been surrounded with an ornamental gilded fence and is the site of great devotion every day of the year. The Bodhi Tree at Buddha Gay in India, the place of Enlightenment, is now a fourth generation tree planted on the spot where the Buddha awakened.

All these main shrines will have around them paved paths for honouring the Buddha by circumambulation. This is done with one's right side towards the sacred object and devotees circle the shrine while repeating sacred texts and they may carry in their hands offerings of candles, incense and flowers. Silent recollection of the virtues of the Buddha, Dhamma, and Sangha is also done at this time. At the time of Buddhist festivals thousands may join in this circumambulation.

Each village has its vihāra, a centre of village activity where a few bhikkhus and sāmaṇeras may live. The buildings are usually less grand than town vihāras but more colourful than those in the forest where meditation is practised. There one finds a great simplification of the buildings. Only a large wooden sālā and a scattering of kuṭis in the forest are needed.[63] The sālā will enshrine a Buddha image and there will be the usual arrangements for seating them but there will be no glitter as in the large town vihāras. Everything is plain, the emphasis being on practicality and simplicity rather than grandeur. The kuṭis are small wooden structures for only one bhikkhu or sāmaṇera and they are set well apart with forest between them. There may be a fire sālā where water can be heated for hot drinks or medicines. Also there may be small lavatories but where the vihāra is newly constructed even this function will be served by pits dug out in the forest. There will be more about the forest and the town vihāras in the next chapter.

In the different Buddhist countries some symbols of the Buddha receive more reverence than others. People in Sri Lanka particularly revere the great Bodhi trees which are found in each vihāra. But in Burma it is rather the stupa (or cetiya) which receives most attention and no vihāra will be complete without a spotlessly whitewashed *zedi*. Thai people, however, rather favour the Buddha-image as the centre of their devotions and many famous bronze images, some very large,

63. In Thailand and Burma wood was used for building in forest monasteries, however nowadays this practice is becoming rare due to scarcity of wood. In Sri Lanka forest monasteries building usually were and are made of stone and brick.

are the object of popular pilgrimages.

To close this chapter some of the ancient and popular Pali verses used in devotions both by bhikkhus and by lay people in Sri Lanka have been translated.

With lights of camphor brightly shining
destroying darkness here,
the three worlds' light, the Perfect Buddha,
dispeller of darkness, I revere.

With this incense sweetly scented
prepared from blended fragrances
Him I revere who is rightly revered,
worthy of highest reverence—

The Buddha I revere with varied flowers,
by this, my merit, may there be release;
even as this flower fades away
so will my body be destroyed.

With those flowers, as long as they last,
colourful, fragrant and excellent,
the Sacred Feet on the lotus
of the Lord of sages, I revere.

All the stupas in every place
wherever they are found,
the bodily relics, the great Bo-tree
and Buddha-images, I revere.

CHAPTER VI

THE LIFE OF BHIKKHUS

The two careers—the town bhikkhu—waking—alms round—what bhikkhus eat—morning chanting—classes—invitations to the houses of laypeople—the forenoon meal—education of bhikkhus—acts of the Sangha—work suitable for bhikkhus—evening chanting—learning in the evening—scholastic tendencies in the different Buddhist countries—the forest bhikkhu—solitude—an Arahant in recent times—Vinaya practice—13 austere practices—meditation—the forest bhikkhu's day—the sālā—alms round—the meal and reflections—the latrine—meditation-walk—work during the day—receiving guests—sweeping—cleaning—water-carrying—a bath—drinks—evening meeting—service to teachers—walking meditation—possessions of a bhikkhu—living alone—"in no long time."

The accounts of bhikkhu life in this chapter are based on experiences in Thailand where there are a good number of differences, though unimportant, even between nearby vihāras or those in the same group. So there are sure to be some ways in which those accounts differ from the lives of bhikkhus in Sri Lanka and Burma. But again the variations are not likely to be of major importance.

Here only two kinds of bhikkhu life are described, that of the bhikkhu who undertakes the work of books and another whose work is meditation. These are the two careers approved of by commentarial tradition but one should not understand that they are completely separate. It sometimes happens that a study bhikkhu decides that he has learnt enough and goes off to practice, while practice bhikkhus have sometimes to abandon their quest and come to the towns for study. Although this separation is to be regretted and certainly was not the Buddha's intention, it is a fact in Buddhist countries. Some Buddhist authors of the present have also noted how inappropriate is this rigid differentiation[64] but change can come only with change in the pattern of education in the Sangha.

Even a century ago the difference between these two sorts of bhikkhus was not so great. In those days travel in Buddhist countries was by foot or in a boat while very few bhikkhus, except those who were aged and greatly respected, will have travelled in palanquins. Bhikkhus were not permitted by the Buddha to use horses or elephants for travel. So if a study bhikkhu from the town wished to travel he had to go by foot and carry with him his own bowl and robes and a few other things. At that time his life closely resembled the forest bhikkhus who have always travelled in this way. The study bhikkhu could then get to know the life of forest bhikkhus from his own experience. Also, cities then were not the sprawling monsters of today. A town bhikkhu's vihāra would be within ten minutes walk of the city wall and the rice fields or fruit plantations beyond. He might be able to see the country quite easily from his kuṭi. Things are different nowadays with town vihāras surrounded by houses, shops and factories, while to get out of the city one must take a bus ride for half an hour at least. So the gap between the two sorts of bhikkhu life has widened now.

It is generally accepted that a town-dweller (*gāmavāsī*) means a bhikkhu concerned with book work (*ganthadhura*), but this is not always so and there have always been a few town-dwelling bhikkhus who are occupied with meditation, or who manage in spite of their responsibilities to progress far in this direction.

The Buddha foresaw that not all bhikkhus would be capable of living the hard forest life, so he did not allow the five points raised by his cousin, the treacherous bhikkhu Devadatta, one of which was that all bhikkhus should live all the time in the forest, never in towns and villages. But those places obviously do not offer the best places for meditation,

---

64. See *The Heritage of the Bhikkhu*, Walpola Rāhula, p. 29f.

they are not so quiet, they have too many people and all sorts of disturbances may be expected there. So the towns became the places for book-study since this requires a less rigorous life-style and less concentration, while the preservation of books is easy there. Bhikkhus who lived in the forest though sometimes attracted to study, have usually been inspired by their teachers and by the quiet of their surroundings to meditate.

First then, the life of a bhikkhu in the (Thai) town.[65] Many more variations are possible in his life since much more happens (outside) than with the meditator, where the principal happenings are interior ones.

In the morning, say about five o'clock, the bhikkhu wakes up. After refreshing himself with a wash and attending to the body's needs he may sit for some time in meditation, or if an examination draws near, open his books and study. Some bhikkhus occupy this time with some chanting since in every kuṭi there is a small shrine with a Buddha-image or picture. Apart from this the total furniture in many kuṭis consists only of a desk, chair and some bookcases. Some small sitting rugs with cushions behind them allow comfortable relaxation and entertainment of other bhikkhus. Many vihāras do not have a bell for rising or any assembly in the early morning. It thus depends on the energy of the individual bhikkhu when he gets up and what he does thereafter.

But when it is fully light, perhaps six or half-past, then there is something that must be done—if he wants any breakfast! He puts on his robes over both shoulders as should be done by bhikkhus when they leave the vihāra, and takes his bowl in his hands. His head is uncovered and he walks barefoot as he goes out "among the houses" to see what generous supporters will offer him[66].

When he leaves the vihāra gate, he does not hurry nor gaze

---

65. For another account, see *Buddhism* by Richard A. Gard, published by George Brazillel Inc., New York.

66. For a fuller account see *The Blessings of Piṇḍapāta*, Wheel No. 73.

about at the houses and shops. To help his inward calm he may be reciting a passage from one of the Suttas he is learning by heart, but in any case the good bhikkhu gives the impression of being mindful and serene. It is early morning, a time when there is not much traffic and the town is still rather quiet. The bhikkhu going for his *piṇḍapāta* (lit, food lumps dropped into the bowl, but normally meaning alms-round) shows an example of inner peace, which the Dhamma has given him. The only times he raises his eyes are to look out for traffic and other possible dangers and to mark where laypeople are giving food.

It is the custom now in Thailand for a bhikkhu to walk silently until he sees a house or shop where food is being given, or until he is requested to stop by a layperson who wants to place in the bowl. This is different from the Buddha-time when the bhikkhu stopped briefly outside each house and if nothing was forthcoming moved on. Piṇḍapāta is still practised in this way in Sri Lanka.

The important thing is that he should do nothing to compel laypeople to give him alms. He may only ask for special foods if he is ill and then it is only proper really to ask laypeople that have invited him to say if he needs something. Normally, he asks for nothing at all but just receives whatever people are happy to offer him. And they offer him the best food they can, at least it will be a portion of the food that they have prepared for themselves and sometimes finer foods than they eat usually. The bhikkhu honours them by passing by their houses and giving them a chance to make good kamma, or merit, by giving generously.

The town bhikkhu though does not always have to go out on piṇḍapāta in the morning. Quite often a bhikkhu has supporters who bring food to him to the monastery, so that it is not necessary for him to find food by wandering to receive it. This is particularly true of senior bhikkhus, such as abbots, but many still go for piṇḍapāta.[67] But bhikkhus look upon this as a duty, as something, which should be done. It was the practice of the Buddha and all the bhikkhus in his days and it has a value far exceeding the collection of food.

It is, of course, good exercise for the body and it promotes in the mind many good qualities such as contentment, humility and gratitude. Moreover it is a way of helping other people, for there is the expression in Thai, to go out to protect beings, which the bhikkhu does by giving them the chance to place food in his bowl and so support his life for another day.

The whole act of placing in the bowl is done in silence. Silently the bhikkhu stops. The layperson silently raises his hands to his forehead in the gesture of reverence. Making no sound the bhikkhu takes the cover off his bowl and just as quietly the layperson, whether woman or man, or a group of people, puts the food gently in the bowl. When finished the householder again raises hands to the forehead in the gesture of *añjali* and the bhikkhu by this knows that the act of giving is finished and quietly closes his bowl and mindfully walks away, usually without a word being spoken. Bhikkhus do not thank the lay donors, some of whom indeed would feel upset if they received thanks. They may sometimes receive a brief blessing like *Sukhi hotu*—May you be happy, or "*Āyu vaṇṇo sukhaṃ balaṃ*—"Long life and beauty, happiness and strength," but truly their thanks is in the good kamma that they have made by being generous and supporting one who leads the Holy Life leading to Enlightenment. Some donors would feel like thanking the bhikkhus for their good example of Dhamma well practised.

A bhikkhu's piṇḍapāta in town takes him past the houses of both the rich and poor and he collects from all whatever they wish to offer, neither greedy for choice morsels nor scorning poor offerings. Also, he must accept whatever is offered, even if he is a vegetarian and people offer meat or fish, he accepts their offering with gratitude and loving kindness. He can always make merit himself by giving away what he does not want! That leads on to a small diversion, for people

---

67. In Sri Lanka few monks go for *piṇḍapāta*. It is the custom for laypeople to bring food to the monasteries.

always assume that Buddhists are vegetarians when this is not usually the case. A few are through their own choice but this is not because they are upholding some tenet of Buddhism. The Buddha did not want his teaching to become a "food religion"—as many religions tend to become in course of time. He gave importance to what came out of the mouth—the words spoken, but not to what was put into it. As he was a bhikkhu he ate whatever people gave and taught other bhikkhus to do the same. This is good for contentment. Laypeople of course can choose their food as they have money but the Buddha said nothing about what they should or should not eat. When they did not kill living beings themselves and so made no evil kammas by killing, they could please themselves with what they ate and what they gave to bhikkhus.

The food is kept separate in the almsbowl by the use of banana leaf wrappings and, these days, by plastic bags and small containers. In this way, curries, sweets, fruit and rice are not all mixed up and only the latter two are usually unwrapped. This differs from the Buddha's days when everything was placed in the bowl unwrapped and so became a mixture which could be rather repulsive and certainly would be only a medicine for curing hunger.

His alms round takes him half an hour, or a bit longer, so that by seven o'clock he should have returned to the vihāra with a bowl half full at least. It is rare for a bhikkhu to get nothing or not enough to eat. If this happens, there is usually some arrangement for providing extra food cooked by lay people in the vihāra, so he does not have to go hungry. And it is a good bhikkhu practice when returning from the alms round, especially when one has plenty, to stop another bhikkhu and give some of the contents of one's bowl to him. Special delicacies are often reserved by bhikkhus to be given to their teachers, the senior bhikkhus in the vihāra. Often he will eat in a group with other bhikkhus and share his food with them.

When he has got back to his kuṭi, perhaps he has a lay pupil or a sāmaṇera who will take his bowl respectfully and arrange its contents in small dishes, leaving the rice in the bowl. The bhikkhu may eat from his bowl; leaving in it just enough rice for himself and then put in whatever he wishes to eat with it, or more likely he will eat from a plate. As the town bhikkhu has two meals a day, he does not make his breakfast too heavy, although it is truly for him *break fast*. He, like all bhikkhus, has not eaten since before midday on the previous day. The evening is the time when the body should be kept light—for meditation or studies are obstructed by an evening meal. Also, as his food is supplied by others out of the generosity of their hearts, he cannot call upon them for evening food as well. Besides, renunciation of sense-pleasures is part of his training and in many parts of the world the big meal of the day is in the evening, so he renounces this so that he may have a mind that is bright in the evening.

His breakfast finished, he may chant a short verse or two rejoicing with the merits of the donors, being glad at the good kamma they have made and extending his loving-kindness to them. Such verses as these may be chanted:

> From all diseases freed,
> from all grief escaped,
> overcome all enmity
> and liberated may you be.
>
> May all distress be averted,
> may all diseases be destroyed,
> may no dangers be for you
> may you be happy, living long.
>
> One of respectful nature who
> ever the elders honours,
> four qualities for him increase:
> long life and beauty, happiness and strength.

Then having washed his mouth it will be about time for the bell to strike summoning the bhikkhus to morning chanting. Bhikkhus and sāmaṇeras make their way to the main temple and upon entering prostrate three times, to the Buddha, Dhamma and Sangha, in the direction of the Buddha-image. The most senior bhikkhu first lights the candles, or lamps and then the incense. Flowers are already arranged there.[68] Then after paying respects to the Triple Gem he leads the bhikkhus to chant: *Namo tassa Bhagavato Arahato Sammā-sambuddhassa* repeated three times. Those words of praise to the Buddha are found in the Suttas and so have now been chanted in his honour for more than twenty-five centuries. *Namo* means homage, honour or reverence and *tassa* is to that.

Bhagavato is usually rendered exalted or Blessed One but really means something like: The Lord who knows how to teach the Dhamma appropriate to different beings out of compassion for them. This word *Bhagavā* therefore celebrates the Great Compassion of the Buddha. *Arahato*—the Arahant, one who is free from defilement, therefore stands for the Buddha's complete Purity. *Sammā*—perfect, *sambuddhassa*—to the Buddha (enlightened) by himself; he is perfectly enlightened by his own efforts and his enlightenment or *bodhi* was not granted him by any other power or person. This stands for the quality of the Buddha's Wisdom, which is unique among the Teachers of this world.

After this the various recollections are chanted. Here are some of them in English translation.

Recollection of the Buddha

Indeed the Exalted One is thus: the accomplished destroyer of defilements, a Buddha perfected by himself, complete in clear knowledge and compassionate conduct, supremely good in presence and in destiny, knower of the worlds, incomparable Master of men to be tamed, the Teacher of devas and men, the Awakened and Awakener, the Lord by skilful means apportioning Dhamma.[69]

---

68. For an explanation of the significance of these offerings, see *Lay Buddhist Practice,* Wheel No. 206–207. BPS, Kandy.
69. For stories illustrating these qualities see Ch. XII *The Splendour of Enlightenment*, Mahamakut Press, Bangkok.

Recollection of the Dhamma

The Dhamma of the Exalted One is perfectly expounded, to be seen here and now, not delayed in time, inviting one to come and see, leading inwards, to be known by each wise man for himself.

Recollection of the Sangha

The Sangha of the Exalted One's disciples who have practised well, who have practised straightly, who have practised rightly, who have practised dutifully,—that is to say, the four pairs of men, the eight types of persons—that is the Sangha of the Exalted One's disciples, worthy of gifts, worthy of hospitality, worthy of offerings, who should be respected, the incomparable field of merit for the world."[70]

Recollection at the time of using the requisites

Reflecting carefully, I use this robe only to ward off cold, to ward off heat, to ward off the touch of gadflies, mosquitoes, wind, sun and reptiles, only for the purpose of covering the sexual organs.

Reflecting carefully, I use this alms food: not for pleasure, not for indulgence, not for personal charm, not for beautification but only for maintaining this body so that it endures, for keeping it unharmed, for supporting the Holy Life; so that former feelings (of hunger) are removed and new feelings (from overeating) do not arise; then there will be for me a lack of bodily obstacles, and living comfortably.

Reflecting carefully, I use this lodging: only to ward off cold, to ward off heat, to ward off the touch of gadflies, mosquitoes, wind, sun and reptiles, only for the purpose of removing the dangers from weather and for living in seclusion.

---

70. For these three reflections explained in detail, see *Path of Purification*. Ch. VII pp. 206–240.

Reflecting carefully, I use these requisites for illness—medicines and utensils: only to ward off painful feelings that have arisen, for the maximum freedom from disease."

Five Subjects for Frequent Recollection

I am of the nature to decay; I have not got beyond decay.

I am of the nature to be diseased; I have not got beyond disease.

I am of the nature to die; I have not got beyond death.

All that is mine, dear and delightful, will change and vanish.

I am the owner of my kamma; the heir to my kamma; born of my kamma; related to my kamma; abide supported by my kamma. Whatever kamma I shall do, whether good or evil, of that I shall be the heir.[71]

These are some of the recollections, which are chanted at this time; the selection varies from one vihāra to another. A section from some famous work expounding the Dhamma or Vinaya may also be read by one of the bhikkhus while the rest listen, their hands held reverently at the level of the heart. At the end, the novices may recite their Ten Precepts.[72]

What happens after this morning chanting depends on the status of the bhikkhu. The youngest (in rains) together with the sāmaṇeras, will go to Dhamma or Pali classes for about one and a half hours from nine until half past ten. More senior bhikkhus will be their teachers. The most senior bhikkhus, such as the abbot and other leading theras, may also teach but usually special subjects and not regularly. Their time is very full with invitations and appointments. Many people come to see them and they are invited frequently to go to people's houses and to other vihāras, sometimes far distant.

Regarding invitations to peoples' houses, some bhikkhus will have been absent from Morning Chanting as they had

71. For more on Buddhist chanting, see *Lay Buddhist Practice* Wheel 206–207 and *Pali Chanting with Translations.*

72. See Appendix II

invitations for breakfast. Usually this means that they would not have gone for Piṇḍapāta. If the house is far away, the owner will send a car or cars for them but if near the bhikkhus walk there. Before they enter the house water is poured over their feet, which are then wiped, often done by the layman inviting them. Inside a number of cushions have been set out against a wall and a clean white cloth is sometimes spread over them. The most senior bhikkhu sits (preferably with his right side, the side showing respect) nearest the Buddha image in front of which candles, incense and flowers are arranged.

When the bhikkhus are seated, the family pays its respects to them with the triple prostration and layman lights the candles and incense. Then they request the Three Refuges and the Five Precepts from the most senior bhikkhu. This is followed by the chanting of auspicious discourses, passages and stanzas that are selected according to the occasion. Upon the conclusion of the chanting the laypeople prostrate again and then serve the bhikkhus with breakfast. This may be in their bowls or on plates and sometimes laypeople provide more food for the bhikkhus to take back to their vihāras for the forenoon meal. In some houses gifts of necessities are given to the bhikkhus who before they go. The bhikkhus then chant the verses of rejoicing in the donors' merits. A short talk on Dhamma may also be given. The bhikkhus then return to the vihāra. What has been said here applies equally to an invitation to the forenoon meal.

But we shall suppose that the bhikkhu whose day we are following has no such invitation and so returns after his classes feeling hot and in need of a wash or shower. In towns, modern vihāras have showers but the traditional bathroom has large pitchers or tanks of water out of which water is scooped and splashed over oneself. The lower robe is kept on and gets washed in the process. Then another dry one is put on over it and the wet one lowered to the floor.

Refreshed from his bath, the bhikkhu goes to wherever the food is served. In part this may be the leftovers from his piṇḍapāta, but there may not be much of this if he has young pupils! Then in some vihāras arrangements are made to supply food cooked in the market to the bhikkhus, a fund supported by laypeople paying for this. In other places and this is the case with many bhikkhus, a lay-supporter will send a tiffin-carrier full of food for the bhikkhus' second meal. It is called the forenoon meal as it must be finished before midday after which bhikkhus do not eat. Apart from this there is nothing special to say about this meal. Sometimes laypeople take food to the vihāra and invite a number of the bhikkhus there, or even all of them. This is often done on birthdays or other special celebrations.

In hot countries and hot seasons it is advisable to take a rest at this time, so from noon until about one o'clock the vihāra is rather quiet. Then the time comes for more classes between one and two for three or four hours in the afternoon. Each vihāra organises its own programme of instruction though some textbooks may be common to all.

The variations of a bhikkhu's schedule, which can take place in the afternoon, are more numerous than in the morning. He can, for example, go to one of the bhikkhu colleges for higher education if his studies are advanced enough. There he learns not only Buddhist subjects but also some other worldly knowledge which may be useful to him. Here there is a difference of opinion between those who want bhikkhus to learn only Pali language, the Dhamma and Vinaya with such related subjects as the life of the Buddha and Buddhist history and those who think that modern education is important for the bhikkhu. The arguments for both sides run like this. Traditionalists say that the Buddha condemned worldly talk (literally animal-talk) and worldly knowledge, while he praised those who were deeply learned, in the Three Baskets for example. Their argument is that bhikkhus should not burden their minds with much worldly knowledge because it will only lead them to worldliness and bad conduct. A bhikkhu has no need, they say, of any of the subjects between algebra and zoology. He will be well equipped if he knows his Discipline well, and the Discourses thoroughly. If in addition he has studied the Commentaries and the Abhidhamma, it will be enough for his own development, also for helping others. Bhikkhus who get their heads stuffed full of worldly subjects which do not show the way to renunciation, neglect both Dhamma and Vinaya and so are easily tempted by worldly pleasures to disrobe. Then their supporters who have kept them supplied with requisites for years are disappointed and become disillusioned with bhikkhus generally so that the Saddhamma is corroded in this way.

Not true,[73] say the modernists. Bhikkhus these days should have adequate knowledge of the world. They should learn psychology, philosophy, also the basic sciences. And they need as well knowledge of modern languages, which will help them to spread the Buddhadhamma. Bhikkhus who know only Pali and Sanskrit and the Buddhist literatures in them will be as fossilised as dinosaurs in the present time. What relevance will they have to a modern man coping with so many new problems and how can he talk to them for they will hardly talk the same language.

As often in such disputes, both sides are right—and in some ways too extreme. The traditionalists are certainly right when they press for a curriculum of Buddhist languages and studies. It is unfortunately correct to say that worldly subjects lead to an increase of worldliness. And the behaviour of bhikkhus may suffer because of this and some do disrobe more quickly if they are not supported by the strength of Dhamma-Vinaya. It is going too far, however, to argue against modern language studies.

Modernists are surely correct when they argue that modern languages, psychology and philosophy are proper for the bhikkhu to study, for these subjects do have some bearing both on communication with others and with Dhamma. But if they assert that it is necessary for bhikkhus to have the same kind of general secondary schooling (or university education) as lay

73. For a modernist view see *The Heritage of the Bhikkhu* by Walpola Rāhula., p. 95f.

people then they go too far also. A bhikkhu does not need many of the things taught in schools—they will not help him nor can he use them to teach Dhamma. They are just distractions wasting energy and time which might have gone into his proper studies. He has the time to specialise in a way, which laypeople can rarely do: he can become master of the Buddha-word. With that unique knowledge of Dhamma he is in a better position to help himself and others, than one with only a smattering of this and that. Certainly, Dhamma is relevant now, so the bhikkhu learned in it is not a "dinosaur." Much will depend on how he learns the Dhamma, whether in a practical way or in some stylised and antiquated fashion. So the debate goes on …

Bhikkhus may also have invitations to a formal act of the Sangha, at this time, perhaps an Acceptance ceremony, or to the fortnightly recitation of the bhikkhus 227 fundamental rules, the code called Pātimokkha[74]. Other matters arise more rarely, such as the consecration of a new boundary (*sīmā*). The afternoon may also be the time when donors come and a chanting ceremony is arranged for them. In some vihāras (in Thailand) where there are crematoria, a bhikkhu may be invited to chant or give a sermon in the presence of the family of the deceased to whom the merits are dedicated. Visits by leading theras (senior bhikkhus) may also provide variety from the usual classes.

When classes end, it will be that good time of the day which is called the cool. It is not evening or twilight, which is very brief in the tropics, but the sun is low and a cooling breeze blows. It is time for another bath and probably a cold drink. These days in the towns there are all sorts of cold bottled drinks, which if they are fruit juices, or simulate fruit juices, are allowable for bhikkhus in the afternoon and evening. They can only take fruit juices, which are strained and clear of fruit particles, otherwise it would be equivalent to eating fruit! Also,

74. See *The Pātimokkha,* Mahamakut Press. BPS ed.: 220 are training-rules; the last 7 cover the legal procedures for settling disputes, etc.

various infusions may be drunk at this time—any kind of tea, or coffee but this must contain no milk, which is counted as a food.

There is no objection to these mild stimulants. Bhikkhus, of course, may not have any kind of alcoholic beverage as this would run counter to the aim of the Holy Life which is to clear the mind of all defilements.

Some free time may follow this but young bhikkhus and sāmaṇeras have the duty to look after their teachers, the theras. So there may be cleaning, robe washing and darning to do besides their own chores. A note on work may not be out of place here. A bhikkhu really should be one with few duties if he is to succeed in the Holy Life. This does not mean he should be lazy or neglect to serve his Teachers and help his fellow-bhikkhus. But it does mean that he should not undertake work, which will burden him unnecessarily. The Buddha when laying down the Vinaya, has ruled out certain occupations so that bhikkhus cannot engage in farming or gardening (as monks of other religions do) nor in mercantile activities. The Buddha often showed how the Brahmins, originally the priests of Vedic religion, had changed their ways and he did not intend bhikkhus to deteriorate in the same way. Here is an extract from a discourse in verses about the way Brahmins had been transformed.

> Whoever among men lives minding cows, Vāseṭṭha,
> you must know as farmer, not as brahmin.
> Whoever among men lives by many crafts, Vāseṭṭha,
> you must know as craftsman, not as brahmin.
>
> Whoever among men lives by a trade, Vāseṭṭha,
> you must know as tradesman, not as brahmin.
> Whoever among men lives by serving others, Vāseṭṭha,
> you must know as servant, not as brahmin.
>
> Whoever among men lives taking things, Vāseṭṭha,
> you must know as robber, not as brahmin.
> Whoever among men lives by archery, Vāseṭṭha,
> you must know as warrior, not as brahmin.

Whoever among men lives as a priest, Vāseṭṭha,
you must know as ritualist, not as brahmin.
Whoever among men owns town and country, Vāseṭṭha,
you must know as rāja, not as brahmin.

(Sn 612–619)

Bhikkhus should only undertake those kinds of work, which they can manage easily, provided they are permissible. The Buddha sometimes found bhikkhus at work repairing kuṭis and vihāras and commended bhikkhus who repaired their own kuṭis. Today one wonders what the Buddha would have said to bhikkhus who were artists, or totally engaged in social service. It may be surmised when we consider that such works are not directly connected with Dhamma-Vinaya, learning or practice.

In the early evening, the time varying in the individual vihāras, the bell will be rung again for the evening chanting. The period of 45 minutes or an hour will not differ greatly from that in the morning, as regards the content of the chanting though some of the longer discourses of the Buddha may be recited at this time. While chanting, the mind should be fixed upon the meaning of what is being said, so that distraction is avoided. For the town bhikkhus who practise little or no meditation, this chanting can concentrate and purify the mind to some extent. Especially, if one knows the meaning of the Pali well, with a concentrated mind, deep faith is stimulated and rapture pervades one's body. The range of chants in the evening time is very wide. From among them here is a set of four traditional verses, possibly originally from Sri Lanka, which are extremely beautiful in Pali, in praise of the Buddha, Dhamma and Sangha.

Seated serene at the Sacred Bodhi's root
having conquered Māra and his serried hosts,
attained to Sambodhi, with Wisdom that is Infinite,
Highest in the universe, that Buddha I revere.

Eight-factored Noble Path for people everywhere,
for those seeking Freedom, the Way that is straight,

this Dhamma fine and subtle making for peace,
leading out of *dukkha*, that Dhamma I revere.

Right worthy of gifts is the Sangha purified,
with pacified senses, all mental stains removed,
one quality alone with which all powers won:
gone beyond desire, that Sangha I revere.

Thus indeed the Highest which is the Triple Gem
should be venerated as revered by me,
and then by the power of this vast amount of merit,
very beneficial, may danger be destroyed.

The closing chant will be a set of verses dedicating the good kammas made by the bhikkhus for the good and happiness of all living beings. They share in this good kamma by rejoicing with the doers of those actions, and thus make good kamma themselves. Here is a translation of a Pali composition of Prince Mongkut (later to become King Rāma IV) when he was Lord Abbot of Wat Bovoranives vihāra in Bangkok:

Wherever there are devas who dwell in this vihāra,
the stupa, the temple, the Bodhi-tree enclosure,
may they be honoured by this gift of Dhamma
and may they bring safety to all in this vihāra.

Senior bhikkhus, new ones and those of middle
standing,
attendants and great donors, all the lay people,
villages and countries, towns and principalities,
all living beings—may they be happy!

Those born from a womb, beings egg-begotten,
born out of moisture, or spontaneously arising,
may they rely on the excellent Dhamma
leading beyond [saṃsāra] and destroying all dukkha.

May True Dhamma long stand fast, and the people
upholding Dhamma.
In concord may the Sangha live for benefits and
happiness.

> May True Dhamma guard me well and all the Dhamma practicers.
> And may we all attain to growth in Dhamma declared by the Noble Ones.

When this has finished, then may follow a few moments of silence. After this, there is no timetable and each bhikkhu spends his time as he likes. Some will have clerical work to do, especially typing documents for the vihāra's administration or the texts of books to be published. Others may spend some time with visitors, perhaps relatives who have come to visit and sit out on the bhikkhu's veranda. Bhikkhus who take up the "work of books" have examinations to pass, so some will be poring over their texts while some in traditional fashion will be learning Suttas by heart. A few may be learning or retaining in their minds by repetition, the Pātimokkha (the 227 Fundamental Rules), which cannot be read out of a book at each fortnightly meeting but must be recited from memory. Such a bhikkhu has to recite part of this text every day and his mindfulness must be strong, otherwise forgetfulness will show in his mistakes while chanting. There are still some bhikkhus who learn whole sections of the Suttas by heart, sometimes all the suttas and most rarely all of the Three Baskets. This is a prodigious feat of memory, which perpetuates the most ancient traditions of the Buddha's days. There are still some bhikkhus in Burma who have accomplished this task. Evening is a time, too, when a bhikkhu can visit his bhikkhu friends in that vihāra and discuss matters with them.

Before sleep, some bhikkhus may spend a short time in meditation, chanting, or both, in front of their own shrines. The mind should be clear and calm before lying down mindfully. One cannot say that bhikkhus go to bed because often they have no bed and in a tropical country, almost no bedding. A mat on the floor is sufficient in the hot weather with a hard pillow and most likely a mosquito-net. Keeping the lower robe on, a bhikkhu lies down mindful on his right side, in the posture seen in recumbent Buddha-images and draws his upper robe over himself. In colder weather a thin mattress may be used and a blanket or quilt. As he goes to sleep, he has in mind rising mindfully in the morning and not submitting to sloth.

This is one ordinary day in the life of a study-bhikkhu, but if all the possible variations were described this chapter would never come to an end! This tradition of study is followed by the majority of bhikkhus though the degrees of proficiency they reach obviously will vary. Some pass only the preliminary examinations as do many of the bhikkhus in the village vihāras while some become great scholars, producing original works on Vinaya or Dhamma, either in Pali or in their own languages. In each Buddhist country there is a great range of literature interesting to lay people and written in the vernacular, the Buddhist novels published in Thailand being an example of such books.

But the scholastic traditions in the three main Theravāda countries are not quite the same. A Thai story has it that an embassy was sent from Ayudhya, capital of Siam, to the King of Sri Lanka requesting a copy of the Three Baskets. That king honoured the Three Baskets by dispatching them each in a separate ship. These became separated on their voyage so that the Vinaya-Piṭaka landed in the Mon country (now lower Burma), the Sutta-Piṭaka reached Siam safely, while the Abhidhamma-Piṭaka landed on the shores of Burma. This is meant to account for Mon bhikkhus' strictness in Vinaya, the interest in Suttas in Thailand and the love of Abhidhamma in Burma. It has also been said, however, that Vinaya is stressed in Thailand, Suttas studied widely in Sri Lanka while certainly the Abhidhamma is most prized in Burma. But like all such generalisations it should not be understood that the remaining parts of the Three Baskets are neglected in any Buddhist country.

Forest bhikkhu life[75] differs from the above account in many ways. One thing that stands out is that forest practice is less gregarious, and a bhikkhu has more time for his own

75. See also the account in *With Robes and Bowl,* Wheel 83/84

practice. Indeed the Buddha praised solitude for those who want to practise Dhamma. Physical solitude is quite easily achieved. Then one should have besides solitude of mind—the completely one-pointed mind able to go deep into meditation, which is not so easy. Finally one should be without any "assets"—belongings, possessions, even this mind and body should not belong or should not be grasped as "myself." This solitariness from assets is equivalent to the enlightened state, to being an Arahant, and this requires great renunciation efforts if it is to be attained.

So the forest bhikkhu's life when well-lived requires great effort and determination. But it is rare to find a Buddhist who without the support of a meditation Master can go to the forest and live a life of striving by himself. Most forest bhikkhus, especially while they are still developing their meditation practice, stay with a Teacher who can guide them.

In Thailand the foremost exponent in modern times of the forest bhikkhu life was the Venerable Phra Acharn Mun (Bhūridatta Mahāthera).[76] He was one of the rare bhikkhus who without much guidance steadfastly practised the Dhamma in the seclusion of caves and forests full of wild animals until he reached Arahantship. Out of compassion for people embroiled in sufferings, he taught great numbers of bhikkhus, sāmaṇeras, nuns and lay devotees. Many who heard his inspiring and eloquent discourses realised great benefits, either while they were sitting there or later through the Dhamma that they were encouraged to practise.

Phra Acharn Mun Bhūridatta Mahāthera died in Buddhist Era 2492 (1949) and among the ashes at his cremation were found the crystalline relics (*sarīrika-dhātu*) which confirmed the fact that he was indeed an Arahant. His life with its descriptions of how he practised, what he attained and the Dhamma he taught, as recorded by his disciple, the Venerable

76. A full and inspiring account of his life is in *Phra Acharn Mun: Meditation Master*, Mahamakut Press, Bangkok, for free distribution. A newer account is in *Venerable Ācariya Mun Bhūridatta Thera: A Spiritual Biography by Ācariya Mahā Boowa Ñāṇasampanno*, Wat Baan Taad, Thailand, 2003.

Phra Acharn Mahā Boowa Ñāṇasampanno, should be read by all Buddhists as an encouragement to practise and attain as much as possible in this life.

A number of his disciples are still alive and are now Teachers themselves. What follows here is a description of the life of a bhikkhu in one of the forest vihāras established by them. There are three important aspects of practice in these forest vihāras: keeping strictly to the Vinaya, undertaking some of the thirteen austere practices allowed by the Buddha and the actual mindfulness and meditation. A few words on each of those are necessary to appreciate the forest bhikkhu's life.

Something has already been said about the Vinaya as laid down in books. In practice it is the way of restraining all one's actions of body and speech so that no evil is done. It is the "leading out" (*vinaya*) of troubles and sufferings, which are the results of evil kammas. Even in small matters, there is the right and the wrong way of doing them and this right and wrong are based on Vinaya and mindfulness. For instance, a bhikkhu puts something down on the floor making a lot of noise. The teacher will reprove him for that because, according to Vinaya all possessions, indeed, all things that a bhikkhu handles, should be carefully preserved and not damaged through negligence. Regarded from the viewpoint of mindfulness his action shows that he was unmindful and so not practising Dhamma. The way of doing everything is important and should agree with the Vinaya tradition. A bhikkhu who thought he knew a better way to do things but one which conflicted with Vinaya, would be thought conceited. If he went against the Teacher's instructions again and again, he might be told to leave the vihāra or would just be ignored by the Teacher and other bhikkhus until he either left of his own accord or changed his ways.

The Vinaya is a reasonable code and its rules all have their reasons and although in general this is to restrain body and speech actions, since these actions are born in the mind, it aids the restraint of greed, aversion and delusion, the three roots of evil from which all defilements spring. The Vinaya alone cannot root out these sources of evil but must be backed up by mindfulness and meditation and strengthened by the austere practices. The reasonableness of the Vinaya rules may not always be apparent but then we must remember that they were framed by the Perfectly Enlightened One whose understanding was rather greater than our own! However to give an example of rules which can be easily comprehended are some of the regulations about food. Not only is a bhikkhu forbidden to dig the ground and to cut or break living plants—and thus he is kept out of agriculture, but also he is unable to buy his own food (as strictly he has no money), or to cook his own meals. Buying one's own food and cooking it gives greed a chance—what one likes and does not like. But when it is obtained by the alms bowl, or through the offerings of laypeople that have come to the vihāra, greed has much less chance while restraint becomes easier. Careful practice of the Vinaya is therefore the basis of the forest bhikkhu's life.

The forest tradition is also where the austere practices are used. We have read already that the Buddha disapproved of both the extremes of sensual indulgence and of bodily mortification, while he taught a Middle Way. Of course, this middle should not be understood as a compromise but as ways and means transcending extremes. The austere practices described below may seem extreme to some people but then they were not intended for all Buddhists, not even for all bhikkhus. They were never made compulsory by the Buddha but were aids to individual training to be used by those bhikkhus who found them helpful.

The aim in the Dhamma is to be free from desires. To attain this goal the multitude of desires, both wholesome and unwholesome, have to be sorted out and the former strengthened while the latter are weakened. Wholesome desires are wishes and intentions to be generous, keep the Precepts, practise meditation and so on. The unwholesome desires (for the bhikkhu) are greed manifesting in desire for sensual pleasures and these can be curbed by the thirteen austere practices. They are concerned with various limitations upon (1) a bhikkhu's robes, (2) his almsfood, (3) his dwelling-place, (4) his posture. They are described here in brief.[77]

A bhikkhu who undertakes the *refuse-rag-wearer's practice* makes up his robes from cloth that he finds thrown away. This he washes, dyes, cuts up, and sews together as his robes. Such a bhikkhu refuses to accept ready-made robes presented by householders, also clean white cloth given by them. This practice is now rare since it has the disadvantage of making a bhikkhu conspicuously different in his patchwork robes. All the austere practices should be undertaken without announcing them to others!

The *triple-robe-wearer's practice* is more common among forest bhikkhus and really essential in the wandering life. If a bhikkhu is wandering on foot, he will be wearing two of his robes while his double thick cloak is folded in his bowl. He will not wish to carry any more robes! Apart from this, the Buddha allowed bhikkhus to have a set of three robes: the inner sarong-like robe, the upper robe to cover the body coming down over the inner robe and the outer cloak of two layers of cloth for use when really cold. Besides these three robes it would be usual to have a bathing cloth, which is permissible according to Vinaya.

In the *alms-food-eater's practice* a bhikkhu eats only what is given in this way. What people place in his bowl, that he later eats. He does not send laypeople out to buy more food, or to cook this or that themselves but is content with the daily offering in his almsbowl, whether little of it or much. This is commonly observed by forest bhikkhus.

The *house-to-house-seeker's practice* involves going to every house in the direction one walks. No houses should be missed, perhaps because they give only poor food or one gets the feeling of being unwelcome, or they are dirty—to each house the bhikkhu with this practice goes and stands silently for a short time before passing on. This is possible still to practise in

---

77. For a full description see *The Path of Purification*, Ch. II—The Ascetic Practices. Also outlined in *With Robes and Bowl*, Wheel 83/84.

Sri Lanka (or even in India) but would now be unusual in Thailand.

If a bhikkhu eats only once in the morning it is called the *one-sessioner's practice.* He does not, like the town bhikkhu, have a second meal at eleven but eats after returning from his Piṇḍapāta at about eight or nine o'clock. This meal is then sufficient for a whole day. Commonly practised by forest bhikkhus.

Bhikkhus in the towns commonly have plates and dishes but one who cultivates fewness of wishes places all his food—rice, curries, sweets and fruits, into his bowl and eats only from that. This is therefore called the *bowl-food-eater's practice.* Again, it is very common among bhikkhus in the forest.

Sometimes when a bhikkhu has already begun to eat, laypeople come late with food they wish to offer. But if a bhikkhu is practising the *later-food-refuser's practice* he does not accept their offering—explaining courteously why he does not do so. When people come from far away to make the offering which has involved them in hard work, then the bhikkhu must decide whether it is not better to lay aside his practice for that day so as not to disappoint those people. This is quite commonly practised specially by individual bhikkhus or at special times such as the rains-residence.

The *forest dweller's practice* is clear—a bhikkhu who undertakes it lives in a kuṭi in the forest, not in a village or town. But "forest" here according to the explanations in "The Path of Purification" rather means anywhere outside a village which should be "500 bow lengths' away, a distance of about half a mile. All forest bhikkhus practise this.

The *tree-root-dweller's practice* is more severe for it means that one gives up living inside a building and lives on a mat at the foot of a shady tree or perhaps upon a little raised bamboo platform. This means that one is not secure from rain, nor from various troublesome creatures like ants, or even snakes. As a bhikkhu must have a roof over his head and four walls round him during the three months of the rains-residence this practice cannot be undertaken then.

Even more severe is the *open-air-dweller's practice.* Undertaking this a bhikkhu renounces even the shelter of trees and lives without any kind of roof and only his robes as protection, a hard thing to do under the tropical sky. This practice also is not for the rains.

A practice which is now not possible as it was in the Buddha's days is the *charnel-ground-dweller's practice.* In those days bodies were often not cremated or buried but simply taken to an outlying stretch of forest and then left there. Bodies in various stages of decomposition and dismemberment would be found there and could be made very good meditation subjects. *The Path of Purification* (Ch. VI) lists the bloated, the livid, the festering, the cut up, the gnawed, the scattered, the hacked and scattered, the bleeding, the worm-infested and the skeleton—as different types of corpses found there. Another list is found in the Discourse on the Foundations of Mindfulness. But in Buddhist culture nowadays corpses are never left to decay but always cremated. The cremation area, a stretch of forest near a village can still be eerie enough and good for both overcoming fear and contemplating impermanence in the shape of the heaps of charcoal and charred bone splinters.[78] This is still widely practised.

The *any-bed-user's practice* is specially suitable for promoting contentment. The bhikkhu who undertakes it is content with whatever kuṭi he is allotted, he does not ask for this or that place. This is another common practice.

Last in the list of thirteen comes the *sitter's practice,* undertaken by the words "I refuse lying down" or "I undertake the sitter's practice." Here a bhikkhu practises meditation and general mindfulness in only three of the four postures, walking, standing and sitting, but not lying down. He sleeps sitting, a practice which limits sleep and cuts down on slothfulness. Widely used by bhikkhus who are striving hard.

---

78. See "A Walk in the Woods" in *Impermanence,* Wheel 186–187.

If a bhikkhu is staying by himself in a cave or at the root of a tree, the practices that he undertakes will be of his own choice, but if he is living in a forest vihāra where there is a meditation master then he will follow the practices generally observed there. All of these practices make for a simplification of life, for being unburdened from possessions and the care that must go into looking after them. The bhikkhu with these austere practices has therefore established himself in the way that leads to non-attachment to material things and the cares they bring while having energy to devote to meditation.

This brings us to glance at the third support for bhikkhus in forest vihāras: the practice of meditation. As this is a vast subject it can only be briefly described asking readers to consult the special books on the subject,[79] or better still, a meditation master. The ordinary mind that we have is "wild" or untamed. It skips about from one sense object to another, interlarding all the sensory data with memories, reflections, ideas, fantasies, hopes, and fears. Mind, in fact, is not one "thing" but a stream of mental processes only some of which we are aware of and we only use a small part of the great potential of the mind. This untamed mind besides being scattered is also weakened through the presence of constituent factors which are called defilements. The greedy mind, the lustful mind, the angry mind, the anxious mind, the conceited mind, the slothful mind, the distracted mind, the confused or depressed mind—these are commonly occurring mental states ruled by defilements. The presence of defilements in the mind means, inevitably, the experience of dukkha—what is unsatisfactory or suffering. So the untamed mind is the source of suffering for oneself and causes suffering to others.

The first requisite for meditation, the purification of the mind, is therefore effort. The effort needed here is to remove the unwholesome states and cultivate wholesome states of mind. We shall see how effort is made by the forest bhikkhu in his life.

---

79. See *The Path of Purification*, Chapters III-IX (BPS), *The Heart of Buddhist Meditation* Nyanaponika Thera, Rider and Co. London. *Contemplation of the Body*, Somdet Phra Ñāṇasaṃvara, Mahamakut Press, Bangkok.

With effort strongly present, awareness or mindfulness grows. The slack and lazy-minded person is also dull and aware of little that goes on in the mind. Now mindfulness is the most important single factor in meditation and if it is not increased and developed, meditation cannot be expected to succeed. So the Buddha has taught the four Foundations of Mindfulness: the body, feelings, mental states and mental factors. Under each of these headings there are exercises listed which sharpen mindfulness.[80] When a person is mindful of, for instance, bodily positions, pleasant, painful and neutral feelings, states of mind with or without specific defilements, and the subtle mental factors which arise and pass away unnoticed by most people, such alertness is the basis for deep and strong meditation.

Until mindfulness is well-established, meditation is more or less a struggle and the meditator finds it very difficult to maintain concentration over long periods of time. But, once mindfulness is made even and continuous, then, distractions and other unwholesome mental factors which disturb concentration can no longer arise. If they do so, then mindfulness is quick to spot the disturbance and use some wholesome Dhamma to cure that trouble.

There are two types of meditation in Buddhist tradition: calm and insight. The meditation on calm or tranquillity can be achieved by the use of many different objects—which should be in some way connected with one's own mind-and-body, but generally not exterior to them. Thus mindful breathing, or the concentration upon loving-kindness in one's heart, or upon coloured light, are examples of one-pointedness of mind. In this type of meditation the mind is continuously aware of only the meditation object and this leads to the experience of bliss and peace. This can be developed so strongly that the meditator is no longer aware of any sensual contact—nothing affects him by way of eye, ear, nose, tongue, or touch, but his

80. See *The Heart of Buddhist Meditation* and *The Way of Mindfulness,* Soma Thera, BPS, Kandy. The latter has a full translation of the Buddha's discourse on the Foundations of Mindfulness with Commentary.

mind is brilliantly aware, calm and full of joy and rapture. Such inward states of peace are called *jhāna* and the meditator who reaches them really meditates, he is no longer "trying to meditate."

But with these states alone Enlightenment cannot be attained for they correspond to a realm of subtle existence and the meditator who dies in one of the jhāna-states just continues to exist, or is "reborn," in that state with a subtle body instead of a gross human one. These heavenly states, called the Brahma-worlds, can be enjoyed as the results of making good kammas—that is of having attained the jhānas and practised them, but like all conditioned things, must pass away eventually. Even though the life span is very long in those heavens, it also comes to an end. Just as a rich man who lives on his capital, making no more wealth for himself, in the end exhausts his money, so with the beings in any of the heavenly planes. They must then be reborn in accordance with previous kammas, perhaps as men again. All that effort to attain the jhānas has then to be made all over again. It has not got them out of the wheel of birth and death.

On the basis of strong calm the second kind of meditation can be developed—and this is unique to the Buddha's Teachings. This is called insight (*vipassanā*) which grows into wisdom (*paññā*) and it is this wisdom which cuts off the basis for future birth and death and opens the gate to Enlightenment. Insight into what? Insight into the three characteristics of all living beings: impermanence, unsatisfactoriness (suffering) and non-self.[81] Though we sometimes know about our own impermanence this undoubted fact is not always clearly present in our minds. As we do not comprehend it all the time, so we grasp at people, possessions, places and experiences as permanent—including our own minds and bodies. So we are deluded and upset when our delusion is made clear to us by impermanence—the loss of loved ones, the breaking or loss of possessions, and so on. And most of all we fear impermanence manifesting in this body.

81. For full explanation, see *The Three Basic Facts of Existence*, BPS, Kandy

Whatever is impermanent, that is also unsatisfactory. No reliance can be placed upon impermanent events; they offer no security. Yet we live in a world of impermanent events which are happenings perceived by way of the five senses and sorted by the mind. Not only the objects "out there" are impermanent but more important, the processes of perception are changing all the time. But we live attached to impermanent things trying to pretend that they are permanent so we experience dukkha, the unsatisfactoriness of the continually passing show.

Now whatever is impermanent and unsatisfactory, that cannot be *myself*. Self or soul is taken to be something permanent. However nothing like this can be found among impermanent and conditioned things. The sense of ownership which we have over this mind and body is therefore useless and deluded. All that is body, feeling, perception, mental formations and consciousness—the sum-total of myself, should be seen with insight-wisdom as not-self. When this has been accomplished there is no identification with these transitory component parts and, instead, "The mind gone to the Unconditioned, to craving's destruction it has come." (See Chapter I) Nibbāna has been attained, Arahantship realized and the miseries of the wheel of birth and death forever extinguished. This is how meditation, in brief, leads to the final attainment which is the goal of the forest bhikkhu.

The day to day life of these bhikkhus is undisturbed by many exterior events but there will be differences depending on whether a bhikkhu stays in a forest vihāra under the guidance of a Teacher, or whether he is wandering in the forest or staying by himself for some time in a cave or other quiet place. As new bhikkhus and sāmaṇeras must stay with a Teacher who will usually be the abbot of a forest vihāra, this mode of life will be described first.

When a new day dawns a forest bhikkhu will just have finished his meditation in his own hut or kuṭi. It is about six o'clock, a little before or after depending on season, and he gathers his things to take them to the hall or sālā. He will have his three robes, the lower one secured with the waistband he has on, the upper one either carried over his shoulder or gathered round him like a shawl according to how cool it is. The outer robe he carries folded up probably in his bowl, in which there will also be a sitting-cloth, wiping-cloth and a clean handkerchief. In the hand not engaged with his bowl he has a water-kettle and a mug. On reaching the sālā he removes his sandals and carefully places them where others will not step on them and goes up the steps to find his place among the bhikkhus. When he has put his bowl down he prostrates thrice to the Buddha image. He must then arrange his sitting-cloth on the floor and his other things neatly in the place to which he is entitled by the order of seniority. The Abbot and Teacher is usually most senior in rains and he has the first seat, raised up by a thin cushion on the floor and another cushion for resting the back. After him the bhikkhus are seated in order of seniority. If new bhikkhus arrive then they are courteously asked about the number of their rains so that they can be seated appropriately. But before all the arrangements can be made for the meal the *sālā* has to be swept, then each bhikkhu lays out his own sitting-cloth and bowl in his right place. The bowls and so on of senior bhikkhus including the Teacher are brought to the sālā by junior bhikkhus, or by sāmaṇeras, and everything is carefully prepared for them before they arrive.

When all this has been finished it is still too early to go to the village. But there is no chatting or wasting time, for the sālā is vigorously polished and dusted till the wooden floor shines. The forest Teachers lay emphasis upon physical vigour, plus mindfulness, as an aid to mental vigour. The defilements cannot be shaken off by one who is lazy and slothful; only the vigorous person has the chance to do that. But though things are done vigorously, there is no noise. Bhikkhus speak softly, do their work quietly where possible and leave it neat and tidy. All this is the good result of mindfulness.

The time for going to the village arrives and the bhikkhus and sāmaṇeras put on their robes and then carefully pick up their bowls in their slings, the strap of which goes on the right shoulder under the robe. Young bhikkhus will also take the bowls of the Teacher and other theras so that they may walk unburdened by them as far as the village.

Walking to the village a mile or two miles away is in silence. The early morning is silent apart from birds and the bells on the necks of the water-buffalo. It is a very good time to practise walking-meditation. Bhikkhus walk as fast as they like—in the cold weather this keeps the blood circulating in the feet—but the fast walkers must wait for everyone else just outside the village. Often the Teacher is one of the last to arrive—which gives him a chance to observe the conduct of his bhikkhus walking to the village. When he comes up to the waiting bhikkhus, the bhikkhu with his bowl gives it to him respectfully and all the bhikkhus follow him in a long line, in order of seniority.

Now their walk is steady, their eyes fixed a plough's length in front as they go round the village streets. Groups of laypeople, both men and women, have gathered outside their houses with baskets in their hands. These baskets are full of the glutinous rice which is the staple of N.E. Thailand and Laos. With their hands they each place a lump of this in the bowls as the bhikkhus pass before them. Occasionally someone will offer bananas as well but usually only the rice is put in the bowl. Some vihāras have energetic small boys, destined to become sāmaṇeras, who collect the curries, vegetables and fruit from the laypeople and put them in tiffin-carriers. In other places some of the laypeople take these things to the vihāra and eat there themselves after the bhikkhus have finished.

Slowly the bowls fill and after going round the village to accept all the offering which people wish to make, the bhikkhus leave. Just as they reach the village outskirts the young bhikkhus and sāmaṇeras run forward and offer to take the bowls of the Teacher and other senior bhikkhus. So the young vigorous bhikkhus have two rather heavy bowls to carry back to the vihāra but they set off at a good pace.

On arriving at the sālā each bhikkhu washes his feet before entering and dries them. Lay people or sāmaṇeras will do this for all the senior bhikkhus at least. Before the bhikkhus are seated they prostrate three times. As the more senior bhikkhus return they will find that everything is ready to begin serving the food. Their bowls have been removed from their slings and placed neatly on their bowlstands. If they have been touched by sāmaṇeras or laypeople then the latter have to offer them back to a bhikkhu. Bhikkhus cannot accept food that has not been offered into their bowls while they are holding them. For the same reason the curries and so on, have to be offered in their various containers.

When all the bhikkhus are seated, the Teacher begins to put into his bowl whatever he wants to eat with the rice, surplus rice having been removed already. Each container he passes on to the next senior bhikkhu—and so all eventually reach even the newest sāmaṇera. Where amounts of some things are insufficient for all, the Teacher may send them down to be shared among the sāmaṇeras, or when the ladling of food into the bowls has ceased he may get up and go to see whether the sāmaṇeras have enough or not. Individual bhikkhus also collect titbits for some of the sāmaṇeras who have been diligent and respectful and send them down the line. Thus everyone has enough.

The aim is to put into one's bowl just the right amount for eating but this is not possible when many laypeople arrive to make merit on the same day or on Buddhist festivals. They offer so many things that even taking a little from each the bowl begins to fill. It is inevitable that food will be left over on these days but it is not wasted for hungry villagers relish it. (Some lay people even suppose that it has special power having been in the bhikkhus' bowls!)

Before beginning to eat and when the last sāmaṇera has finished with the last dish, the Teacher begins to chant the verses of "Rejoicing-with" in which the bhikkhus join in some vihāras. This is quite brief and usually followed by some minutes of silent contemplation.

What do the bhikkhus reflect on at this time? One text they may bring to mind is, "Reflecting carefully I use this almsfood..." (See p. 115.) Another subject they can bring to mind is the loathsomeness of food (which will have been easier to see when the almsfood was spooned into one's bowl in the Buddha's days, all mixed together, but is more difficult now, specially when choice things are prepared)! The Buddha advised bhikkhus to have moderation in eating and to control greed by reflecting on loathsomeness. A chapter in—*The Path of Purification*—elaborates on this theme. The Buddha himself compared almsfood to one's son's flesh. He told the story of a couple that was travelling across a desert with their only son, a child of tender age. Part way across their food ran out and they considered slaying their own son in order to survive but he died of exhaustion first. Then they cut up his body and dried the flesh and, sustained on this diet, crossed the desert. The Buddha asked the bhikkhus, "Will they eat this with greed and craving, or will it be only just enough to sustain them?" The bhikkhus replied that they would eat moderately and not with greed. Thus, the Buddha said, should almsfood be eaten.[82]

The food is eaten with the right hand from the bowl and while this is going on there is no talking, unless the Teacher has something to say to the laypeople. Mostly there is silent concentration on the reasons for eating food. Each bhikkhu eats as much as he feels is necessary "so that former feelings of hunger are destroyed and new feelings from overeating do not arise." As soon as each bhikkhu is satisfied he washes his hand in his bowl lid and then tips the water into the spittoon. Then he rises and takes out his bowl and spittoon for washing. Also he takes the bowls of bhikkhus senior to him and their spittoons. When they have been carefully washed and then dried in the sālā they are set in the sun's heat for a few moments to dry off any remaining moisture. A bhikkhu must not be negligent and let his bowl rust. The requisites of the theras are returned to their kuṭis and arranged properly after which the bhikkhu takes his own things back.

Perhaps at this time he has to visit the latrine. If the vihāra has been built a long time, it is likely to have enamelled

82. See *The Four Nutriments of Life*, Wheel No. 105/106.

squatting-type latrines over a pit dug by the sāmaṇeras and laymen with the bhikkhus helping. The inside is spotlessly clean, another area where the Vinaya regulations are carefully applied. A leading meditation master in Northeast Thailand has said that one may know a good vihāra by two facts: Are the novices (sāmaṇeras) respectful? Are the latrines clean? The first of these points means that if the sāmaṇeras, the youngest and least trained element in the vihāra, are respectful, then everyone else will be so and the vihāra harmonious. As to the latrines, they are used by everyone but do not belong to anyone. People who are not mindful do not clean up after themselves or they do not see to it that supplies of things are renewed there. But where everything is in good order in such a place, the rest of the vihāra is likely to be well run and peaceful. A small walled and roofed latrine contains a large water-jar with a top on it to prevent mosquitoes laying eggs there and a scoop for washing oneself when one has finished. Soap and a candle and matches will also be found. In some places there is paper but most vihāras still have the narrow strips of smooth bamboo used with the water for cleansing.

More primitive arrangements are simple pits in the forest with some wood over the top. The contemplation on the changes wrought on that delicious food can be continued by regarding the filth below seething with maggots.

The bhikkhu after his meal will probably pace up and down on his meditation walk for half an hour or so. The Buddha mentioned that this path has five benefits: "It hardens one for travelling; it is good for striving; it is healthy; (its use) tends to good digestion after one has eaten and drunk; the concentration won upon a meditation-path lasts a long time" (AN 5:29. Adapted from Hare's rendering in *Gradual Sayings* III).

His meditation-path is some way from his kuṭi and preferably surrounded by shady trees so that it can also be used during the day though mostly used at night. When he has dispelled any sleepiness from the meal he sits down under his kuṭi or nearby to make various articles used by bhikkhus. He may make toothpick-brushes out of a log of bitter-tasting wood.

This is bashed on one end with a stone so that the fibres curl down. When plenty of fibre has been exposed, slivers are cut off the log and smoothed, one end to a fine point, the other being the fibrous "brush." Bundles of these are presented to one's Teacher, to visiting theras and to bhikkhu-friends. Some bhikkhus are skilled at making the large umbrellas that forest bhikkhus carry and from which a mosquito net is hung so that a bhikkhu has a secure "tent" to meditate in. Another thing which is made skilfully from bamboo growing in the vihāra is the bamboo broom used everyday for cleaning the grounds. After an hour or two of these small works a bhikkhu may rest during the heat of the day.

Occasionally bhikkhus have some heavy work to do, a new sālā or kuṭi to erect, fencing or gateposts to see to, or individual bhikkhus seeing rust in their bowl decide to oxidize them afresh. This involves stripping the old oxidized layer and collecting plenty of firewood, an old but clean oil drum, and one or two friends to help. The bowl is placed upside down on sandy ground supported by stones with the drum fitting over it and made airtight. Then the bamboo or wood is heaped up around and lit, five fires being made in this way in the course of the day. When the evening comes and the last fire has burnt low, the embers are removed and the drum very carefully taken off. And there, if he is lucky, is a beautiful silver-grey surface inside and outside the bowl—which should prevent rust for another five years with careful handling.

Another all-day job which comes up from time to time is making robes. A number of forest bhikkhus are skilled at sewing, these days using a machine, although one can still find bhikkhus who can sew a set of robes by hand, usually for presentation to some revered Teacher. An upper robe, cutting the material in strips, marking the seams and cross-pieces and sewing together, takes about one day to make. An outer robe which is double-thick and more difficult to make can take nearly two days. It is usual to cut robes from bolts of white cloth (given by lay supporters), so afterwards they have to be dyed the yellow-brown obtained from boiling up jak-wood.

Every week or two, depending on the season, there is a washing day when fires are lighted, jak-wood chips boiled up and all bhikkhus bring their robes for washing and re-dyeing. Teachers and senior bhikkhus of course are served by the younger members of the Sangha. This is also a job needing all the morning and some of the afternoon.

Then every month, on the day before Full Moon, it is time to shave the head. Bhikkhus generally shave each other. The one who is shaving taking care not to cause any cuts with his open razor, a thing rather disgraceful if it happens since it indicates a lack of mindfulness and skill, while the one being shaved reflects perhaps upon impermanence—the falling of his hair. Solitary bhikkhus shave themselves with the same "cut-throat" type of razor and show their skill and perfect mindfulness by their perfectly shaved heads. One slip of mindfulness means one cut!

A rest during the midday would be normal for those bhikkhus who try not to sleep at night—which is the best time for meditation. They rest from about ten o'clock when the sālā has been cleaned until about three in the afternoon. This is a quiet time in the vihāra and few bhikkhus can be seen then. There will be one or two sāmaṇeras staying under the sālā in order to receive any guests who may happen to come at this time.

Receiving a guest in the proper way is an important part of bhikkhu training. If he is a senior bhikkhu, his reception will cause a stir, even though it is during the quiet time. Sāmaṇeras will go to receive his bowl and shoulder bag. Someone will pour water over his feet from the pot at the entrance of the sālā and they will then be dried. Meanwhile up in the sālā, bhikkhus and sāmaṇeras, some alerted by the sound of an approaching vehicle, have hurried about and set out an appropriate sitting-place with at least a bottle of water, a glass and a spittoon. Sometimes other drinks are offered together with betel and areca-nuts for chewing. When the thera has reached his seat he pays respect to the Buddha image and the pictures of enlightened Teachers before he sits down. His upper robe is taken by sāmaṇeras to spread out and dry, while in hot weather he will be fanned. The abbot of that vihāra will hasten there and pay his respects to the visitor if the latter is senior to him and all other bhikkhus do likewise. Even if the guests are a party of people from a local village they are invited into the sālā where mats are spread and water set out to drink.

The first noise which marks the end of the midday period is a gentle but insistent one: the swish of the long bamboo brooms over the sandy paths. When a senior bhikkhu begins to sweep, the sound is heard by his neighbour in a kuṭi perhaps fifty yards away so that he begins sweeping—and so it spreads all over the vihāra. Bhikkhus first sweep their own kuṭis, a job done every day.

All the paths and open spaces too have to be swept each day. This is partly so that the vihāra is neat and clean but also because dead leaves on the ground can harbour dangerous insects and reptiles which the forest-bhikkhu, with bare feet, does not want to tread upon. Sweeping is also fine exercise for the body and a good time to exert the mind with one's meditation subject. The Parivāra, the fifth book of the Vinaya, gives five advantages of brooms: "one calms one's own mind; one calms the minds of others; the devas are glad; one accumulates kamma that is conducive to what is pleasant; at the breaking up of the body after dying one arises in a good bourn, a heaven world." In a further five benefits, the first three are the same, and then "the Teacher's instruction is carried out; people coming after fall into the way of (right) views."[83] Brooms are much esteemed! The whole vihāra, round about each kuṭi, the winding paths and the open space about the sālā may take an hour to sweep.

As sweeping raises dust, the open-sided sālā has to be cleaned before the next piece of work. This is to fill all the

83. trans. *The Book of Discipline* VI p. 207, I.B. Horner, P.T.S.

water pots in the various latrines and those smaller ones outside each kuṭi. (The latter are used when a bhikkhu will enter his kuṭi which he cannot do with dirty feet, or for washing his face, etc.). The water comes from a well and is raised by a number of manually operated devices. Teachers generally do not approve of machines being used for this, partly because they are noisy, partly because bhikkhus lose some chance for good exercise. The water is carried round the vihāra in large tins suspended from a bamboo pole borne on the shoulders of two bhikkhus. When all the pots are full it is time for a bath.

The Teacher usually has his own bathroom but all the other bhikkhus bathe round the well-head from buckets of water which they tip over themselves, soap and then more water. The bathing cloth is used at this time in accordance with the Buddha's instructions that bhikkhus should not be naked in a public place.

Cool and refreshed the bhikkhus may then go to the fire-sālā, a small open building with a room for storing tea, coffee, cocoa and sugar—and any other things that bhikkhus can take as medicine after midday. Such things as myrobalan, an astringent plum-like fruit, pickled in brine with chilli (a purgative!), garlic, salt and various dried stems or roots which can be used for different complaints. But this hot drink may not be available every night. If bhikkhus have had to work during the morning and early afternoon then the Teacher will allow some refreshment. On other days there is nothing except plentiful supplies of rain water from the tanks round the sālā. This is true for every day of the year in the more remote vihāras. Those near to "progress" may have the benefits of bottled drinks as well but they have also to put up with a lot of visitors!

Even when bhikkhus gather, as at this time, conversation is limited to necessary subjects, which are discussed both quietly and briefly. Teachers discourage much talking which tends to turn to worldly things. Absolute silence, or vows to remain silent cannot be made, the Buddha having criticized some bhikkhus who did so, comparing them to horses, cows and sheep! Soft, gentle speech which is to the point is commended.

Evening has come. Some vihāras have a regular evening meeting at which all the bhikkhus and sāmaṇeras led by the teacher do the evening chanting with laypeople joining in if any are present. At other places the teacher does not like to have meetings so often and they may be held on each Holyday (the four phases of the Moon), or even only on the two Uposatha-days (the Full and New Moon days). In some vihāras there is no chanting and the bhikkhus gather and sit in silence until the Teacher arrives when they pay their respects to him and he begins his discourse.

However that discourse begins, it is not usually based, like a town-bhikkhu's sermon, on a quotation from the Buddha-word. Usually the teacher takes up some incident of that day, or recently, and makes that the basis for his talk. Perhaps he has seen someone breaking a Vinaya-rule, or he knows the mind of another bhikkhu which is going on the wrong path of practice, thinking the wrong sort of thoughts. If laypeople are present, the Dhamma talk may be addressed to them—all about events in the local village, or how to live at peace with others, encouraging them to make merit as the basis of happiness, or explaining sets of Dhammas which they will find useful in everyday life. In any case, there is complete silence on the part of the bhikkhus and the laity. No one even coughs or moves any part of the body while the discourse is going on. Everyone listens intently. This intent listening to the Dhamma can be the foundation of Enlightenment when the Dhamma spoken is exactly suited to the minds attuned to it.

When the discourse has ended—and sometimes it may go on for hours—all pay respects to the Buddha, Dhamma and Sangha, after which all the bhikkhus and sāmaṇeras honour the Teacher with three prostrations. Sitting mats, bottles of water and glasses are quietly put away and the candles extinguished on the shrine. All disperse silently to their kuṭis.

The night is the time for *samaṇa-dhamma*. "Samaṇa" is "one who makes himself peaceful in mind, speech and body," hence a bhikkhu or nun, while Dhamma is what should be practised to bring this about. But, before a bhikkhu goes to meditate, he may have something to do for his Teachers. It is common at this time, especially if the Teacher is old, to massage his legs and back. This gives bhikkhus a good chance to ask personal questions about meditation or other ways of conduct. And the Teacher in answering may refer to other Teachers, perhaps to the venerable Tan Acharn Mun Bhūridatta Thera, or to other great Teachers and their lives. A small group of bhikkhus and sāmaṇeras kneel around their Teacher and listen to his words, sometimes late into the night...

Returning to the kuṭi invigorated by the Teacher's words, a bhikkhu does not feel like sleeping but just to ward off sloth he may decide to do walking-meditation. If there is no moon he lights some small candles and places them on tree-stumps or rocks at either end of his walk so that he will not tread on a snake or any other creature. For when the wind blows, he has made himself a small collapsible cloth lantern in which candles can be fixed. Before beginning his walk he places his hands together reverently and recollects the Triple Gem and then begins steadily pacing back and forth, at each end checking that the mind is fixed on the meditation subject. His walking can go on for hours, indeed some bhikkhus prefer this to sitting meditation, but usually after an hour or two a bhikkhu will change to the sitting posture in his kuṭi or outside on its veranda.

Night is the time when it is good to meditate. In the tropics it is cooler, it is also much quieter then. But the greatest advantage at this time is that the defilements become manifest more clearly. Slothfulness is an obvious example, specially at one or two in the morning! Also desires of various kinds raise their heads and can be recognized with mindfulness. Fears too come on with the night: darkness, snakes, tigers or just the unknown. The forest bhikkhu trains himself to face them and so become fearless. At night he is out of sight even of fellow-bhikkhus. He is the doer of heroic deeds, the true hero who conquers himself.

Though one conquers on the battlefield
a thousand times a thousand men,
yet should one conquer just oneself
one is indeed the greatest conqueror. (Dhp 103).

Now if we go on to consider the forest bhikkhu life outside a vihāra, it is much simpler by comparison with the account above. A bhikkhu has only eight possessions or requisites, whether he lives in town or forest: three robes (lower, upper and outer cloak), a waistband, a bowl, a water-strainer, a razor, and needle and thread as the eighth. There will be few other things that a wandering bhikkhu wishes to carry. These days, he will have besides them: a shoulder-bag (for handkerchief, small medicines, penknife etc.), a water bottle in a sling and a *klot*—umbrella-mosquito net also in a sling. Already he has quite a load! In the days of the Buddha (and in other Buddhist countries apart from Thailand) the *klot* and shoulder bag are not used though a forest bhikkhu can have a very hard time trying to meditate while surrounded by swarms of hungry mosquitoes!

So fewness of possessions marks the wandering bhikkhu. Few possessions means few troubles. While the bhikkhu in a forest vihāra has to clean his own kuṭi and sweep all the vihāra grounds each day, the lone bhikkhu in forest or cave has no such duties. This does not mean that he can be lazy: on the contrary, he must be more alert, more aware, more mindful, since he has so much more time to himself. For this reason, only experienced bhikkhus of more than five rains go off by themselves for long periods. Newer bhikkhus stay with a Teacher until their practice is strong enough to live in the wilds.

To live content in a cave or on a little platform in the forest, or among some rocks, is the mark of a bhikkhu whose mind has turned away from worldly comfort. He finds happiness from his practice and from possession of very few things. A meal once a day is plenty and sometimes if his meditation is going well he does not bother with that. Some water to drink; his robes to keep off heat or cold; a *klot* to shelter in and the simple medicines which trees and plants offer to cure at least minor sickness—with these he lives as though in an abundance of riches.

Loneliness is something he enjoys for it helps him to develop one-pointedness of mind and finally to attain that security from the defilements which the mind reaches at the moments of seeing the Path and knowing Nibbāna. But his aloneness is not that of the misanthrope, for part of his practice is developing mettā or loving-kindness so vast that it embraces all the worlds and planes of existence.

But to attain this goal of Enlightenment requires, at least, very great efforts in this life. Helpful too for its accomplishment will be a stock of good kammas made in past lives. It is true that there are some people who have only to hear a few words to set them on the path to Enlightenment but they have always been few. Others require only a single discourse to inspire them and gain the Noble Paths and Fruits but they are rare too. Most of us, if we are to get anywhere, must have repeated instruction after which we must practise hard for many years before attainment comes. Finally, there are those for whom "words are the highest"—meaning that because of blockages from past bad kammas they cannot attain anything in this life however hard they may try.

There is a phrase in the Pāli Canon often repeated in the stock passage which describes the enlightenment of a bhikkhu: "in no long time" he attained Arahantship. (See for instance the Discourse about Raṭṭhapāla in the Appendix). The Commentary says that this "No long time" spent in the wilds was in Raṭṭhapāla's case, twelve years. Most people these days when so many things are "quick" or even "instant" would certainly call this a long time. They might be prepared to do a seven day course, or one lasting a fortnight, even a month, but the number who would spend a year or longer at systematic and careful application of Dhamma and Vinaya, are few indeed. Short periods of practice are useful for those who have no time for more extended efforts but they can never replace the single-minded devotion and renunciation exemplified by the forest bhikkhu.

His way of life now is not very different from that of bhikkhus in the Buddha-time among whom there were so many Arahants. It is not surprising therefore, that some who have made the Dhamma their very own by penetrating its truth in their own hearts, are still to be found among forest bhikkhus today.

CHAPTER VII

BHIKKHUNĪS AND BUDDHIST NUNS NOW

Kamma and rebirth as woman with more dukkha—attraction to works and faith—position of women in India—history of bhikkhunī-saṅgha—Eight important points—dangers of sex and conceit—double ordination—novices—special rules—some bhikkhunīs of the Buddha-time—Asoka's daughter a bhikkhunī—bhikkhunīs in Sri Lanka to China—Are there bhikkhunīs now?—upāsikās (nuns) and their support—their life—Westerners becoming nuns—The foundation of Thai nuns and its work—nuns in Burma and Sri Lanka

Having described the different sorts of bhikkhu life, it is now the turn of the bhikkhunī, as the original Buddhist nuns were called. Their Sangha was formed six years after the first bhikkhus' and to appreciate their position in India at that time, before giving their history, the Buddhist teaching on rebirth should be clarified. The point that we shall be interested in is why one is reborn specifically as man or woman.

Kamma (in Sanskrit, karma), is the key to understanding about rebirth generally. In the present time we are constantly deciding, I shall go ... or I like ... or I hate ... or any number of other decisions. Many of the varied kinds of minds, which pass in a stream (and which I call collectively my mind') are concerned with decision-making. Every time a decision is made, always with reference to the fictional self—the "I" or ego—this is called kamma, the work of the mind. This work bears fruits, just as work done with the hands, and the results or fruits it bears are manifest in different ways—as happiness or suffering. Kamma is good when beneficial to oneself and others, that is, it leads to growth and purification of one's own mind and to the benefit of other people. When that kamma fruits, its fruits will be happiness; but bad kammas, actions done for one's own deterioration and others' harm bear the fruits of suffering. Not all kammas fruit in the present life. We may see good people whose goodness seems to come to no good fruit, while there are evildoers who get away with everything and never seem to come to harm. Their present kammas are not fruiting yet, obstructed by previous kammas giving different results.

When a person comes to die, craving is usually part of the character which is craving to exist, to continue experiencing. With strong craving in the stream of mind and having made much kamma not yet come to fruit, a person is bound to continue in the wheel of birth and death. The next birth depends on the last moment of consciousness before death and that in turn is dependent upon what sort of kammas one has made during life. A person dying with human thoughts in mind destines himself for rebirth as a human being. Death with thoughts affected by the roots of evil—greed, aversion or delusion, produces rebirth of various sub-human varieties, including birth as animals. On the other hand, if the last moment is occupied by thoughts of religion, or thoughts purified and inspired by religious practice, the mind being uplifted "above" ordinary human level, then rebirth takes place in the super-human heaven realms.

Nothing is permanent here. There are no permanent states of existence because the kammas giving rise to them are conditional, so rebirth states are conditioned too. And there is no entity, which is unchanging and passes from life to life, a soul or atman, or call it what you will. We discover no such "being" either through rational investigation, or by meditation experience: only conditional factors are found. This means that there is nothing essentially human, such as a soul. At present, the mind flows along the human channel—except when we are lustful or angry, when it becomes sub-human; or when we exercise loving kindness, compassion or generosity, when it is super-human. So mind varies, becoming different with the different mind of which it is composed. There is no special human particle, nor can we talk about an abiding masculinity or femininity.

If we take the case of a woman who in a past life has led a rather ordinary life—she has married, had children, brought up the family, looked after the house, we can see how much of her time will have been taken up with typically feminine activities. These centre around having a body which is capable of giving birth, suckling children and generally caring for their needs. Where so many kammas are made centred about female activities, it will not be surprising if at death, assuming that her mind is not raised or lowered by factors mentioned above, she grasps at rebirth as a woman again. Some women who become tired of the work bound up with a woman's body, grasp instead at birth as a man.

Now if we compare honestly, a typical man with a typical woman, it becomes clear that a woman has more sufferings to bear then a man. By the very nature of her body she has menstruation and the difficulties that this brings. The body's workings are geared to motherhood—with its pains and sufferings which can be increased a thousandfold by death of children and the other mishaps that may befall them. Here are some of the Arahant Kisāgotamī's verses on this subject:

> "Woman's state is painful,"
> declares the Trainer of tameable men,
> a wife with others is painful,
> and once having borne a child,
> some even cut their throats,
> while others of delicate constitution
> poison take, than pain again,
> And then there's the baby obstructing birth
> killing the mother too. (Th216–217).

Also, as women have this function of bearing children they crave usually for a secure environment to raise their family. Usually this means depending on a man who will gain a livelihood and provide that security. It is generally true to say, too, that women are less physically strong than men and require more protection than a man does, though there are obvious exceptions.

More difficulties, more sufferings, more *dukkha,* means from a Buddhist point of view, a less favourable birth, one which is created by kammas made with attachment to the continuity of existence. When the Buddha finally allowed women to go forth, and when he had to make special rules for them, probably the factors discussed above influenced his rulings.

There are other factors, too, which should be considered, especially the inclination of many women even when given the chance to lead the Holy Life, to be drawn towards faith and the sort of pious expressions of it combined with household activities which might well be called holy domesticity. It is noticeable that wherever a religion gives room for these things, there are many nuns, indeed they can outnumber monks. Examples of this can be found among Roman Catholics, also in Chinese Buddhism. But original Buddhist teachings emphasise the cultivation of mind, speech and body kammas through wisdom, meditation and moral conduct—an all-round and balanced development, not a one-sided approach through faith. It is easy to have faith (in a God, Buddhas or Bodhisattvas) but it is another thing to balance it with wisdom so that finally by knowing and seeing impermanence, *dukkha* and non-self, one goes beyond faith. The Arahant is called faithless—he no longer believes anything, instead he or she knows Dhamma. As women generally have more potential for belief and faith than men, it may be more difficult for them to pursue the Holy Life in the original Buddhist teachings which goes beyond the usual objects of belief (gods, devas, Buddhas, etc.).

Another and very important factor obstructive to the Holy Life among women was their position in India at the time of the Buddha. A Western woman who knows nothing of the sort of restrictions imposed by the Brahmins upon women, especially those of high caste, in India, cannot appreciate the significance of the Buddha's actions when he allowed women to become bhikkhunīs. The brahminical attitude towards women is summed up in the well-known verse which says, "Their fathers protect them in childhood, their husbands protect them in youth, their sons protect them in age: a woman is never fit for independence."[84] This means obviously, that the Brahmins held strongly that a woman's place is in the house. (It is still this way among orthodox Hindu households where women keep house, prepare food, bear children, preferably sons and get very little education or none at all). The teaching of the Brahmins, the priests of the Aryans who invaded India, did not favour spreading knowledge—they themselves and the noble-warrior caste shared power while the rest of the people, farmers, workers and outcasts, supported them. Their theory of a four-caste society made no allowances for people to leave home and seek a path through meditation in the forest. This teaching, of going forth, was not Aryan in origin but part of the religion practised by the pre-Aryan civilisations of India.[85] When Brahmins came into contact with this practice, they did not approve as it went beyond their system. Eventually, they incorporated it into the later classification of the four stages of life: celibate student, householder, retreat from social life and renunciation, which would mean that a man would only be able to go forth in old age, when he was weak and too conditioned to household life to make it practicable. Nothing is said about women going forth, and in fact modern Hinduism has almost no nuns.

Women coming from the little republics and federations with a more or less elected leadership where the power of the Brahmins was not yet consolidated, as in the Sakyas and the Licchavis, may have had more freedom, even those of noble lineage. But as brahminical teachings spread, with the growth of kingdoms and the disappearance of other forms of government, women of high caste became more and more restricted. Of course in the lower ranks of society, farmers and other poor folk, women still had the right—it was a necessity—to leave the house, go to market, plant the fields, and so on.

84. *The Laws of Manu* (*Mānavadharmaśāstra*), Ch. IX, 3.
85. See, *Brahmanism, Buddhism and Hinduism*, Wheel 150–151, BPS.

These women too will have had little education.

What is very important to realise is that women then had no chance to organise anything for themselves. This is in sharp contrast to our times when there are numerous ways in which women can come together and organise their energies to achieve their ends. So this is another point to remember when reading below the regulations laid down by the Buddha upon bhikkhunīs. In Chapter III we mentioned that some rules for bhikkhus are subject to the principle of time-and-country and it could be that this principle would apply also to bhikkhunīs, too, if they came into existence now instead of two thousand five hundred years ago.

People may say that it is because women have been trained from childhood to depend on men that they have an inferior position. No doubt this is partly true, in particular for the Indian scene but this view only takes account of the present life and does not realise that the tendencies made in past lives may have influence, too. It is possible that the facts presented so far and the account of the establishment of the Bhikkhunī Saṅgha below may displease some women. The truth, however, is not always palatable and pleasing. In case displeasure or anger should arise, such manifestations of aversion should be examined to see from where do they arise? Wounded vanity? Damaged pride? Such conceit would be a mental factor as far from the practice of Dhamma as humility is near to it. More will be said about this below.

Now, what is the history of the Bhikkhunī Saṅgha? The Commentaries say that when Prince Siddhattha left his palace at the time of his Great Renunciation, cut off his hair and donned yellowish brown robes, Yasodharā his wife, hearing that he had done these things, resolved to live in the same way in her palace. She shaved her head and wore rough patchwork robes, ate once a day from a bowl and slept on a low, hard bed. No doubt she strove also to develop her mind through meditation.

So even before there were any nuns formally ordained, Yasodharā out of devotion to the way shown by the prince, led a nun's life. When the Buddha, a year after his Enlightenment, returned to Kapilavatthu at the request of his father, Yasodharā had an opportunity to pay her respects together with the other Sakyan ladies, foremost among whom was Queen Mahāpajāpatī Gotamī, the Buddha's aunt and foster-mother. This lady became a Stream-winner upon hearing the Buddha's teaching while King Suddhodana won the third Path and Fruit of Non-returning.

Four or five years then passed before the Buddha again visited the Sakyan people. This time he went there because his father was gravely ill and he taught him Dhamma upon his deathbed so that the King attained to Arahantship.

At this time Mahāpajāpatī Gotamī went to him and asked if women might also get the chance to go forth into homelessness. The Buddha's reply is interesting, as it is not a flat refusal, "Enough Gotamī, do not ask for the going-forth from home to homelessness in the Dhamma-Vinaya declared by the Tathāgata." And though she asked three times the reply was the same, so she thought, "The Exalted One does not allow it" and she was sad and unhappy. If the Buddha wished to prohibit the formation of the Bhikkhunī Saṅgha, he could have used much more forceful language, such as, "It is impossible, Gotamī, it cannot happen that ..." All he told Mahāpajāpatī Gotamī was "enough, do not ask ..." and these words may be assumed to be a test of the sincerity of that lady and her companions. The life led by bhikkhus, at the beginning of the Buddha's teaching, was a hard one, hard even for the aristocratic men from the various princely and Brahmanical families who joined the Sangha: then how much harder would it not be for ladies from a sheltered palace life! Since the Buddha was aware of the intentions people had in their minds, he must have known that Mahāpajāpatī Gotamī intended to go forward with her idea but as she had not yet demonstrated her unshakeable resolve he did not grant permission.

We are told that after the Buddha left Kapilavatthu he went to Vesālī, a distance of 200 or 300 miles. "Meanwhile Mahāpajāpati had her hair cut off and put on the yellow cloth.

With a number of Sakyan women, she set out for Vesālī. On arrival there she went to the Peaked Gable Hall in the Great Wood, and she stood there outside the porch. Her feet were swollen, her limbs covered with dust, and she was sad and unhappy with tears on her face and sobbing. Sakyan ladies of rank were not accustomed to travel in this manner for they usually journeyed by palanquin or upon elephants. Then venerable Ānanda, who was especially compassionate with the troubles of women, saw her and asked what she did there. She told him that the Exalted One had not allowed her to become a bhikkhunī, so he offered to ask the Buddha again. The answer was still the same but venerable Ānanda was not deterred by this for he thought, "But suppose I asked the Exalted One in another way?" So he asked if it was possible for women to attain to the noble Paths and Fruits after Going-forth? Could they attain Arahantship? The Buddha replied that it was possible for them to do so. From this we can know that the Buddha saw nothing innately inferior in a woman's mind, though the Holy Life might be more difficult for her physically. Then venerable Ānanda pleaded the case of Mahāpajāpatī Gotamī in these words: "... (she) has been exceedingly helpful to the Exalted One when as his mother's sister who was his nurse, his foster-mother, his giver of milk, she suckled the Exalted One when his own mother died. Since that is so, Lord, it would be good if women could obtain the Going-forth."

The Buddha then permitted women to become bhikkhunīs, (rather because they could attain Arahantship, not because of venerable Ānanda's plea), provided that certain points were accepted. Mahāpajāpatī Gotamī could count as her Going-forth and Acceptance the following eight important points:

1. *"A bhikkhunī who has been accepted even for a hundred years must pay homage to, get up for, reverentially salute and respectfully greet a bhikkhu accepted that day."*

This means that a senior bhikkhunī (a therī) must bow down thrice even to a newly ordained bhikkhu. This is not pleasing to some women these days whose idea is to be free from male domination. But when the Buddha laid down this rule he knew that some principle of respectful relations must be established between bhikkhus and bhikkhunīs. Later, Mahāpajāpatī Gotamī requested that juniors, male or female, pay respect to senior bhikkhus or bhikkhunīs without distinction. The Buddha however, replied that no bhikkhu should pay homage to a bhikkhunī. Certainly he had no feelings of male superiority or of female inferiority (which, after all, are just extensions of the basic conceit I am'), but he took into a account how this matter would appear to laypeople. In that day and age, men in lay society hardly acknowledged female ability, certainly did not bow down to them! To permit this would be too great an inversion of the social norm and could be a cause for the decline of the Buddhist religion. The Buddha was already making a great innovation by allowing women to go forth but to allow equality of respect was probably too much for that time. In the Vinaya (the Lesser Chapter, bhikkhunī-section), the Buddha actually refers to other religious groups and how they do not permit salutation of nuns by monks. This would seem to support the argument here. We shall return to the question of conceit and humility below.

2. *"A bhikkhunī must not spend the rains in a place where there are no bhikkhus."*

Bhikkhunīs were made dependent upon bhikkhus in a number of ways as we shall see in the following points. This rule was also for the bhikkhunīs' safety since unscrupulous men might molest a nun if she was alone but they would think twice about it if she lived near to bhikkhus.

3. *"Every half-month a bhikkhunī should expect two things from the Bhikkhu Saṅgha: the appointment of the Uposatha-day each half-month and the visit for exhortation."*

The Buddha-time was without calendars and almanacs, and it was learned bhikkhus who calculated the phases of the moon and worked out when the Uposatha-days would fall. The visit for exhortation was in part a Dhamma-talk given by an eminent bhikkhu to the bhikkhunīs, (see the Exhortation by Nandaka to the bhikkhunīs in the MN 146) and partly an exhortation regarding these eight important points. The bhikkhu who gave it had to be agreed upon by the Bhikkhu Saṅgha, he had to be a thera with twenty or more rains and he had to give the talk during the day, before the sunset. Otherwise, the bhikkhunīs should not be approached by a Bhikkhu to teach them Dhamma unless one of their numbers was ill. The Buddha while seeing that it was necessary that the bhikkhunīs depend somewhat on bhikkhus, also saw the danger of too many contacts between the two Sanghas and so limited this. The fact that a great Teacher from among the bhikkhus would give the fortnightly exhortation did not mean that the bhikkhunīs had no Teachers among themselves. In this connection the section on the bhikkhunīs who were declared "foremost" in different abilities in the Book of the Ones, Numerical Collection, should be noted, besides which there are the many beautiful verses of the Enlightened bhikkhunīs in the Therīgāthā (Verses of the Elder Nuns). Discourses spoken by bhikkhunīs, some of them Arahants, are found scattered throughout the collections of Discourses.

4. *"At the end of the rains a bhikkhunī must invite the admonition of both Sanghas with regard to three matters; that is, whether any thing untoward in her conduct has been seen, heard or suspected."*

Bhikkhus have to invite admonition on the last Full Moon day of their rains-residence (usually in October) from the rest of the Sangha. This ceremony is held in place of the recitation of the Pātimokkha wherever a minimum of five bhikkhus have kept the rains. If anyone among them has seen or heard or suspected that one of the others has done some wrong which has not been confessed he can speak at that time. It also means that bhikkhus invite such admonition from other bhikkhus for the future. They make themselves admonishable by doing so and know that their teachers and friends will therefore help them with good advice. The bhikkhunīs have to make this declaration in the presence of both Sanghas, first to her own and then to the bhikkhus. This is no doubt to help the restraint of the bhikkhunīs and to assist the good government of the Bhikkhunī Saṅgha.

5. "*When a bhikkhunī has committed an offence entailing initial and subsequent meeting of the Sangha, she must do the penance before both Sanghas.*"

This is a group of thirteen offences for bhikkhus (already outlined in Chapter III) but for bhikkhunīs they number seventeen. A number of these thirteen, as well as of the extra bhikkhunī rules, concern sexual misconduct, and it would surely be a grave deterrent for a woman to have to confess them in the presence of bhikkhus after she had done so in front of the bhikkhunīs. Like a bhikkhu, she has then to practise the penance for seven days plus a period of probation equal to the time of concealment if her offence has been deliberately concealed.

6. "*A probationer who seeks Acceptance must do so from both Sanghas and after training in the six things for two years.*"

A probationer (*sikkhamānā*) was a special kind of female novice (*sāmaṇerī*). The latter has ten precepts just as a sāmaṇera but on reaching the age of eighteen, that is, two years under the age for Acceptance, the Bhikkhunī Saṅgha could announce a motion to give her permission to train (specially) in the first six rules: not killing living creatures, not taking what is not given, no unchaste conduct, not speaking falsely, no intoxicants causing carelessness, and no eating at the wrong time (after noon until dawn). If during the following two years she does not break any of these six precepts then she can seek Acceptance by the Bhikkhunī Saṅgha first. (If any are broken, the two-year probation period has to begin again). Then she is taken to the Bhikkhu Saṅgha who ordains her by proclamation and without investigation. She is then a fully ordained bhikkhunī. But if she gets only the Acceptance ceremony from the bhikkhus, or she gets it from the bhikkhunīs and does not go to be re-ordained by bhikkhus, then she is only a once-accepted-bhikkhunī, not fully-fledged according to the Vinaya.

When twice ordained however, she is called a both-accepted-bhikkhunī and fully-fledged. This has an important bearing on the present day as we shall see below.

7. *"A bhikkhunī must not find fault with or abuse a bhikkhu in any manner at all."*

Here again the aim is to stop malicious gossip and promote concord between the two Sanghas. A bhikkhunī could, of course, report a bhikkhu to his Teacher or abbot if his actions went against the Vinaya and damaged the good name of the Sangha but she should not directly speak against that bhikkhu to his face or behind his back.

8. *"From today onwards it is not allowed for bhikkhunīs to address discourses to bhikkhus but it is allowed for bhikkhus to address bhikkhunīs."*

As we have seen a bhikkhu was expected to exhort the bhikkhunīs at least twice a month but a bhikkhunī should not teach Dhamma to bhikkhus. No doubt this rule was also to curb conceit in bhikkhunīs and help them in their training.

The Buddha finished his eight points saying, "These eight things are to be honoured, respected, revered and venerated and they are not to be transgressed as long as life lasts. If Mahāpajāpatī Gotamī accepts these eight important points, that will count as her full Acceptance."

Five of these eight points, if transgressed, are offences of expiation, which are righted by confession to another bhikkhunī.

Mahāpajāpatī Gotamī accepted these eight points joyfully and so became the first bhikkhunī. The fact that she did so joyfully shows her humility. Her wisdom led her to accept these points seeing that they would be helpful in Dhamma-training. This point should be carefully noted. On this occasion, the Buddha pointed out to venerable Ānanda that since trouble could be expected when women were allowed to go forth, he had appointed the eight important points in advance to them: "As a man might construct in advance an embankment so that the waters of a great reservoir should not cause a flood, so I, too, have made known in advance these eight important points for bhikkhunīs not to be transgressed as long as life lasts."

These eight important points are compared by the Buddha to an embankment so we may ask what was the flood that he sought to prevent by means of it. If we examine these points, all eight have one thing in common: they deal with various sorts of contact between bhikkhunīs and bhikkhus, either as sanghas or individually. The flood that the Buddha tried to stem was probably that unregulated contact between members of the two sanghas could easily give rise to gossip and slander even when actions were innocent of any wrongdoing. In fact the Vinaya gives many examples of laypeople who were not Buddhists, exclaiming that the bhikkhunīs were obviously the bhikkhus' wives. This sort of misapprehension or slander, whichever it was, had to be avoided at all costs for the good name of both bhikkhus and bhikkhunīs. Opponents the world over of any religious movement have never hesitated to use the smear of sexual relations as the most potent method of discrediting celibates.

It appears, too, that part of the flood was conceit. Then it may be asked whether women on the whole have more conceit than men and whether they are more in need of humility. Generalizations of this sort are difficult to make since some women have more humility than others, but woman's preoccupation with cultivating and preserving bodily beauty is evidence of conceit. Conceit in a Buddhist sense means how one conceives oneself, as superior to others, equal to them, or inferior. As far as beauty is concerned women like to be at least equal or superior to other women, an attitude which is rooted in attracting men and binding them by attachment. This conceit cannot be allowed to manifest in a celibate order and there are actually many rules laid down by the Buddha about bhikkhunīs, that neither their persons nor their robes should be adorned in any way. Perhaps such restraint is more difficult for women than for men. A nun in Thailand in the present day has declared that she believes that women require the rules which are directed against conceit as aids for their own training.

After these digressions we should continue to follow the history of the bhikkhunīs. Mahāpajāpatī Gotamī became the first of them just by accepting the Eight Important Points. Her first question to the Buddha was how the Sakyan ladies who had accompanied her and who included Princess Yasodharā, the Buddha's former wife, should be given the Acceptance. The Buddha instructed that the Bhikkhu Saṅgha should give them Acceptance as bhikkhunīs. We know that a large number of this first group of bhikkhunīs, including Mahāpajāpatī Gotamī and Yasodharā, became Arahants.

Later, when an applicant was questioned by bhikkhus during the Acceptance-ceremony, she became shy and the Buddha then said that the Bhikkhunī Saṅgha should ordain the applicant first, asking the usual questions, after which the Bhikkhu Saṅgha should give the Acceptance again without asking any questions. It seems likely that this dual acceptance would make more difficult the entry of undesirable elements into the Bhikkhunī Saṅgha.

As time went on, unruly elements in the Bhikkhunī Saṅgha did things which were unsuitable for the Holy Life so that the Buddha had to lay down rules of training specially for the bhikkhunīs. Many of the bhikkhus' training rules applied to them as well but they had also precepts which had no application to bhikkhus, amounting in all to 311 training-rules, compared with the 227[86] for bhikkhus. These rules were recited at the Uposatha ceremony every lunar fortnight and constituted their basic rule. Together with the stories of how they originated and their elaboration, they constituted the second book of the Vinaya Basket, as we saw in Chapter IV.

A senior bhikkhunī or therī, that is one who had spent twelve rains in the Sangha, was entitled to be an ordaining teacher but it happened that young bhikkhunīs were not trained properly (which points out a lack of capacity for organization at

---

86. Actually, there are only 220 training-rules. The last seven cases in the Pātimokkha are covering legal procedures. (BPS Ed.)

that time) so that the Buddha had to limit Acceptance to one pupil every other year for each bhikkhunī-teacher. There was no limit in the Bhikkhu Saṅgha. This meant that the spread of the bhikkhunīs was limited both by the above limitation and by their more difficult disciplinary code. No bhikkhunī could live or travel alone but had to have, all the time, a bhikkhunī companion. Even their living places had to be limited to towns where they could be properly sheltered from molestation by violent men. Forest-dwelling bhikkhunīs existed only in the earliest days and were later forbidden after the rape of the Arahant Therī Uppalavaṇṇā.[87] She was one of the great Teachers in the Bhikkhunī Saṅgha and was praised by the Buddha as foremost in supernormal powers.

During the Buddha-time, many thousands of women became bhikkhunīs from all levels of society. Here the verses of just ten of them, with their stories in brief, will be presented. Some of the verses of Kisāgotamī Therī have been quoted already, while those of the venerables Muttā and Rohiṇī will be given below. To begin with, here is the verse of the Arahant Dhammadinnā. She was born in a wealthy family and married to Visākha, a leading citizen of Rājagaha. He heard the Buddha teach and attained the Fruit of Non-returning and so, having no sexual desire left at all, gave Dhammadinnā the choice of remaining in the house and enjoying the wealth there, or of returning to her own family, but she chose to become a bhikkhunī and soon reached Arahantship. Her verse was uttered before this, while she was still a Non-returner striving in a solitary place. Later, she was praised by the Buddha as "foremost (of the bhikkhunīs) among the Dhamma-preachers."

> One with a wish for the Final End,
> with a mind exhilarated,
> a mind unbound from pleasures of sense,
> an Upstream-goer[88] she is called. (Th 12)

---

87. See her story in the Dhammapada Commentary (*Buddhist Legends* Vol. II, p.127f.). King Pasenadi of Kosala urged that nuns should live in cities where they could be protected from such violence.

Next, *Sakulā,* born in a brahmin family. She was also married and acquired faith in the Buddha at the time when he accepted the Jeta Grove as a monastery. One day she listened to the teaching of an Arahant bhikkhu and was deeply stirred at which she requested the Going-forth. Later, as an Arahant, the Buddha assigned to her pre-eminence among those with the Divine Eye.

> As I was living in my house
> I heard a bhikkhu teaching Dhamma,
> Dhamma I saw, stainless then—
> Nibbāna, the unchanging state.
>
> I left my son, my daughter too,
> my wealth as well, my stored-up grain
> and having had my hair cut off
> I went forth to the homeless state.
>
> Then was I a probationer
> developing the path that's straight,
> I abandoned lust, aversion too
> and the pollutions linked to them.
>
> Accepted as a bhikkhunī
> I remembered former births
> having made pure the Eye Divine,
> spotless it is and well-developed.
>
> The conditioned as other[89] having seen,
> arising causally, dissolving away,
> the pollutions all I abandoned then,
> Quenched, I have become quite cool.[90] (Th 97–101)

Son was also born into a good family and eventually became the mother of ten sons and daughters, so that she was known as

---

88. One who goes against the stream of birth and death, a Non-returner to human birth but sure to attain Arahantship in the Pure Abodes.

89. Having seen mind and body both conditioned, as not self or "other."

90. *Pollutions, abandoned, quenched* and *quite cool* all signify attainment of Nibbāna and Arahantship.

the many-childrened. After her husband had become a bhikkhu, she gave over the wealth of the family to her children, keeping nothing for herself. But soon her children ceased to show her any respect, so she went forth among the bhikkhunīs, thinking, I have gone forth in my old age, I must make great efforts. So she practised all night, every night and became known for her energy. The Buddha one night projected a vision of himself and spoke these words:

> Though one should live a hundred years
> not seeing the Deathless State,
> yet better is life for a single day
> seeing the Deathless State.

At these words, she attained Arahantship. The Buddha one day declared her to be foremost among bhikkhunīs who strive energetically. Reflecting one day upon her experience she spoke these verses:

> Ten children having borne
> from this bodily conglomeration,
> so I, now weak and old,
> approached a bhikkhunī.
>
> The Dhamma she taught me—
> groups, sense-spheres and elements.[91]
> Her Dhamma having heard
> I shaved my hair, went forth.
>
> Then a probationer
> I purified the Eye Divine,
> former lives I knew
> and where I lived before.
>
> One-pointed, well-composed,
> the Signless[92] I develop—

---

91. The five groups (or aggregates), the twelve sense spheres and the eighteen elements—see *Buddhist Dictionary*, BPS, Kandy, for definitions.
92. One of the three Gates to Freedom, the other two being the Desireless and Emptiness. See op. cit.

immediately released
unclinging now and quenched!

The five groups knowing well,
exist, their roots are cut,
unmovable am I
on a stable basis sure,
now rebirth is no more. (Th 102–106)

Reborn in a brahmin family, *Somā*'s father was officiating priest to King Bimbisāra. While still in her own house she came to have confidence in the Buddha, and hearing Dhamma her mind became deeply stirred so that she became a bhikkhunī. Thus she did not marry. After practising for some time she attained Arahantship. Then dwelling in the bliss of Freedom she went one day after the alms-round to the Dark Wood and sat there in solitude. Then Māra (the personification of evil) spoke these words to her:

That which sages may attain,
the Firm State very hard to reach,
a woman with two fingers' worth
of wisdom cannot win.

And she replied with these verses showing how she could not be shaken:

What's it to do with a woman's state
when the mind is well-composed
with knowledge after knowledge born
sees into Perfect Dhamma clear?

For who indeed conceives it thus:
a woman am I, a man am I
or what indeed then am I—
it's worthwhile Māra's speech. (SN 5:2).

Ubbirī was reborn in her last existence in the family of an important citizen of Sāvatthī. She was extremely beautiful and so was invited to the palace of King Pasenadi of Kosala. After some time a daughter was born to her whom she named Jīvā and when the king saw the child he was so pleased that he had Ubbirī raised to the status of a queen. But the little girl died and the mother went daily to the burning ground in grief. Near there the Buddha met her and told her that innumerable daughters of hers (in past lives) had been burnt there and pointing out the places where this one and that one had been cremated or cast away, he spoke as follows:

> Mother! you who wail in the wood,
> come to yourself, O Ubbirī!
> Eighty-four thousand daughters of yours
> all with the name, Jīvā,
> have been burnt in this funeral fire,
> for which of them do you wail?

Then and there because she had the requisite conditions, she attained Arahantship and replied in these verses:

> Truly has he removed the dart,
> hard to see, that nestled in my heart,
> Grief for my daughter he drove away
> in me who was overcome by grief.
>
> Now is the dart plucked out by me,
> not yearning now and fully quenched.
> To the Buddha, Dhamma and Sangha too
> to the Wise One I for refuge go. (Th 51–53)

Then there was another mother, Vāsiṭṭhī, who for grief of her dead son went quite mad. Born in a good family and married to a young man of equal status, she lived happily with her husband and bore one son. When able to run about he died, and while relatives were consoling the father, Vāsiṭṭhī ran away raving and wandered about until she came to Mithilā. There she saw the Buddha and at the sight of the Great One, regained her normal mind. Hearing Dhamma in brief, she asked to become a bhikkhunī and soon after, she became an Arahant. Reflecting on her attainment, she exulted in this way:

With my mind deranged, crazed by grief
for my son and out of my senses,
naked, with dishevelled hair
I wandered here and there.

On heaps of rubbish from the streets,
on charnel-grounds and chariot-roads,
there I lived for three long years
given over to hunger and thirst.

Then I saw Him, the Sugata,[93]
come to Mithil's city
the tamer of the untamed,
Enlightened, without fears at all.

Having then regained my mind,
I bowed to him and sat nearby
and out of compassion did Gotama
teach me Dhamma, which having heard
I went forth to the homeless state.

Devoted to the Teacher's Word
I realized the State Secure,
all griefs completely cut right out,
abandoned, brought to an utter end,
for known to me are the causes
from which all griefs are born. (Th 113–138)

Due to her past bad kamma, *Vimalā*[94] was born to a prostitute and herself followed that trade when she grew up. One day she saw the left-hand chief disciple of the Buddha, venerable Mahā-Moggallāna, walking for almsfood in Vesālī. Feeling desire for him she went to his dwelling and tried to seduce him. She could not succeed as he was an Arahant, but he succeeded in humbling her pride of beauty with verses ending with this one:

93. The Well-farer, one whose going was always auspicious, in this world and beyond all worlds.

94. Ironically her name means "pure"—which of course she was, eventually.

See this body beautiful,
a mass of sores, a congeries,
much considered but miserable
where nothing is stable, nothing persists.

She was ashamed of her actions and became a lay-follower, later a bhikkhunī who after effort and striving won Arahantship. Her verses of exultation are as follows:

Proud of my good complexion and figure,
my beauty and my fame as well,
haughty because of my youth
other women I despised.

Having adorned this body,
well decorated, deceiving fools,
at the brothel door I stood
like a hunter laying a snare.

Showing off my attractions,
much of my secrets revealing,
various jugglery I performed
and many people laughed loud.

Today for almsfood having walked
shaven-headed, wrapped in my robe,
sitting down at the foot of a tree
I have obtained the non-thinking mind.[95]

All ties completely cut away
Whether for gods or men
and all pollutions having destroyed,
quenched, I have become quite cool. (Th 72–76)

Vaddhamātā, the name means Vaddha's mother—parents often being nicknamed after their children, was born in a good family in the town of Bhārukaccha (Bharoch). When married, she bore one son who was known as Vaddha. After hearing a bhikkhu teach Dhamma she handed her child over to relatives and

95. The attainment of the 2nd absorption (*jhāna*) in which thought processes are completely stilled.

became a bhikkhunī. Afterwards she won Arahantship, and in due course her son became a bhikkhu, learned and eloquent in preaching. One day, negligently, he went alone with only his upper and under robes to see his mother.[96] She rebuked him for both these things so that he returned to his own quarters and sat in meditation there, attaining Arahantship.

This incident is interesting in view of the prohibition on bhikkhunīs instructing bhikkhus (see above, Eight Important Points, 8), but perhaps this prohibition only covers formal sermon-type instruction and not more informal conversation of this sort:

Mother: Do not, Vaddha, ever get entangled
in jungle-lusts[97] regarding the world!
My son, do not again and again
become a sharer of dukkha!

Happy indeed are the Wise Ones, Vaddha,
having no craving, cut off doubt,
become quite cool, taming attained,
unpolluted now they live.
The way that Seers have practised
for attaining insight,
for putting an end to dukkha,
that, Vaddha, you should develop.

Vaddha: You have spoken confidently to me
concerning this matter, mother.
I think, indeed, my mother,
no jungle-lust in you is found.

Mother: Whatever conditioned elements are,
whether middling, low or high[98]
for them not a speck, even an atom,

---

96. A bhikkhu must take a companion when going to see the bhikkhunīs, and on a journey he must not be separated from his three robes. Vaddha had left his outer double-thick robe behind.

97. One word in Pāli means both jungle and lust and refers generally to the tangle of sexual passions.

of jungle-lust in me is found.
My pollutions, all destroyed
by meditating diligently,
possessed of triple knowledge
done is the Buddha's Sāsana.

Vaddha: Splendid is the goad indeed,
these verses on the Highest Goal,
which out of her compassion
my mother has applied to me.

Having heard her words,
the instructions of my mother,
I was aroused in Dhamma
to reach security from bonds.

I resolved to exert myself,
unrelaxing, day and night;
incited by my mother
I touched the Peace Supreme. (Th 204–212)

As a result of pride in former lives, *Puṇṇikā* was born in the household of Anāthapiṇḍika, to a domestic slave. After hearing a discourse by the Buddha called the (Lesser) Lion's Roar (MN 11), she became a Stream-winner. After the incident described below, Anāthapiṇḍika freed her so that she could gain Acceptance as a bhikkhunī. In no long time she attained Arahantship and one day reflecting on this attainment, uttered these verses of exultation:

Puṇṇikā: I am a water-carrier who,
even in the cold, goes down into the water
fearful of ladies' blows,
harassed by fear of blame.

What is it, brahmin, that you fear
always going down into the water?
Why with shivering limbs
do you suffer bitter cold?

---

98. This world, all worlds, everything known through the senses and the mind, is conditioned. The Unconditioned is Nibbāna.

Brahmin: Already you know, Miss Puṇṇikā,
the answer to what you ask:
Making wholesome kamma
while annulling evil kamma.

Whoever, whether young or old,
evil kamma makes,
even he from evil kamma's free
by baptism in the water.

Puṇṇikā: Who has told you this,
O ignorant of the ignorant—
that truly he's from evil kamma free
by baptism in the water?

If this is so all turtles, frogs,
serpents, fish and crocodiles,
all that live in the water,
all will go to heaven!

Butchers of sheep and swine,
fishermen and trappers,
robbers and murderers too,
all who make evil kamma,
even they by water-baptism
will be free from evil kamma!

And if these streams could bear away
the evil formerly done by you,
then your merits they'd bear away
leaving you stripped and bare!

That of which you're frightened,
and so go into the waters,
that thing, brahmin, do not do;
let not the cold pierce your skin.

Brahmin: From the practice of the wrong path
to the Noble Path you've led me!
This cloth for water-baptism
now I give to you.

Puṇṇikā: Let the cloth be yours,
no desire for cloth have I.
If you are afraid of dukkha,
if dukkha is not dear to you,
then make no evil kamma
either openly or in secret.

But if you make, or you will make,
all kinds of evil kamma
then you'll not be free of dukkha,
even by flying or running off.

If you are afraid of dukkha,
if dukkha is not dear to you,
go to the Buddha who is Thus[99]
as refuge, to Dhamma and Sangha too,
undertake the training-rules,
for your benefit that will be.

Brahmin: I go to the Buddha who is Thus[100]
as refuge, to Dhamma and Sangha too;
I undertake the training-rules;
for my benefit that will be.

Formerly Brahma's kin,
today a brahmana true,[101]
possessed of triple knowledge,
learned and washen pure. (Th 236–251)

The brahmin became a bhikkhu and shortly afterwards an Arahant when he repeated joyously these verses.

Sumaṅgalamātā (Sumaṅgala's mother) is the last of the bhikkhunīs whose stories and verses are given here. She was born in a poor family and in due course, married to a rush-plaiter. Her first child was called Sumaṅgala who grew up,

99. See Ch. II under Brahmadatta.
100. See Ch. II under Brahmadatta.
101. Brahmins boasted that they were the kin of Great Brahmā but the Buddha taught that a true brahmin is one who is rid of defilements.

became a bhikkhu and attained Arahantship, while she became a bhikkhunī. One day, reflecting on her sufferings as a lay-woman, insight quickened and she attained Arahantship, afterwards exclaiming:

> Well freed am I, well freed indeed,
> thoroughly free from my pestle,
> from my shameless man, the sunshade maker,
> from my poverty and cooking pots.
>
> I live with lust and aversion completely cut off
> and having gone to the foot of a tree
> meditate on this happiness—
> 'Ah! happiness indeed!' (Th 23–24).

We do know that the good name of the bhikkhunīs lasted far beyond the Buddha-time, supported by the embankment that he had constructed. There were many Arahants among the bhikkhunīs and some of their discourses survive in the Basket of Suttas. Their inspired poems spoken often at the moment of Enlightenment have also survived in Pāli. How these were included in the Canon is not clear since there is no mention of bhikkhunīs taking part in the First Council: only five hundred Arahants are mentioned and they are all said to be bhikkhus. But perhaps some bhikkhunīs did participate, for the records of both first and second Councils are lacking in details.

In the reign of the Emperor Asoka the bhikkhunīs must have had a good name both in learning and in practice, for the Emperor's daughter, Saṅghamittā, joined their Sangha. Later, she embarked with many bhikkhunīs for Sri Lanka bearing the southern branch of the Bodhi Tree under which the Buddha's Enlightenment took place. This was reverently planted in the capital of Anurādhapura and, still, more than two thousand years later, is accorded great devotion.

The Bhikkhunī Saṅgha continued to flourish in Sri Lanka for many centuries and the construction of nunneries by various Sinhalese kings is recorded in the Great Chronicle (*Mahāvaṃsa*), even up to the reign of Kassapa IV (898–914 C.E.). Bhikkhunīs were treated with respect as the king's wards and in Sri Lanka their nunneries were in the Inner (Royal) City. This fact may have led to their disappearance during the conquest of the island by the Cholas, from south India in the tenth century. The Bhikkhu Saṅgha could survive as it was scattered over the whole land but the bhikkhunīs, concentrated in a few cities and towns, would have been vulnerable to destruction. When peace later returned to Sri Lanka the kings of those times were either not interested in restoring the Bhikkhunī Saṅgha, or more likely, were unable to do so for lack of pure bhikkhunīs. There is even less record of the history of the bhikkhunīs in India and we do not know now whether their sangha perished before its extinction in Sri Lanka, or continued right up to the final end of the Buddha's teachings there.

However, long before the lineage of the bhikkhunīs died out in Sri Lanka, their sangha was established in China, as recorded in the Chinese work, *Lives of Bhikkhunīs*:

> In the sixth year of Yuan Chia (429 C.E.) the foreign ship-owner Nandi arrived from the Lion Country (Sri Lanka) bringing with him some bhikkhunīs.[102] They went to the Sung capital (Nanking) and lived in the Ching-fu Convent. After a time they asked the (partly-ordained) nun Seng-kuo[103] whether any foreign bhikkhunīs had ever come. "Then how did previous nuns manage to have bhikkhunīs as well as bhikkhus to conduct their ordination (acceptance)?" asked the bhikkhunīs from Ceylon. "We were ordained by a senior bhikkhu", said Seng-kuo. "Any woman whose nature prompted her to take the vows was accepted. The earnest desire of the candidates gave rise to this expedient, which is in some measure justified by the case of (the Buddha's aunt)

102. The translation of this passage (from *Buddhis Texts through the Ages* Bruno Cassirer, Oxford, translated by Arthur Waley) has "nuns" but as bhikkhunīs are meant here, in order to avoid confusion with the partly-ordained Chinese "nuns," this substitution has been made.

103. This nun and others like her had only Acceptance from a Bhikkhu Saṅgha headed by a senior bhikkhu. It is for this reason that the question arises of "re-ordination" (really completing the Acceptance) with the real Bhikkhunī Saṅgha.

Pajāpati, who was admitted to the Sangha on the strength of her Eight Declarations of Reverence, and afterwards she in turn acted as Sīla-upādhyāya (preceptress in the rules) to five hundred ladies of the Sakya clan."

Such was Seng-kuo's reply. But in her heart of hearts she was not very happy about the situation and consulted the Master of the Three Baskets Guṇavarman, who supported her contention. She also asked him if it was possible for nuns who had been ordained already (only by a Bhikkhu Saṅgha) to be re-ordained (with a Bhikkhunī Saṅgha). "Morality, meditation and wisdom", he said "are all progressive states. If an ordination is repeated, so much the better."

In the tenth year (433 C.E.), the ship-owner Nandi came again to China bringing the Sinhalese bhikkhunī Tessarā and ten other bhikkhunīs from Ceylon. The bhikkhunīs who had arrived previously could now speak Chinese. They asked the Indian bhikkhu Saṅghavarman to reordain with their assistance three hundred Chinese nuns ... at the Southern Forest Monastery (at Nanking), receiving them in batches. (Takakusu, *Lives of Bhikkhunīs*, 939).

This brings us to the question of whether there are bhikkhunīs in the present day. If you ask a Chinese Buddhist from Taiwan, Hong Kong or a Korean from the South, or a Vietnamese, they would reply, Yes, there are Bhikkhunīs. These ladies are certainly nuns for they keep the Holy Life. They have their own nunneries as the bhikkhunīs of ancient times had their *upassaya*, the special name for their vihāras. Their Dhamma-study of course, as they come through the Chinese tradition, is largely of Mahayana texts, as their dress is in Chinese-style robes.

They are not judged to be bhikkhunīs by this or that style of robes but according to the lineage of their Acceptance. It seems these days that bhikkhunīs, wherever they are ordained, take Acceptance only from the Bhikkhu Saṅgha. They do not have the dual Acceptance laid down in the Vinaya which means that they can be counted, at best, as once-accepted-bhikkhunīs.

Then the question arises whether such partial bhikkhunīs can rightly be called bhikkhunī for they are not passing on their lineage through ordination at all. This Bhikkhunī-Saṅgha is being constantly re-created by the Bhikkhu Saṅgha. In fact their position is not much different from the nuns of Theravāda Buddhist countries who are also given their precepts by senior bhikkhus, though not as an act of the Sangha.

There have been a few Westerners ordained as Bhikkhunīs in this way but in the light of strict Vinaya practice they could well doubt their true status. Then someone might ask, Well, will it ever be possible for women to become bhikkhunīs in Theravāda lands? It is difficult to see how this could be done. A Sangha of bhikkhus led by responsible theras would have to recognize that the bhikkhunīs are perhaps not quite extinct and then reordain them in Theravāda tradition. Many problems would arise since there have been no bhikkhunīs for such a long time and ways of doing things have been forgotten. More serious than this, however, would be the danger of causing a schism in the Sangha. In fact, the Bhikkhunī Saṅgha could only be restored properly by majority approval of the theras in Theravāda countries of the Sangha. In northern Buddhist lands, a different attitude could be taken to this question.

Meanwhile, though there are no bhikkhunīs in Theravāda, there are ladies who live the Holy Life as nuns. This has been the case since the Bhikkhunī Saṅgha disappeared and since there was no sangha for them to join, they have lived with the Eight or Ten precepts as their rule. They shave their heads and wear robes of differing colours according to their country of ordination—white in Thailand[104], yellow in Sri Lanka and pinkish-brown in Burma. Generally they live in special sections of vihāras though in some places they have established their own nunneries. Such independence usually indicates the presence among them of learned nuns, or those highly developed in meditation.

104. There are also small groups using dark brown and yellow robes.

The Pāli name for these nuns is *upāsikā*. This word means literally (a woman) who sits down near to (a Teacher) but as this is a word used also for laywomen devotees living the household life, the word nun will be used here. And this is how many nuns come to be ordained, having been attracted to the Dhamma taught by a famous bhikkhu-teacher. In Thailand they are called *mae chee,* literally mothers (an honorific for women') who are ordained." In Burma, they are known as *thila-shin,* literally possessors of the precepts, while in Sri Lanka they are called *silmātavaru* (lit. mothers (honorific) observing the precepts).'

Their status in Buddhist countries now does not usually approach the esteem in which bhikkhus are held by most people. In the popular way of thinking, bhikkhus have 227 precepts but nuns only eight, therefore bhikkhus are more virtuous! Sometimes it is not considered that a lax bhikkhu can be excelled in both learning and practice by a diligent nun. And no one has thought that as a bhikkhunī had 311 precepts, she was therefore much more virtuous than a bhikkhu! Popular estimation of the worth of nuns is based on their usual lack of Buddhist education in the past. In some places the nuns were pious ladies who had finished with family life and wished to devote the rest of their existence to making merits. This meant that they cooked food and offered it to the bhikkhus there, swept the temple compound and made various decorations for the shrine. They were not expected to study or to be learned and their practice would be limited generally to keeping their eight or ten precepts pure and some devotional chanting twice a day. And where younger women shaved their heads this was not always for the highest reason—poverty or the desire for a quiet uncomplicated life were (and are) sometimes causes. (But such reasons apply to some bhikkhus too).

This brings us to consider how a nun is supported. Bhikkhus usually do not have too many difficulties here as robes are offered, food comes from the alms-round or from invitation, dwellings are given and medicines provided, all by generous lay-supporters. But nuns are rarely supported in this way and while a few may have laypeople who guarantee support, most of them must rely upon small alms from their families or upon their own savings. It is true that in some country areas (in Thailand) nuns do go upon alms-round with bowls just as bhikkhus do, but this is the exception rather than the rule. The writer remembers seeing a small group of nuns who used to do this in Bangkok and how their mindfulness contrasted with some rather distracted looking bhikkhus! Materially, therefore, the life of a nun can be more difficult than that of a bhikkhu.

This is not always a disadvantage, especially if a nun has just enough. She will not suffer at any rate as some bhikkhus do, from excess of support and too much attention from wealthy laypeople. While a bhikkhu may be spoiled by this, a nun need not be in the limelight and so not involved with the dangers to the Holy Life which this entails. Another of these "negative" advantages is that nuns have fewer possibilities for their livelihood if they disrobe, than bhikkhus. This fact and perhaps the generally stronger faith-element in women makes disrobing among them much less frequent than it is with bhikkhus.

The popular reason why nuns get less support is based on the misapprehension of numbers of precepts mentioned above. The fruit or result of kamma made by giving to a bhikkhu is thought to be greater than can be expected from gifts to a nun. This could be quite wrong, for instance if the bhikkhu is not careful with his Vinaya while the nun is pure-hearted, even a Stream-winner or more.

These attitudes are beginning to change as a result of more attention paid to nuns and their education. In some places they have their own institutions and organizations which will be described below.

Now we should say something about the life of nuns in Thailand, the country most familiar to the writer.[105] A nun there can either engage in studies in a town vihāra, or meditate

105. Some of the information above and much of it below I owe to a letter from Upāsikā Cirañāṇī (Evelyn Spencer), an Australian who was a nun in Thailand. The quotations below are from her letter.

with a Teacher in the forest.

It is not necessary to describe her daily life in detail, as it will to some extent resemble that of bhikkhus but with the addition of such work as food preparation and gardening. Recently, another kind of livelihood has opened for nuns: teaching and other social services. More will be said about this below.

Nuns, wherever they stay, in town or country, live usually in special compounds within the vihāra grounds. In the towns these have fences and gates surrounding the nuns' kuṭis, sālā and gardens, but in the country a line of trees and bushes separates these quarters from the rest. In some vihāras a certain amount is charged for food each month and nuns must be able to find this in order to stay there. Other vihāras give them the second choice of the bhikkhus' piṇḍapāta food after the latter have taken what they want. As the alms-round usually produces more than enough the nuns may be quite well provided for. However, when all food requirements are taken care of there still are other expenses. Some vihāras provide the area for the nuns while the *kuṭis* that they live in have been erected by generous laywomen. In other vihāras, nuns must pay for the construction of their own kuṭis. As my informant says after commenting on nuns and how they must be self-supporting: However, there are still stationery expenses, books, soap, washing powder, etc. to buy... Elsewhere she remarks that nuns have a little help from their families, but —"It is not a life of comfort for nuns."

This brings us to consider a Western woman becoming a nun. There are now only a very few by comparison with the number of Western men who join the Bhikkhu Saṅgha. What are the reasons for this? One factor, financial support, has been mentioned already. However as far as Western women are concerned they have generally cut themselves off from their families, or have been cut off by their families, so they have no income on which to subsist, so they have no means to live if they become nuns. After all, one must eat, wash and so on.

Another difficulty is the differences between Western and eastern women who become nuns. The former are "independent types, already well-travelled, often well-educated, worldly, etc." But often Asian women who become nuns in Buddhist countries may have a poor education and very little experience of the world as they will have led a much more sheltered-life. It is difficult for people so different to relate to one another, and the only way of doing this is through the common interest in Dhamma. Even here, the meeting-ground can be narrow enough because a Western woman will have an enquiring attitude to Dhamma while many Asiatic Buddhists have a more traditional approach. Great patience and perseverance, as well as adaptability, are needed by a Western woman to succeed as a nun in Asia.

And humility is very important too. Another point about Western women is that there are women's-libber types who are definitely not happy[106] in the East, where women are subservient to men. For myself, I take the attitude that there is nothing in the world except *nāma* (mind, mental states) and *rūpa* (body, material qualities) and, therefore, if offence arises at having to pay respect first to a man, then it is only because the ego that is offended or unhappy. With an ego attitude no progress will be possible, whether for a bhikkhu or for a nun.

One of the dangers of a nun's life, a feature unlikely to appeal to Westerners, has been mentioned already—"holy domesticity." Having given up household life, shaved the head and put on robes, a large part of life can still be household chores. Bhikkhus are precluded from such involvement by their rules, but nuns have their own food to buy and prepare (in some vihāras) and gardening to do—they raise some of their own vegetables and provide flowers for the temple and do cleaning work—all of which can distract the mind far from Dhamma. The bhikkhunīs of olden times were glad to be rid of their household burden. Here is the venerable Arahant Muttā Therī's verse:

---

106. "*Mai sabai jai*" in the letter, meaning "not happy (or contented) mind" (Thai).

O free indeed! O gloriously free
am I in freedom from three crooked things:
from mortar and pestle, from my crooked lord.
Free am I from birth and death!
What leads to becoming is destroyed! (Thī 11)

It is easy to go from one sort of bondage to another but hard to go from bondage to real Liberation, to ownership of nothing at all, even of mind and body.

After all these difficulties it may be good to present the positive developments which have taken place amongst the nuns in Thailand. The position in other Buddhist countries will be dealt with later. The following information, for example, is a summary made by Upāsikā Cirañāṇī of the aims and projects so far of *The Foundation of Thai Nuns*:

Founded 28th of August, 1969. Number of members now, in 1979, is 5,000 (coming from 500 nunneries). Number of nuns in Thailand: 70,000. (Although only 5,000 of the 70,000 nuns are members, they are an excellent nucleus. Such a Foundation is worthy of support, for without it there may result a dissipation of energies leading to a lowering of Vinaya and standards generally).

The Annual General Meeting has been held in Bangkok, in the convocation hall of Mahamakut Buddhist College (where a number of nuns study). H.M. the Queen of Thailand has opened the proceedings. The President and Secretary are both nuns and the Committee which includes laywomen is elected for a three year period.

The Aims of the Foundations are:

To promote the activities of the Foundation.

To improve the status of nuns.

To assist nuns and others who need assistance.

To build a school and university for nuns to enable them to study Dhamma, Pāli and other allied subjects so that they can teach others and be useful to society generally.

Achievements so far:

Increasing numbers of nuns are now studying Dhamma and Pāli.

Nuns are currently helping in schools and hospitals in country districts with the cooperation of the Ministry for the Development of Rural Areas.

Nuns who have reached an acceptable level of education are now teaching Pāli to other nuns while there are some who have reached degree level and are at present doing their theses for doctorate in India.

Plans for the achievement of the aims:

One lady donated a piece of land about 100 rai (40 acres) at Rajburi for the establishment of a study centre to include a school and university. Though the land is available money is needed to commence building.

Another piece of land has been given in another locality about four hours drive from Bangkok where a few nuns are already living permanently, others going there on a rota basis. The object in this village is to be as useful as possible in helping to overcome delinquency problems among teenage girls. The nuns educate small children who come to the nunnery every day. Some older girls come along to the nunnery where they are gradually learning useful things from the nuns. The nuns are establishing a good name for themselves in the locality among the villagers.

The Foundation puts out a well-produced magazine four times a year. This is quite a big undertaking as the standard is high. This publication, called simply "Mae Chee Sara" ("The Nuns' Epitome") and costs 20 baht (50p) a year. There is a mailing list and many hundreds of copies are rolled and sent off.

The magazine is the main medium for the nuns to let others know of the success or otherwise of their various works. It is also the way in which interest may be aroused to give financial support for realizing the educational programme. Since its inception six years ago, the Foundation has been instrumental in giving nuns the incentive to coordinate their activities. During this period the people generally have increased in their respect for nuns recognizing their seriousness and devotion.

In Upāsikā Cira's nunnery, a quiet compound within one of the larger vihāras in Bangkok, all the nuns go to study in one of two other vihāras where there are special classes for them in Abhidhamma and the Pāli language. This is on all days of the week except Holy Days (Full and New Moon days and two quarter moon days). Also in the nunnery there is a rota of nuns who help to teach under-five-year old children in the vihāra school. The children come from the very poor people living around the vihāra. They make up two large classes which are taught by bhikkhus and nuns.

There is morning and evening chanting in Pāli with Thai translations, phrase by phrase. This is helpful for nuns who have not learnt Pāli (also found in some forest vihāras where bhikkhus chant in this way) but it is slow and rather tiresome if the meaning is already known.

The nunneries in Bangkok emphasize study rather than meditation, reflecting the atmosphere of the vihāras and many nuns come from the countryside to study and then return to their own provinces when they have finished their education. They are then in charge of instructing other nuns there.

Among nuns in the country there are some who teach meditation, such teachers having their own independent nunneries which are also centres where laywomen can go to practise meditation. Those centres which are in the countryside will have conditions and a way of life resembling those of forest bhikkhus.

As a contrast with Thailand where nuns live mostly in special sections of the Wats, in Burma most nuns have their own institutions. Nuns there (Mae Thila or Thila-shin) live in independent nunneries called Thila-shin-kyaung which are quite often of large size. Their present well-established place in Burma is a result of royal patronage by the queens of the Alompra dynasty, as well of course, of their learning and good practice. Originally, as in Thailand, nuns wore white robes but in course of time these have changed to the pinkish-brown ones worn now, together with a brown "shoulder-clot." Quite a number of these nuns can be found in Rangoon, and a large nunnery there will soon be described, but their real centre is in the Sagaing Hills where there are many famous nun-teachers of both learning and practice.

Hanthawady Thila-shin-kyaung is one of the best nunneries around Rangoon. When one sees the considerable area covered by the building, pleasantly shaded by many flowering trees and bushes, it is not hard to understand that this nunnery is very well supported. Many nuns living in smaller institutions have a much harder time, some being really very poor. Those in this nunnery are well provided for and well educated. The main building with classrooms and two large halls, the one downstairs for ordinary gatherings, the upstairs one for a shrine-temple, would have been a substantial structure in any educational institution, if one excepts the shrine. Separate buildings are the dormitories, kitchen and dining-hall. Nuns, or ladies who help them, maintain the grounds and see to the preparation of food.

A nun's day begins with the rising at 4 a.m., with morning chanting half an hour later. Early breakfast is served as soon as it is dawn, about half past five. During the morning the nuns study Buddhist subjects until half past ten when the main meal is served. On some days this is provided by lay donors who supply enough food for all the nuns in residence, one hundred and fifty during the period of rains-residence and a hundred or so at other times. More study follows in the afternoon with evening chanting at six o'clock. No formal meditation is practised by the nuns at Hanthawady since those who wish to practise can easily go to a meditation centre. The shrine-hall where their chanting was done is very beautiful and evidence of their great devotion.

Apart from donations to the foundation supporting this nunnery and meals supplied by donors, nuns here, as elsewhere in Burma, go out to collect food two days each week, that is, the two days before each phase of the moon. They carry a flat bamboo basket on their heads balanced on a roll of pinkish cloth. They also have a small bowl to receive the offerings of uncooked rice and money which are made to them. While receiving the offering they chant good wishes, ("May you be happy! May you attain Nibbāna!"). Nuns in Burma never use big bowls like those of bhikkhus, nor do they always go on an alms-round to receive cooked food. In Hanthawady nunnery it is only necessary for the younger nuns to go out to collect alms.

Nuns often receive invitations to chant the discourse of protection in the houses of laypeople. It is customary to offer them a meal, like bhikkhus, on this occasion. This contrasts with Thailand where no such invitations are given to nuns.

The teaching of Dhamma by nuns is usually restricted to the instruction of other nuns and the laywomen who stay in the nunneries. Although they have among them many learned teachers, they do not teach laypeople as a whole. This is also true of meditation.

Social works are limited to the invitations that nuns may receive from schools, hospitals, prisons and so on. Nuns do go to help when they are invited in this way but there are no permanent arrangements for work of this kind.

At the Hanthawady nunnery, ordinations, the Eight Precepts, are given by a Sayādaw (a learned senior bhikkhu). Any girl or woman can get ordination after a probation period of fifteen days. During this time, the applicant's character is assessed to see whether she will be suitable for the nun's life. An applicant need not bring any monetary contribution, but robes, bowl, tray and bedding, are usually provided by their families or other supporters. In case of great poverty, the Teacher-nuns can supply these things through their own lay-supporters. It is the custom for many young girls, before puberty, to be ordained temporarily for a few weeks. As ordination involves shaving the head, if women are ordained, it will usually be for longer periods or sometimes even for life.

In Sri Lanka,[107] sometime after the disappearance of the Bhikkhunī Saṅgha there came into existence a band of female disciples of the Buddha who left their households and led a celibate life. One of the first few nunneries which arose as a result, was Lady Blake Nunnery in Kandy. A few other nunneries of this type, though smaller in size, were founded in places like Galle, Colombo and Ratmalana.

These nunneries were and are a source of inspiration for women which increased as time went by. As a result there are at present about two hundred and fifty nunneries in Sri Lanka. Anurādhapura, Biyagama, Colombo, Kelaniya, Kurunegala, Galle, Matara, Kalutara, Pitipana, Akuressa, Mellagala and Navgala are some of the places where nunneries are found today.

While in some nunneries we find around twenty to thirty nuns, there are more where only two or three may dwell. These nuns are known as *silmātavaru* or *silmaenivaru* (i.e. Mothers (used as a honorific) observing sīla or precepts).

Such Buddhist nuns practise the ten precepts and spend their time in studying Buddhism, practising meditation, attending to Buddhist rites and duties teaching the Dhamma to both adults and children, the latter mostly in Sunday Schools, and conducting classes in meditation. They lead a pure and celibate life having given up entirely the pleasures and wealth usually found in worldly existence, devoting themselves to the practice of the Buddha's teachings.

The Buddhist lay disciples offer alms and other requisites and pay homage to these virtuous beings as they do to bhikkhus. The nuns (*silmātavo*) in return perform the great service of directing these lay disciples to the practice of meritorious deeds.

The number of nuns living in Sri Lanka now is estimated at three thousand. Before becoming a nun one has to live in

107. The following is based upon an account kindly written by Sister Sudhammā, a Sinhalese Buddhist nun in Colombo.

association with an elder nun and at the same time study the Dhamma, practise meditation, and observe the usual precepts. After some time, the applicant gets the opportunity of becoming a nun herself, thus attaining greater heights by the fulfilment of the noble and sacred duties both day and night.

There have been various attempts to reintroduce the Bhikkhunī Saṅgha into Sri Lanka so that the nuns there could be reordained as bhikkhunīs. These have not been successful.[108] It has been said that although there are great advantages for women in Sangha life, one wonders whether they are not better off without the load of 311 precepts. If these are undertaken as a bhikkhunī then they should be strictly kept—which involves such difficulties as bhikkhunīs travelling together and living together (never one by herself) as well as the ban on living in the forest (they must live in a secluded urban environment). Generally with all precepts it is better to undertake those which one knows can be kept. It is certainly more meritorious—better kamma—to undertake eight or ten and observe them purely rather than burdening oneself with three hundred and eleven, not all of which one can keep.

To close this chapter, here are the verses of the Arahant Rohiṇī Therī who recollects how, before her Enlightenment, she explained to her unbelieving brahmin father the virtues of samaṇas, meaning bhikkhus here. Her father was so moved by her praises that he both permitted her to become a bhikkhunī and became a Buddhist himself, later being accepted as a bhikkhu and attaining Arahantship.

Father: See the samaṇas, lady, you say,
you want me to know these samaṇas,
only samaṇas do you praise,
perhaps a samaṇa you will be?

---

108. In the meantime full bhikkhunī ordinations have taken place in Sri Lanka. They are carried out in Dambulla with the assistance of the bhikkhus of the Rangiri Dambulla Chapter of the Asgiriya Chapter of the Siam Nikāya. (BPS Editor)

On these samaṇas you bestow
very abundant food and drink,
I ask you, Rohiṇī, therefore,
why are samaṇas dear to you?

Lazy and not liking work
and living off others' gifts,
hopeful, desiring delicacies,
why are samaṇas dear to you?

Rohiṇī: For long indeed, father, you have asked
me about these samaṇas,
now shall I commend to you
their wisdom, virtue and energy.

Not lazy they, but liking work,
doers of the noblest work—
lust and aversion they forsake,
hence are samaṇas dear to me.

They remove the three Evil Roots
making all pure within,
abandoned all their evil,
hence are samaṇas dear to me.

Pure are their bodily kammas,
just the same their kammas of speech,
their mental kammas too are pure,
hence are samaṇas dear to me.

Spotless as the mother of pearl,
purified both within and without,
full of radiant qualities,
hence are samaṇas dear to me.

Deeply learned Dhamma-experts,
Noble, those who Dhamma live,
the Goal and Dhamma do they teach,
hence are samaṇas dear to me.

Deeply learned Dhamma-experts,
Noble, those who Dhamma live,
mindful, with one-pointed minds,
hence are samaṇas dear to me.

Deeply learned Dhamma experts
wise their words without conceit,
the end of dukkha that they know,
hence are samaṇas dear to me.

When they walk the village street
they gaze at nothing longingly,
wishless, they go walking on,
hence are samaṇas dear to me.

Keeping nothing in a storeroom
neither in basket nor in jar,
their quest is for the Final End,
hence are samaṇas dear to me.

No silver do they grasp at,
neither at gold nor yet at coin,
supporting themselves with present things,
hence are samaṇas dear to me.

From various families they Go Forth,
coming from various countries,
still each to the other one is dear,
hence are samaṇas dear to me.

(Th 271–285)

Chapter VIII

Westerners in the Sangha

The Yonakas or Greeks?—Geographical and religious obstructions to the spread of Dhamma-Pride of empire—the first Western bhikkhus—difficulties of Westerners in the Sangha—why become a bhikkhu (or upasikā)—not for everyone—the Holy Life unnatural?—what causes a person to take up the Holy Life?—faith or confidence—four types of people having faith—advice for those who would like to go forth—the Sangha in Western countries?

Possibly the first people of Western origin recorded to have entered the Sangha are some bhikkhus whose names have been recorded in the Great Chronicle (*Mahāvaṃsa*) having also the epithet *Yonaka*. This word is the Pali equivalent of Ionic, hence Greek. But one may doubt how much Greek blood was in their veins as *yonaka* was applied to any citizen of the Greek type of city and such cities were found from the Mediterranean to Northwest India. It is possible that a Buddhist centre existed in Alexandria (Egypt) where Indian merchants were known to trade. This would not have lasted through the fanatical Christianization programme following the adoption of that religion by Constantine.

Between Egypt and India lay at different times the various countries having Zoroastrianism as their state religion. The powerful priesthood of this religion persecuted other faiths from time to time so that Buddhism could not gain much ground in Persia though numbers of Persians from central Asia became bhikkhus. Prevented from spreading westwards overland, Buddhism turned north through Central Asia and then east to China and Japan.

Even if Buddhism had reached the Mediterranean countries after Constantine's fateful choice, it could not have become established there since Dhamma cannot be planted or kept going when opposed by brute force. The attitude of the churches, once they gained power, was to use compulsion forcing all to baptise or to suffer death, with the destruction of all religious movements which ran counter to them. Heterodoxies were rigorously suppressed and freedom of religion, which had existed, to a very considerable extent in the Roman Empire, became a thing unknown. Men's minds were drilled to accept certain dogmas—of creation, salvation, and so on, as true and unquestionable. Indeed, it became a sin to question such doctrines in such a narrow and stifling religious climate, which continued, aided by the fire and sword of secular power for 1,700 years or so, the gentle but penetrating truth of the Dhamma had no chance.

It was only with the decline of church power in the eighteenth and nineteenth centuries that there was any possibility of eastern thought reaching westwards. By then however, a new obstacle arose in many Western minds: pride of empire. People who have empires always look down upon those they conquer but this attitude ensures that nothing can be learnt by the conquerors from the subject population. It is assumed that power to conquer means natural superiority in every respect, such conceit shutting the door against knowledge, which could otherwise be absorbed. But Western nations not only felt their weapons to be superior but their religion too. They saw themselves as light-bringers to the darkness of backward peoples. Their industries and mass-made products were soon to bring about a Golden Age of peace and prosperity and the ignorant natives of Asia had to play their part as cheap labour. Such attitudes as these guaranteed a lack of interest, even a derision of Asian culture. And Buddhism was the religion of the conquered, so what could be learnt from it?

Of course there were a few wise men that were interested both in the Pāli manuscripts on *ola* palm leaves from Sri Lanka and Burma, and in other Buddhist Sanskrit writings found in Nepal. In this way, a comparison also became possible for scholars between the earlier and simpler Pāli accounts and the later more embroidered versions found in Sanskrit.

One of the first Europeans to spread knowledge of the Buddha's teachings outside the circle of scholars and their journals was Schopenhauer.[109] It is quite possible that the first Westerner known to have become a bhikkhu, an Austrian whose name could not be traced, had read about the Buddha's teachings in the writings of this German philosopher. At the time of his ordination, c. 1870, he was employed by the Siamese government. He temporarily ordained as a bhikkhu at Wat Pichaiyat in Thonburi, during the reign of King Chulalongkorn (Rāma V).

Siam was never conquered by any colonial power, so his ordination ceremony was no doubt regarded with favour in government circles. But in Sri Lanka and Burma (as in Cambodia and Laos) the idea of Westerners "going native" to such an extent as to ordain was looked upon with horror.

Things have now changed a great deal. No longer do Western and semi-Christian countries have empires in the east, so pride of empire has had to be relinquished. And, again, many people now have second thoughts about industrialisation and its benefits. They are very doubtful whether the Golden Age will dawn through fast factories, mass-produced articles and the pollution which results. So now a great many young people turn to look at the eastern cultures and see what they have to offer to their hearts and minds starved of spiritual teachings.

That people are able to go now to Buddhist countries and find some institutions there which have relevance to their needs is due to the pioneers, who, from the beginning of this century, were courageous and sought acceptance in the Sangha. We shall not attempt here to give outlines of many of these pioneers, only three of the most famous will be mentioned, two British and one German.

In order of ordination, Allan Bennet was the first (though not the first Englishman in robes). His interest in Dhamma was

---

109. See *Schopenhauer and Buddhism*, Wheel 144–146, BPS

awakened by reading *The Light of Asia*, Sir Edwin Arnold's famous poem on the Buddha. So moved was he by this that he went to Sri Lanka in 1901 where he became a sāmaṇera with the name Ānanda Metteyya. The next year he went to Burma where it appears he was accepted as a bhikkhu. While studying and practising in Burma he founded *Buddhism*, an illustrated magazine of very high standard, which could hardly be matched in the Buddhist world today. In this organ, which had a worldwide circulation, plans were published for a Buddhist Mission to the West partly financed by generous Burmese lay-supporters, partly by the newly established Buddhist Society of Great Britain and Ireland. Bhikkhu Ānanda Metteyya arrived in Britain in April 1908 and began his work propagating the Dhamma. He experienced great difficulties as at that time Buddhism even as a word was hardly known to many people. Progress of the mission was not so rapid as had been expected. In the autumn of the same year, he returned to Rangoon and stayed there until 1914, but the bhikkhu's health deteriorated due to severe asthma, so he disrobed, returned to Britain and led a more retired life until 1923, the year of his death from that disease. His dying wish was to give his last few pence to a beggar he heard passing beneath his window. He was the author of *The Wisdom of the Aryas* and *An Outline of Buddhism*, besides many articles on the Dhamma.[110]

The second Westerner was Anton Gueth, a German, who was a bhikkhu for no less than 53 rains with the name of Nyanatiloka. He met with Buddhism in Germany and from there made his way to Sri Lanka, though it was in Burma that he became a sāmaṇera in 1903 and a bhikkhu in 1904. Then, he returned to Sri Lanka where he established a hermitage upon an island in the midst of a lagoon near to the south coast of the country. He lived an ascetic life quite unafraid of the many snakes that were his neighbours. The villagers nearby brought

110. See *Ānanda Metteyya: The First Buddhist Emissary of Buddhism*, E. J. Harris, Wheel 420/422

him alms food by boat every day, erected a *kuṭi*, hut, for him and treated him with great respect. Gradually he became known more widely, especially as other Westerners came to join the Sangha and took up residence under his guidance.

A number of his Western pupils have spent all their lives in the Sangha as he did, such as the venerable Vappa Mahāthera and Nyanasatta Mahāthera. Venerable Nyanaponika Mahāthera also is well known as a translator, author and founder of the Buddhist Publication Society in Kandy, while the late Nyanamoli Thera's name will live upon the many books he translated from Pāli.

Venerable Nyanatiloka Mahāthera was a great scholar who wrote and translated very many books, both in English and German. The most famous and influential of his works is the invaluable *The Word of the Buddha,* a sutta anthology on the Four Noble Truths (published by the BPS, Kandy).He also contributed to the Sixth Buddhist Council held in Burma. Such was his eminence that the Government of Ceylon made him a distinguished citizen in 1950. After his death in 1957 the government accorded him the honour of a State funeral. His last wish was to be reborn in Sri Lanka and to become a bhikkhu again.[111]

Last to be mentioned here is J. F. McKechnie whose bhikkhu name was Sīlācāra. His first contact with the Dhamma was through a copy of *Buddhism,* the magazine produced in Burma. This interested him so much that he went to Burma in 1906 and there became a bhikkhu. He studied Pāli and helped to produce the magazine, later writing a number of books himself and translating some more from Buddhist works in German. He was the translator also of the first hundred of the Buddha's *Middle Length Discourses* in two volumes, which he condensed and tried to put into easily understood English. He disrobed as a result of poor health and returned to England in 1925 to help there with *The British Buddhist,* the magazine of the British Maha Bodhi Society. He died in Bury, Lancashire in 1951.

---

111. See *The Life of Nyanatiloka Thera,* which contains his autobiography, biography and bibliography, BPS, Kandy.

Westerners entering the Sangha in more recent times still have to face a number of difficulties in Buddhist countries. If their confidence in the Triple Gem is not strong enough, these difficulties will soon find their weaknesses. Among them are such things as differences of climate, a trouble which can only be overcome by patience; and of food, where contentment with what one gets is needed. Another unwanted experience is that of the tropical diseases which afflict some aspirants. On such trouble as these the Buddha's Discourse on All the Troubles may be consulted in the Appendix. Language is another problem and it is essential to master the tongue spoken by one's Teachers as soon as possible. Other changes affect some people who cannot adapt to the religious and cultural environments of the Buddhist people to whom they go to learn. It is one thing to read a few Buddhist books, often not the words of the Buddha but various ideas of modern authors, but it is another to be in Buddhist surroundings and to have to discipline oneself accordingly. Western nuns will have to face even more difficulties, as have been outlined in the previous chapter.

One difference between many eastern Buddhists and Westerners, which can be a cause of difficulty, is the way they approach Dhamma. For the Buddhist, born and brought up in a Buddhist environment, Buddhism is coloured by traditional practices, ceremonies and festivals, which most do not question or ask what they mean and are inclined to accept the words of their Teachers as true. This is not to say that everyone is undiscriminating but rather that faith outweighs wisdom in many cases. Such an attitude can even be found in the Sangha, although this may be changing as a more Western-oriented youth grows up. The Westerner, by contrast, has no traditional Buddhist background and often discovers the Dhamma as the result of a personal search. He wants to know "Why?" Sometimes, there are Westerners who enter the Sangha with critical attitude founded on superiority-conceit. While it is right to inquire, this should be done with humility at the right time. While some Westerners start from an attitude of total scepticism and others begin from blind faith, these are two extremes to be avoided, however—the first leading quickly out of the robes and the second leading who knows where? To overcome these extremes, confidence should be developed by the sceptical questioner and wisdom by the traditional follower.

The question may be asked, "Well, why become a bhikkhu (or an upāsikā)?" The explanation runs like this—"If it is so difficult and there is the possibility of ruining one's health, well, just stay here at home and practise Dhamma!" This has to be the course of action for those who are tied-down to worldly responsibilities of family and so on. But if one is free of these burdens then learning the Dhamma "at home," with a small Buddhist centre nearby, is only a very second-best. In Western countries usually one can go to only one Teacher and so may miss the great variety of Teachers and Teachings found in the East. It is even more likely that no bhikkhus may be found near home and that one's practice must be based upon books and intelligent guesswork, which can never be a substitute for a good Teacher's presence. Where there is a Buddhist Society, this can be helpful, depending on those running it and what their understanding of Dhamma is like but it is not uncommon for unguided Buddhist groups to be more a source of confusion than enlightenment! Moreover, surrounding most Westerners there is a culture, materialistic and based on defilements, opposed to Buddhist aims, making them more difficult to realise. (This is not to say that Buddhist Countries are a paradise where Enlightenment will fall into one's lap!) But by learning thoroughly the language of the country one goes to and by living with Teachers and talking to them, appreciation of Dhamma is broadened and deepened in a way that cannot come about if one is a stay-at-home.

The West still has too few really great Teachers in the Buddhist tradition, and for the guidance of Enlightened minds one has to travel to the East. The effort and sacrifice may be great but the results can be greater still, depending on one's own reaction in the presence of Teachers. The best results are never attained without effort. Of course, it all depends how far one wishes to go but generally it is true to say that little effort towards training oneself means little result. And training oneself alone has a severe limitation: there is no one to tell one how to deal with defilements, or to point out the blind spots in one's conduct. Teachers, when one has humility, have compassion for one and guide one through the tangles of inner defilement and outer misbehaviour. So there is certainly some reason for seeking them out rather than going it alone.

If one finds a Teacher who has good Dhamma, then one thing is necessary so that the Dhamma can enter one's own heart: stay with him long, years will be better than months!

Then of course, for the easiest practise of Dhamma, ordaining as a bhikkhu or a nun is the best thing to do. Lay people have to fight on two fronts—the material, to keep themselves alive and the spiritual, against the defilements invading the mind. Those who wear robes, being supported by faithful laypeople, have only to fight the defilements. They have all their days and nights to do this, and they are protected by their Vinaya against situations which make Dhamma practice difficult or impossible.

The life of a bhikkhu or upāsikā is of course not for everyone (An old chestnut is the question, "But what would happen if everyone became monks and nuns?"—as if this is ever a possibility!) Many people in the Buddha-time and since then have even attained the Paths and Fruits by steady practice while leading the household life. Does this not contradict what was said above about renunciation? No, because those who can practise to levels of attainment as householders must have made much good kamma in the past. They have striven already, even if they do not remember doing so, but the numbers of such people are few. It is more common to be impeded by household life when on a spiritual path, than helped by it. Of course, one should never assume that one is a person of great merits who does not need to give up anything—for this would look rather like a conceit!

Other people say that the chaste life is unnatural, using analogies such as, "We have eyes so we are meant to see—and all the other organs including those of sex, so who are meant to use them." This kind of statement suffers from an assumption: that someone means us to act in some way rather than another. This is assuming the existence of a God and a plan that he has for the world. Buddhism shows that such assumptions are founded upon a misinterpretation of the evidence. There is no Creator and so no plan.[112] There are other objections too, which come out more strongly when people say, I have a stomach and so I eat, lungs and so I breathe, sex organs and so I have intercourse. But here of course, eating and breathing are necessary for the life of the body while sex certainly is not. Further, breathing is an automatic function and in no way connected with greed, while eating is not automatic and often involves kamma linked to greed, but sex is also a deliberate action (=kamma) and always rooted in greed (= lust, desire). Kamma rooted in lust or desire is not good kamma and its fruits are to strengthen craving for existence, for more life—and more death. So if one wants to make great efforts at Dhamma-practice in this existence the Holy Life is the most "natural" one to adopt. It favours becoming rid of defilements; it is near to or goes naturally towards renunciation and to Nibbāna.

What are the factors, which cause people to take up the Holy Life in the Buddha's teachings? The prime causes are two, one of which is experienced by all living beings while the other is only strong in some of them. The first of these experienced by all is *dukkha*,[113] unsatisfactoriness, pain, anguish, all kinds of unwanted mental and physical experiences whether gross or subtle. But not everyone has the second causal factor—wisdom (*paññā*), the understanding of how *dukkha* arises, of what conditions its existence. When a wise person reads the Four Noble Truths—(1) *Dukkha* (its existence), (2) Causal Arising (by way of craving—ignorance), (3) Cessation (by removal of craving = Nibbāna), (4) the Path to

---

112. See, *Buddhism and the God-idea* Wheel 47, BPS. For those who want something more substantial there is, *A Buddhist Critique of the Christian Conception of God*, by Gunapala Dharmasiri, Lakehouse Publications.

113. See, *The Three Basic Facts of Existence—II—Suffering*, Wheel 191–193, BPS

this cessation (the Noble Eightfold Path), he realises that much of his *dukkha* is made by himself and if he changes the course in his life, he can find peace and happiness. So *dukkha* impels people with wisdom (*pa*) to practice Dhamma.

If people have not seen much *dukkha* in this life, or they have seen it but not known that anything could be done about it, they are unlikely to be interested in the Buddha's teachings. *Dukkha,* the Buddha said, should be thoroughly known. This means that one should know it as such whenever it occurs, and as it is of various forms gross and subtle, not all of it will be obvious from the beginning. The subtle *dukkha,* of reliance upon this impermanent world (including mind-body) for instance, is only thoroughly known in the higher levels of insight meditation. This Buddhist teaching contrasts with the attitude of most people to *dukkha*—to try to ignore it constantly.

When people have *dukkha*—everyone has, but it is being really piled up in the West now—and wisdom too that appreciates the Noble Truths, then confidence (*saddhā*) is born. Confidence means trust in the Buddha who has discovered the way out of *dukkha* through his Enlightenment; in Dhamma as that Way which leads out of *dukkha* towards Nibbāna; and in the Sangha of Noble Ones who by following the Way have got rid of the causes of *dukkha* in themselves and reached to Enlightenment. These three factors then, *dukkha,* wisdom and confidence are the prime causes for Westerners ordaining.

A Pali Commentary lists four types of people who have confidence. (I do not use the word faith as in Buddhist contexts real *saddhā* is always allied to wisdom or understanding—*paññā*. Only the fourth type possesses true *saddhā* as we shall see.)

The first type of person gains faith through seeing something magnificent or beautiful. Such a person is said to measure by seeing. What they see may be a religious procession full of colour and pageantry, priests robed gorgeously, mighty cathedrals—or, great Buddha-images covered with gold. They are impressed by what they see.

In the second case, it is not seeing but hearing which is the basis for the arising of faith. People hear divine singing, or chanting, without knowing its meaning, or they recite a mantra, usually a meaningless word or collection of words, in the company of others, becoming carried away by the sound in any case. Their faith is established in this way.

The third group of people gain faith through appreciation of rough, coarse or common things. They "measure by coarseness." What does this mean? This means gaining faith through seeing an ascetic or monk who uses such things. It is based on the thought, "I love and use beautiful things but this ascetic is content with coarse things. Therefore he must be holy." In an Indian setting it applies to admiration and confidence on seeing a dusty, bearded ascetic with patched robes, or none at all. In Buddhist countries it is also found as when town-dwelling laypeople admire a forest-dwelling bhikkhu with his dull-coloured robes and other signs of asceticism.

It is rather obvious that none of these criteria are really safe for the development of confidence. One can see or hear things, which will lead one's understanding astray. What use is a religion, which encourages one's faith with gorgeous ritual and divine music but approves of persecution and power politics? One may be equally mistaken with the signs of coarseness in an ascetic's articles. Perhaps he is a hypocrite displaying such marks to win admiration or he may be just a dullard who does not care that his things are rough. All three fail through lack of wisdom, of that understanding, which, in this case, arises after thinking in terms of cause and effect.

So the fourth sort of person has faith, or better call it confidence, because he has used his wisdom. When he encounters religious splendours of eye and ear he is not taken in by them; such things, he knows, are all conditioned and imply no standard for truth. And he is not deceived by plainness or coarseness but asks why—is it for show or is it because of contentment and lack of desire for beautiful things? He "measures by wisdom" and uses his mind to test and ask questions. And he is not satisfied with a teaching if he is told that such questions should not be asked, or that they have no answers which we can understand. He believes only after repeated questioning, not being satisfied until his questions are answered with complete clarity. His understanding of the conditional arising and passing away of all things not only satisfies the intellect but is supported by practice of the Dhamma, particularly meditation. He is not satisfied if assumptions are presented to him for his belief, such assumptions as a Creator or an eternal soul, because such concepts can never be incontrovertibly demonstrated and do not agree with either sense-experience or with the evidence of meditation when investigated in the light of the Three Characteristics[114]—impermanence, *dukkha* and non-self, of all living beings. Such a person does not have to keep his faith apart from the conditionality which rules in the empirical world, indeed his wisdom (*paññā*) derived from observing conditionality, supports his faith in the Triple Gem; while that faith balances his wisdom so that the latter is not just intellectual knowledge. This type of person will be a good Buddhist, being both intellectually pleased with the clarity of Dhamma and emotionally satisfied with the good results, which come from practice.

A person like this may want to take up the Dhamma full-time, to give mind and body to the study and practice of the Dhamma. What should such a person do? What follows is the text, in revised form, of a little booklet published in Bangkok[115] for the information of people writing to find out about ordination and what is entailed by this step.

1. Become a Buddhist.
2. Understand clearly: Why do I wish to go forth to homelessness?
3. Consider: Can I lead the Holy Life honourably?
4. Question oneself: Am I free from obstacles to ordination?

---

114. See, *The Basic Facts of Existence*, BPS.

115. *Brief Advice to those wishing to Go Forth from home to homelessness*, (by the present writer), Mahamakut Press.

5. Decide: How shall I use my time when I have gone forth?
6. Practical needs for an applicant.
7. Necessary virtues in an applicant.
8. The Aim of the Holy Life.

(1) Become a Buddhist

One may think it unnecessary to start with this point as one might assume that everyone who wished to go forth was a Buddhist already. However, this is not always the case and there have been some people who though not really Buddhists but holding to their own views, still wish to be ordained. So what is a Buddhist? A Buddhist is one whose ideals are embodied in the Triple Gem, the most precious things in this world:

The Buddha as the Enlightened Teacher.
The Dhamma as the Path of practice leading to Enlightenment.
The Sangha as those who have attained Enlightenment by practising that Path.

To these Gems or Treasures a Buddhist goes for Refuge finding in them an incomparable security from the limitless variety of *dukkha,* which can be experienced in the world. From the manifold sufferings and fearfulness of the world with its cycle of birth, decay, disease and death, its instability and insecurity, a Buddhist goes for Refuge to Buddha, Dhamma and Sangha which are all aspects of Enlightenment and ultimately, through practice, to be found in his own heart. Without a good understanding of what the Triple Gem is, at first gained by study, no one can go for Refuge sincerely. And without this faith grounded on understanding, practice of the Dhamma is not possible nor will one possess the confidence needed to sustain one in the homeless life. One should be able to say, without any reservation of one's previous views, theistic, pan-religious, or whatever they may have been—throwing them all away, "To the Buddha I go for refuge. To the Dhamma I go for refuge. To the Sangha I go for refuge."

(2) Understand clearly: Why do I wish to go forth to homelessness?

Having become a Buddhist, one should then ask oneself this question to understand clearly whether one's motives for desiring ordination are correct or not. Some wrong reasons for this include such aims as: wishing to learn magic or gain supernormal powers, wanting a life of idleness or wanting to escape from personal difficulties or family responsibilities which should not be evaded, desiring fame or craving to become a Teacher after only a few months of ordination, desiring the respect shown by laypeople to those following the Holy Life, and so on. Right motivation includes: wishing to lead the Holy (chaste) Life as a way to go beyond the unsatisfactory world, seeing that such a life is free from worldly cares and gives one the chance to practise Dhamma fully devoting all one's time to the Triple Gem. Wrong reasons are based on the mental defilements of greed, pride, fear and so on, while the correct reasons arise from excellent qualities such as renunciation, wisdom, devotion and humility. The homeless life requires learning and steady practice for many years under the guidance of good Dhamma-teachers. Only when one has attained great practical experience of the Dhamma, will it be the time to teach others.

(3) Consider: Can I lead the Holy Life honourably?

When one knows that the reasons for undertaking the homeless life are straightforward, then one should ask a further question about one's abilities to keep to the Discipline (Vinaya). Whatever code of rules one undertakes (bhikkhus have 227, nuns 8 or 10), one should be able to keep them pure. These rules are to help one practise the Dhamma, a fact which can be understood from the name of those rules collectively: the Vinaya, meaning that which leads out of worldly sufferings towards peace of mind and purity of heart. Therefore one has the right attitude when one determines to keep all the training-rules carefully, not dropping those which impede one's own comfort and convenience. From such effort to keep all the training-rules pure, one becomes very careful of all actions of mind, speech and body. This awareness or mindfulness is the keystone in the arch of Buddhist training and, unless it is developed in the homeless life, one will give up the quest for Dhamma. The person with the right attitude understands the value of this awareness and is diligent in practice of the training-rules but does not expect to be free from all faults and failings. Whenever one falls into offences against those rules, then they should be confessed promptly so that the heart having been opened in this way, there is no burden of guilt but the restoration of purity. After ordination, one wears robes which are symbols of striving in the Holy Life and devotion to the Triple Gem. The good person determines to be worthy of them.

(4) Question oneself: Am I free from obstacles to ordination?

There are five obstacles to ordination as a bhikkhu: one is not a male, is not yet 20 years old (from conception), lacks organs or limbs so. One he is not a complete man, has committed very serious crimes such as murder or has committed the most serious offences against the Vinaya, such as the four defeating offences when previously ordained as a bhikkhu. Also one has been a bhikkhu in the past but held wrong views and gone over to and got ordination in another religion. When one has any of those five obstacles, bhikkhu ordination is not possible. Further, during the ceremony of Acceptance (ordination as a bhikkhu) the aspirant will be asked these questions[116]: Are you afflicted with diseases like these—leprosy, boils, eczema, consumption, epilepsy? Are you a human being? … a man? … a free man? Are you without debt? Are you exempt from government service? Have you the permission of your parents? Are you fully 20 years old? (Under this age one may be ordained as a sāmaṇera or novice). Are your robes and bowl

116. See, Appendix II.

complete?" (This is arranged by supporters at the temple where the ordination will take place). To the questions about diseases he must be able to reply truthfully, "No, venerable sir." To all the others with truth he must reply, "Yes, venerable sir." If these questions cannot be answered in this way, then he is not free from obstacles to ordination. The man who is free from them can be ordained a bhikkhu. In the case of a woman who wants to become an upāsikā or nun, she is required to have shaved her head, put on the nun's robes and be able to keep the Eight (or Ten) Precepts, the taking of which constitute her ordination. She will also require the necessary support for her life as upāsikā (see 6).

(5) Decide: How shall I use my time when I have gone forth?

A bhikkhu is supported by the offerings of faithful laypeople and does not work for money. He is able therefore, to give all his time to the Dhamma, learning and practising it so that he is worthy of lay support, not idling or wasting his time. To spend a fruitful life in the Sangha one must have good roots in the Dhamma. When the roots are weak the tree is easily blown down, such a bhikkhu quickly disrobes and returns to lay life. The roots that one must have are either in the path of book-study and the practice of the Vinaya in the town vihāras, or in the path of meditation in forest vihāras where strict discipline, the austere practices and meditation are the basis of life. Which way one takes depends upon one's character. In the first he must be able, very largely, to plan his own studies though there are some classes now for non-Thai bhikkhus. However, knowledge of Thai[117] is indispensable for easy communication with Teachers. Along with this language, Pāli should be learnt if one wishes to know the Buddha's words in his original tongue. Although there are many translations of the Buddha-word in English, older renderings are often unreliable and misleading. There is plenty of room for improved translations

117. (Or the language of whatever country one goes to for training).

of the Buddha's words. If one's aim is meditation, only knowledge of Thai, and Pāli technical terms used in the Dhamma, will be needed. A bhikkhu will certainly get help from his Teachers but this will still leave him with a great deal of time to fill. There is no rigid timetable that one has to follow so that self-discipline is very important. The few fixed events in a bhikkhu's day are an alms round, one meal or two finished by noon, chanting in Pāli in the temple once or twice a day, sweeping and cleaning, with perhaps a class or Dhamma-talk from the Teacher in the afternoon or evening. As it is rare to get the chance for ordination a man or woman who is so fortunate to be free from all obstacles should use the time for study or practice diligently and to the greatest advantage.

(6) Practical needs for an applicant

Obviously an applicant for ordination must have the means to get to the country and the vihāra where ordination will take place. But he or she must also have enough money to pay for a return ticket in case, before or after ordination, one decides not to continue in the homeless life. It will be a great advantage to have contacted the venerable abbot of a vihāra before arriving so that he may have some idea about oneself and the advisability or otherwise of going-forth. When contact has been made, a brief biography of oneself with details of education and a recent photograph are usually appreciated. On arrival at the vihāra, one should be prepared to stay there as a lay person (keeping the Eight Precepts) for a month or so while Teachers observe one's conduct. If it is decided that the ordination should go ahead, then during this time the Pāli ordination procedure should also be learnt. A man will require at least enough money to support himself for this period, buying perhaps his two meals, toilet requisites, and providing for any travelling that he may undertake to other vihāras. A woman, unless she has a definite supporter, will require just enough to keep herself in food and other necessities while she is in robes, at least for the first few years. She will probably get support after that when she has shown her firm intention to continue in the Holy Life. During this preliminary period one should wear clothes which are easily washable and in good repair. White is a colour favoured in Buddhist tradition, while bright colours are inappropriate.

(7) Necessary virtues in an applicant

Success in the Holy Life is possible when a person has, or makes efforts to develop certain good qualities. Faith in the Triple Gem has already been mentioned but though an applicant has this, yet if he or she is given to harshness, not much can be expected. So loving kindness in deeds and words is very important. A Buddhist is gentle and concerned not to harm other living beings; especially this is the mark of one in robes. Along with gentleness must go humility, that mildness of character, which welcomes instruction. If one supposes that one knows it all, which is just pride and conceit, and then one does not want to be told what to do or how it should be done. Humility opens the mind's door to knowledge, while conceit slams it shut. With humility, patience is necessary too. It is not likely that the aims of the Holy Life can be quickly achieved and patience is necessary for that. The mind has been defiled for a long time and it must take some while to cleanse and purify it. Though the ancient accounts of the Buddha's discourses speak of people becoming Arahants (Enlightened) in "no long time" one should remember that commentaries tell us that this sometimes meant as long as twelve years. Patience too is needed to deal with various obstacles, which may break the smooth course of the Holy Life. The Buddha has praised this quality most highly. Persevering effort should go along with patience. It is not enough to be patient, effort also is needed, a steady effort, not one of erratic leaps with indifference in-between. Effort is needed to cultivate all aspects of the Buddha's way in oneself, to change oneself from the ordinary ways of the world to act according to Dhamma, in mind, speech and body. These virtues are opposed to the defilements and while the latter only lead to more sufferings, the former are the basis for steady growth in the Dhamma.

(8) The Aim of the Holy Life

This may be divided into one's immediate aims and the ultimate aim. The immediate aims, which are in accordance with Dhamma, include becoming a better-disciplined person with the Vinaya as one's support, or gaining more knowledge of the Buddha's teachings through study of the Dhamma. To remove the troubles and difficulties in one's character can be also an aim, which will be realised as one progresses in the attainment of Nibbāna, the Ultimate aim. The Buddha frequently urged those who had gone forth not to rest content with the lower aims but with energy to press on to the attainment of higher goals, until Nibbāna was reached. That this is the ultimate aim should not be forgotten while one is in training, or after that, though the world of the senses makes it easy to do so. Although there is a fast express line direct to Nibbāna, it is easier to get shunted off this to some quiet siding where effort is no longer needed! The effort needed to conquer sloth and other dull mental states and the restraint necessary to guard one's actions from the defilements, bring happiness to those who lead the Holy Life, as the Buddha has said:

> By yourself incite yourself!
> By yourself restrain yourself!
> Thus mindful and self-guarded too,
> Happily, bhikkhu, you will live. (Dhp 379)

This is the end of the small booklet from Thailand and nearly the end of our book upon the Sangha. One thing remains to be said: While the Sangha flourishes the Buddha's teachings will spread for the happiness and benefit of mankind. But if the Sangha should not survive, either in the prisons of communism or in the madhouses of Western materialism, then the disappearance of Buddhism will shortly follow. The position of the Sangha in the Theravāda Buddhist countries of Asia is unsure. Already Cambodia and Laos have communist governments and communism, a product of Western intolerance, has not so far shown much favour to any kind of religious order. The future, then, in Asia is uncertain. It is also uncertain whether Theravāda will put down viable roots in the various Western countries in which it now has small centres. If it is to do so this will largely depend upon Western bhikkhus and nuns from those countries. This is not to say that the efforts of venerable bhikkhus from Asia are unappreciated because they have been the pioneers in establishing the vihāras that exist now in Western countries. But they do have difficulties with both language and cultural background, which are very different in their countries to conditions in Western lands.

As my revered Teacher, venerable Somdet Phra Nyanasangvorn, Lord Abbot of Wat Bovoranives vihāra in Bangkok, has said in a letter concerning the recently established Buddhist vihāra, Wat Buddharangsee, in Sydney, According to my opinion to construct a temple is much easier than to form a native Sangha in that temple, doing their proper work, stable and well established. In the West in general and Australia particularly, we must try to form the Sangha from among the people native to those countries and there should be bhikkhus from those countries who spend all their lives in the Sangha. If the Dhamma is practised well the venerable Somdet's vision will be realised. As he ends his letter-:

> May True Dhamma long stand fast
> and the people upholding Dhamma
> In concord may the Sangha live
> for benefits and happiness.
>
> May True Dhamma guard me well
> and all the Dhamma-practicers.
> And may we all attain to growth
> in Dhamma declared by the Noble Ones.

Appendix I—Discourses to or about Bhikkhus

Discourse on Setting in Motion the Wheel of Dhamma

Thus have I heard. At one time the Exalted One was staying at Benares in the Deer Park at Isipatana (the Resort of Seers). There he addressed the bhikkhus of the group of five:—

Bhikkhus, these two extremes ought not to be cultivated by one gone forth to homelessness. What are the two? There is devotion to indulgence of pleasure in the objects of sensual desire, which is inferior, low, vulgar, ignoble, and leads to no good; and there is devotion to self-torment, which is painful, ignoble, and leads to no good.

The middle way discovered by a Perfect One avoids both these extremes: it gives vision, it gives knowledge, and it leads to peace, to direct acquaintance, to discovery, to Nibbāna. And what is that middle way? It is simply the Noble Eightfold path, that is to say, right view, right intention, right speech, right action, right livelihood, right effort, right mindfulness, right concentration. That is the middle way discovered by a Perfect One, which gives vision, which gives knowledge, and which leads to peace, to direct acquaintance, to discovery, to Nibbāna.

Suffering,[1] as a noble truth, is this: Birth is suffering, ageing is suffering, sickness is suffering, death is suffering, sorrow and lamentation, pain, grief and despair are suffering, association with the loathed is suffering, dissociation from the loved is suffering, not to get what one wants is suffering—in short, suffering is the five grasped-at groups.

The origin of suffering, as a noble truth, is this: It is the craving that produces renewal of being, accompanied by enjoyment and lust, and enjoying this and that; in other words,

---

1. This is *dukkha*, as used in the body of the book.

craving for sensual desire, craving for being, craving for non-being.

Cessation of suffering, as a noble truth, is this: It is remainderless fading and ceasing, giving up, relinquishing, letting go and rejecting, of that same craving.

The way leading to cessation of suffering, as a noble truth, is this: It is simply the noble Eightfold path, that is to say, right view, right intention, right speech, right action, right livelihood, right effort right mindfulness, right concentration.

"Suffering, as a noble truth, is this": such was the vision, the knowledge, the understanding, the finding, the light, that arose in regard to dhammas not heard by me before. "This suffering, as a noble truth, can be diagnosed": such was the vision, the knowledge, the understanding, the finding, the light, that arose in regard to dhammas not heard by me before. "This suffering, as a noble truth, has been diagnosed": such was the vision, the knowledge, the understanding, the finding, the light, that arose in regard to dhammas not heard by me before.

"The origin of sufferings, as a noble truth, is this:" such was the vision ... "This origin of suffering, as a noble truth, can be abandoned": such was the vision ... "This origin of suffering as a noble truth, has been abandoned": such was the vision ... in regard to dhammas not heard by me before.

"The cessation of sufferings, as a noble truth, is this:" such was the vision ... "This cessation of suffering as a noble truth, can be verified": such was the vision ... "This cessation of suffering, as a noble truth, has been verified": such was the vision ... in regard to dhammas not heard by me before.

"The way leading to cessation of suffering as a noble truth, is this": such was the vision ... "This way leading to cessation of suffering, as a noble truth, can be developed": such was the vision ... "This way leading to cessation of suffering as a noble truth, has been developed": such was the vision, the knowledge, the understanding, the finding, the light, that arose in regard to dhammas not heard by me before.

As long, bhikkhus, as my knowledge and insight according to reality was not quite purified in these twelve aspects—in these three phases of each of the four noble truths—I did not claim to have discovered the full awakening that is supreme in the world with its gods, its angels of death and high divinity, in this generation with its monks and divines, with its princes and men. But as soon as my knowledge and insight according to reality was quite purified in these twelve aspects—in these three phases of each of the four noble truths—then I claimed to have discovered the full awakening that is supreme in the world with its gods, its angels of death and high divinity, in this generation with its monks and divines, with its princes and men. Knowing and seeing arose in me thus: My heart's deliverance is unassailable. This is the last birth. Now there is no renewal of being.

Thus spoke the Lord. Delighted, the bhikkhus of the group of five rejoiced in the Exalted One's words.

Now, during this utterance, there arose in the venerable Kondañña the spotless, immaculate vision of the Dhamma: Whatever is subject to arising, all that is subject to cessation.

When the Wheel of Dhamma had thus been set rolling by the Exalted One, the earth-gods raised the cry, "At Benares, in the Deer Park at Isipatana, the incomparable wheel of Dhamma has been set rolling by the Exalted One, not to be stopped by monk or divine or god or death-angel or high divinity or anyone in the world."

On hearing the earth-gods' cry, all the gods in turn in the six paradises of the sensual sphere took up the cry till it reached beyond the Retinue of High Divinity in the sphere of pure form. And so indeed in that hour, at the moment, the cry soared up to the World of High Divinity, and this ten-thousand-fold world-element shook and rocked and quaked, and a great, measureless radiance surpassing the very nature of the gods was displayed in the world.

Then the Exalted One uttered the exclamation, "Truly Kondañña knows! Indeed Kondañña knows!" and that is how that venerable one acquired the name, Aññā-Kondañña—Kondañña who knows.

(SN 56:11. Based on the translation by Ñāṇamoli Thera.
See Wheel 17, BPS.)

Appendix I

Discourse on the Noble Lineages

Thus have I heard. At one time the Exalted One was staying near Sāvatthī at the Jeta Grove, Anāthapiṇḍika's monastery. Then the Exalted One addressed the bhikkhus, saying, "O bhikkhus." "Lord," they replied. The Exalted One spoke thus:

Here (in this Teaching), bhikkhus, are these four lineages of the Noble Ones, known as highest, known as oldest, known as the (true) lineage, pure from ancient times, unstained of old, neither suspect now nor will they be suspect in future, and not despised by Samaṇas, brahmins and (other) wise men. What are the four?

1. Here, a bhikkhu is content with this or that robe and he speaks in praise of contentment with any sort of robe. For the sake of a robe he does not go about seeking it wrongly, in an unbecoming way. If he does not obtain a robe he is not worried while if he gets it he is not attached, not infatuated, not in bondage to it but seeing this danger he knows how to use it as a support (for his life). Yet he does not exalt himself because of contentment with any sort of robe, nor does he disparage others. Whoever is skilful in this matter, not lazy but clearly understanding and mindful, he is called a bhikkhu who stands firm in this ancient and highest lineage of the Noble Ones.

2. Then again, a bhikkhu is content with this or that alms food and he speaks in praise of contentment with any sort of alms food. For the sake of alms food he does not go about seeking it wrongly, in an unbecoming way. If he does not obtain alms food, he is not worried while if he gets it he is not attached, not infatuated, not in bondage to it, but seeing this danger he knows how to use it as a support. Yet he does not exalt himself because of contentment with any sort of alms food, nor does he disparage others. Whoever is skilful in this matter, not lazy but clearly understanding and mindful, he is called a bhikkhu who stands firm in this ancient and highest lineage of the Noble Ones.

3. Then again, a bhikkhu is content with this or that lodging and he speaks in praise of contentment with any sort of lodging. For the sake of a lodging he does not go about seeking it

wrongly, in an unbecoming way. If he does not obtain a lodging he is not worried while if he gets it he is not attached, not infatuated, not in bondage to it but seeing this danger he knows how to use it as a support. Yet he does not exalt himself because of contentment with any sort of lodging, nor does he disparage others. Whoever is skilful in this matter, not lazy but clearly understanding and mindful, he is called a bhikkhu who stands firm in this ancient and highest lineage of the Noble Ones.

4. Then again, a bhikkhu enjoys development (of good mental states[2]) and delights in it; he enjoys abandonment (of evil mental states) and delights in it. Yet because of his enjoyment and delight in development and because of his enjoyment and delight in abandonment he does not exalt himself, nor does he disparage others. Whoever is skilful in this matter, not lazy but clearly understanding and mindful, he is called a bhikkhu who stands firm in this ancient and highest lineage of the Noble Ones.

These, bhikkhus, are the four lineages of the Noble Ones, known as highest, known as oldest, known as the (true) lineage, pure from ancient times, unstained of old, neither suspect now nor will they be suspect in future, and not despised by samaṇas, brahmins and other wise men.

A bhikkhu having these four lineages of the Noble Ones may dwell in the East or in the West, in the North or in the South and wherever he dwells, aversion (to wholesome mental states, boredom with helpful environments) does not overpower him but he overcomes aversion. For what reason? The steadfast sage, O bhikkhus, has overcome both aversion and delight.

Thus spoke the Exalted One, the Welfarer, the Teacher then further said:

> Not by aversion is the steadfast sage overcome,
> not by aversion, for the sage is steadfast, firm.
> The steadfast sage aversion overcomes,
> indeed is the sage aversion's conqueror.

---

2. Including meditation.

What obstructions can there be,
for him, all kamma rejected, given up?
Who could blame him as worthy as
an ornament of Jambu gold—
even the devas praise him,
even by brahmas he is praised! (AN 4:28).

Discourse on Six Ways of Conduct To Be Remembered

Thus have I heard: At one time the Exalted One was staying near Sāvatthī at the Jeta Grove, Anāthapiṇḍika's monastery. Then the Exalted One addressed the bhikkhus, saying "O bhikkhus". "Lord," they replied, and the Exalted One said: "Bhikkhus, these six ways of conduct are to be remembered, to be cherished and held in great esteem as conducive to sympathy, to unbroken and harmonious concord. What six?

Bhikkhus, here a bhikkhu's friendliness in bodily action is ever present towards his fellow-monks, openly and in private. This is a dhamma (way of conduct) to be remembered, to be cherished and held in great esteem, conducing to sympathy, unbroken and harmonious concord. (1)

Again, bhikkhus, a bhikkhu's friendliness in verbal action (speech) is ever present towards his fellow-monks, openly and in private. This is a dhamma to be remembered, to be cherished and held in great esteem, conducing to sympathy, unbroken and harmonious concord. (2)

Again, bhikkhus, a bhikkhu's friendliness in mental action (thought) is ever present towards his fellow-monks, openly and in private. This is a dhamma to be remembered, to be cherished and held in great esteem, conducing to sympathy, unbroken and harmonious concord. (3)

Again, bhikkhus, a bhikkhu in respect of whatever he receives as due offerings even to the contents of his bowl, does not make use of them without sharing them with virtuous fellow-monks. This is a dhamma to be remembered, to be cherished and held in great esteem, conducing to sympathy, unbroken and harmonious concord. (4)

Again, bhikkhus, a bhikkhu in company with his fellow-monks trains himself, openly and in private, in the rules of conduct, which are complete and perfect, spotless and pure which are liberating, praised by the wise, uninfluenced (by mundane concerns) and favourable to concentration of mind. This is a dhamma to be remembered, to be cherished and held in great esteem, conducing to sympathy, unbroken and harmonious concord. (5)

Again, bhikkhus, a bhikkhu dwells with his fellow-monks openly and in private, preserving the insight that is noble and liberating, and leads him who acts upon it to the utter destruction of suffering. This is a dhamma to be remembered, to be cherished and held in great esteem, conducing to sympathy, unbroken and harmonious concord. (6)

Bhikkhus, these six ways of conduct are to be remembered, to be cherished and held in great esteem as conducive to sympathy, to unbroken and harmonious concord.

Thus spoke the Lord. Delighted, those bhikkhus rejoiced in the Exalted One's words.

(AN 6:12)

Discourse on Seven Conditions for Non-Decline of Bhikkhus

Thus have I heard: At one time the Exalted One was dwelling at Rājagaha, on Mount Vulture Peak. Then the Exalted One addressed the bhikkhus, I shall teach you seven conditions for non-decline, listen well and attend to what I shall say.

Yes Lord, replied those bhikkhus in assent to the Exalted One. Then the Exalted One, spoke thus:

And what, bhikkhus, are the seven conditions leading to non-decline?

So long, bhikkhus, as you will assemble frequently together and assemble in large numbers, so long bhikkhus may be expected to prosper, not to decline. (1)

So long, bhikkhus, as you will meet in concord, disperse in concord and tend to the affairs of Sangha in concord, so long bhikkhus may be expected to prosper, not to decline.(2)

So long, bhikkhus, as you will appoint no new rules and

will not abolish the existing ones, but will proceed in accordance with the rules of training as laid down, so long bhikkhus may be expected to prosper not to decline.(3)

So long, bhikkhus, as you will respect, honour, esteem and venerate the elder bhikkhus, those of long standing, long gone forth, the fathers and leaders of the Sangha, and will deem it worth-while to listen to them, so long bhikkhus may be expected to prosper, not to decline (4)

So long, bhikkhus, as you will not come under the power of producing craving that leads to fresh becoming, so long bhikkhus may be expected to prosper, not to decline (5)

So long, bhikkhus, as you will be delighted with forest dwellings, so long bhikkhus may be expected to prosper, not to decline. (6)

So long, bhikkhus, as you will establish yourselves individually in mindfulness, so that virtuous fellow-monks who have not yet come, might do so, and virtuous fellow-monks already come might live in peace, so long bhikkhus may be expected to prosper, not to decline. (7)

So long, bhikkhus, as these seven conditions leading to non-decline shall endure among the bhikkhus and the bhikkhus shall be known for them, then so long bhikkhus may be expected to prosper, not to decline.

Thus spoke the Lord. Delighted, those bhikkhus rejoiced in the Exalted One's words.

(AN 7:21)

Discourse on Ten Dhammas

Thus have I heard: At one time the Exalted One was staying near Sāvatthī at the Jeta Grove, Anāthapiṇḍika's monastery. Then the Exalted One addressed the bhikkhus, saying, "O bhikkhus!" "Lord," they replied. The Exalted One spoke thus:

"These ten dhammas should be constantly reviewed by one gone forth. What ten?"

"I have come to a classless state,[3]" should be constantly reviewed by one gone forth.

"My livelihood depends on others," should be constantly

reviewed by one gone forth.

"Different is the way I should behave," should be constantly reviewed by one gone forth.

"Do I reproach myself for my moral conduct (precepts)?" should be constantly reviewed by one gone forth.

"Do wise companions in the Holy Life, considering me, reproach me for my moral conduct (precepts)?" should be constantly reviewed by one gone forth.

"All that is mine, dear and delightful, will change and vanish," should be constantly reviewed by one gone forth.

"I am the owner of my kamma, the heir to my kamma, born of my kamma, related to my kamma, abide supported by my kamma; whatever kamma I shall do, whether wholesome or unwholesome, of that I shall be the heir" should be constantly reviewed by one gone forth.

"How do the days and nights fly past for me?" should be constantly reviewed by one gone forth.

"Do I delight in a, lonely place?" should be constantly reviewed by one gone forth.

"Have I arrived at any superhuman state of knowledge and insight worthy of the Noble Ones, so that if questioned in my last hours by companions in the Holy Life I shall not be embarrassed?" should be constantly reviewed by one gone forth.

These, bhikkhus, are the ten dhammas which should be constantly reviewed by one gone forth.

Thus spoke the Lord. Delighted, those bhikkhus rejoiced in the Exalted One's words.

(AN 10:48)

Discourse on All the Troubles

Thus have I heard. At one time the Exalted One was staying near Sāvatthī at the Jeta Grove, Anāthapiṇḍika's monastery. Then the Exalted One addressed the bhikkhus, saying: "O Bhikkhus."

---

3. By cutting off hair and beard, wearing plain robes and no ornaments, etc.

"Lord," they replied. The Exalted One spoke thus:

Bhikkhus, I will expound to you the method of controlling all the troubles. Listen well and attend to what I shall say to you. Yes, Lord, replied the bhikkhus in assent.

Then the Exalted One spoke thus:

Bhikkhus, I say that the getting rid of troubles is (possible) for one who knows and who sees, not for one who does not know and does not see. What must one know and see so that the getting rid of troubles may be possible? Wise reflection and unwise reflection. For a person who reflects unwisely there arise troubles which have not yet arisen and those which have already arisen increase. But for one who reflects wisely, troubles which have not yet arisen do not arise and those already arisen disappear.

Bhikkhus, there are troubles to be got rid of by insight; there are troubles to be got rid of by restraint; there are troubles to be got rid of by practice, there are troubles to be got rid of by endurance; there are troubles to be got rid of by avoidance; there are troubles to be got rid of by removal; there are troubles to be got rid of by development.

Bhikkhus, what are the troubles got rid of by insight? Bhikkhus, the uninstructed ordinary man, who does not see the Noble Ones, who is unversed in the Dhamma of the Noble Ones, who is untrained in the Dhamma of the Noble Ones, who does not see good men, who is unversed in the Dhamma of good men, who is untrained in the Dhamma of good men, does not understand what things should be reflected on and what things should not be reflected on. Not knowing what things should be reflected on and what things should not be reflected on, he reflects on things that should not be reflected on, and does not reflect on things that should be reflected on.

Now, bhikkhus, what are the things that should not be reflected on but on which he reflects? If, while reflecting on things the unarisen pollution of sensual pleasure arises and the arisen pollution of sensual pleasure increases; the unarisen pollution (of desire) for existence arises and the arisen pollution (of desire) for existence increases; the unarisen pollution of unknowing arises and the arisen pollution of unknowing increases, then these are the things that should not be reflected on, but on which he reflects.

Bhikkhus, what are the things that should be reflected on, but on which he does not reflect? If, while reflecting on things, the unarisen pollution of sensual-pleasure does not arise and the arisen pollution of sensual-pleasure disappears; the unarisen pollution (of desire) for existence does not arise and the arisen pollution (of desire) for existence disappears; the unarisen pollution of unknowing does not arise, and the arisen pollution of unknowing disappears, these are the things that should be reflected on, but on which he does not reflect.

By reflecting on things that should not be reflected on, and by not reflecting on things that should be reflected on, pollutions that have not yet arisen arise while pollutions that have already arisen increase. Thus he reflects unwisely in this way: Did I exist in the past? Did I not exist in the past? What was I in the past? How was I in the past? Having been what did I become in the past? Shall I exist in future? Shall I not exist in future? What shall I be in future? How shall I be in future? Having been what shall I become in future? Or, now at the present time he is doubtful about himself: Am I? Am I not? What am I? How am I? Whence came this person? Whither will he go? When he reflects unwisely in this way, one of the six false views arises in him: I have a self: this view arises in him as true and real. I have no self: this view arises in him as true and real. By self I perceive self: this view arises in him as true and real. By self I perceive non-self: this view arises in him as true and real. By non-self I perceive self: this view arises in him as true and real. Or a wrong view arises in him as follows: This is my self which speaks and feels, which experiences the fruits of good and bad actions now here and now there, this self is permanent, stable, everlasting, unchanging, remaining the same for ever and ever.

This, bhikkhus, is what is called caught in views, the jungle of views, the wilderness of views, the struggling of views, the agitation wilderness of views, 'the fetter of views." Bhikkhus, the uninstructed ordinary man fettered by the fetters of views does not liberate himself from birth, decay and death, from sorrow, lamentation, pain, grief and despair; I say he is not freed from suffering (*dukkha*).

But, bhikkhus, the instructed noble disciple, who sees the Noble Ones, who is versed in the Dhamma of the Noble Ones, who is well trained in the Dhamma of the Noble Ones, who sees good men, who is versed in the Dhamma of good men, who is well trained in the Dhamma of good men, knows what things should be reflected on and what should not be reflected on. Knowing what things should be reflected on and what should not be reflected on, he does not reflect on things that should not be reflected on and he reflects on things that should be reflected on.

Now, bhikkhus, what are the things that should not be reflected on which he does not reflect? If the unarisen pollutions of sensual pleasure, (desire for) existence and unknowing arise and the arisen pollutions increase, these are the things that should not be reflected on, and on which he does not reflect.

Bhikkhus, what are the things that should be reflected on, and on which he reflects? If ... the unarisen pollutions of sensual-pleasure should be (desire for) existence and unknowing do not arise and the arisen pollutions disappear, these are the things that reflected on and on which he reflects.

By not reflecting on things that should not be reflected on, and by reflecting on things that should be reflected on, the pollutions that have not yet arisen do not arise, and the pollutions that have already arisen disappear. Then he reflects wisely: This is dukkha (suffering). He reflects wisely: This is the causal arising of dukkha. He reflects wisely: This is the cessation of dukkha. He reflects wisely: This is the path leading to the cessation of dukkha. When he reflects wisely in this manner, the three fetters—the false view of self, uncertainty and attachment to vows and rites—fall away from him. Bhikkhus, these are called the troubles got rid of by insight.

Bhikkhus, what are the troubles got rid of by restraint? A bhikkhu, reflecting carefully, lives with his eyes restrained.

Now, whatever troubles, destructive, and burning, there are for him when he lives without restraining his eyes, those troubles do not exist for him when he does so.

Reflecting carefully, he lives with his ears restrained ... with his nose restrained ... with his tongue ... with his body and his mind restrained. Now whatever troubles, destructive and burning, there are for him when he lives without restraining his ears ... mind, those troubles do not exist for him when he does so. Bhikkhus, these are called the troubles got rid of by restraint.

Bhikkhus, what are the troubles got rid of by practice?[4] A bhikkhu, reflecting carefully, uses his robes—only to ward off cold, to ward off heat, to ward off the touch of gadflies, mosquitoes, wind, sun and reptiles, only for the purpose of covering the shame-causing sexual organs. Reflecting carefully, he uses almsfood—not for pleasure, not for indulgence, not for personal charm, not for beautification but only for maintaining his body so that it endures, for keeping it unharmed, for supporting the Holy Life; so that former feelings (of hunger) are removed and new feelings (from overeating) do not arise; then there will be for him a lack of (bodily) obstacles and living comfortably. Reflecting carefully, he uses his lodging—only to ward off cold, to ward off heat, to ward off gadflies, mosquitoes, wind, sun, and reptiles, only for the purpose of removing the dangers; from weather and for living in seclusion. Reflecting carefully, he uses supports for the sick, medicines and utensils only to ward off painful feelings that have arisen, for the maximum freedom from disease. Bhikkhus, whatever troubles, destructive and burning, there are for him who does not practise thus, these troubles do not exist for him when he does so. Bhikkhus, these are called the troubles got rid of by practice.

Bhikkhus, what are the troubles got rid of by endurance? A bhikkhu, reflecting carefully, puts up with cold and heat, hunger and thirst, with gadflies, mosquitoes, wind, sun and reptiles, abusive and hurtful language, he becomes hardened

4. "Practice" and "use' are different translations of the same Pali word.

to bodily feelings which are painful, acute, sharp, severe, unpleasant, disagreeable, and deadly. Bhikkhus, whatever troubles, destructive and burning there are for him when does not endure, those troubles do not exist for him when he does so. Bhikkhus, these are called the troubles got rid of by endurance.

Bhikkhus, what are the troubles got rid of by avoidance? A bhikkhu, reflecting carefully avoids a savage elephant, horse, bull or dog, avoids a snake, the stump (of a tree), a thorny edge, a pit, a precipice, a refuse-pool, or a cesspool. Also he does not sit in such places, nor frequent such resorts, nor associate with such bad friends that intelligent fellow-monks might suspect that he fixes his mind on evil things. Bhikkhus, whatever troubles, destructive and burning, there are for him when he does not avoid such things those troubles do not exist for him when he does so. These are called the troubles got rid of by avoidance.

What are the troubles got rid of by removal? A bhikkhu, reflecting carefully, does not tolerate but rejects, discards, destroys and extinguishes thoughts of sense-pleasure which have arisen in him; he does not tolerate ... thoughts of ill-will ... he does not tolerate ... thoughts of violence ... he does not tolerate but rejects, discards, destroys and extinguishes whatever evil and unwholesome thoughts have arisen in him. Bhikkhus, whatever troubles, destructive and burning, there are for him when he does not remove (these thoughts), those troubles do not exist for him when he does so. Bhikkhus, these are called the troubles got rid of by removal.

Bhikkhus, what are the troubles got rid of by (mental) development? Bhikkhus, a bhikkhu, reflecting carefully, develops mindfulness, a factor of Enlightenment dependent on seclusion, passionlessness, cessation, and maturing to renunciation; reflecting carefully, he develops investigation of Dhamma ... effort ... joy ... tranquillity... collectedness ... equanimity, a factor of Enlightenment dependent on seclusion, passionlessness, cessation, and maturing to renunciation. Bhikkhus, whatever troubles, destructive and burning there are for him when he does not develop (these factors), those troubles do not exist for him when he does so. Bhikkhus, these are called the troubles got rid of by development.

Bhikkhus, a bhikkhu in whom the troubles to be got rid of by insight have been got rid of by insight; the troubles to be got rid of by restraint have been got rid of by restraint; the troubles to be got rid of by practice have been got rid of by practice; the troubles to be got rid of by endurance have been got rid of by endurance; the troubles to be got rid of by avoidance have been got rid of by avoidance; the troubles to be got rid of by removal have been got rid of by removal; the troubles to be got rid of by development have been got rid of by development. Bhikkhus, it is this bhikkhu who is said to have restrained all the troubles; he has cut off craving, struck off his fetters and by fully penetrating conceit has put an end to suffering.

Thus spoke the Lord. Delighted, those bhikkhus rejoiced in the Exalted One's words.

(MN 2)

Discourse about Raṭṭhapāla[5]

Thus have I heard. At one time, when the Exalted One was wandering in the Kuru country together with a large sangha of bhikkhus, he eventually arrived at Thullakoṭṭhita, a town of the Kurus.

The brahmin householders of Thullakoṭṭhita heard this, The samaṇa Gotama, a son of the Sakyans who went forth from a Sakyan clan, it seems has been wandering in the Kuru country with a large sangha of bhikkhus and has come to Thullakoṭṭhita. Now a good report of Master Gotama has been spread to this effect: He describes this world with its gods, its Māras, and its Brahma divinities, this generation with its samaṇas and brahmins, with its princes and its men, which he himself realised through direct knowledge. He teaches Dhamma that is good in the beginning, good in the middle,

5. Honoured by the Buddha as the bhikkhu "foremost among those who went forth out of faith."

and good in the end, both in the spirit and in the letter. He proclaims the Holy Life, altogether perfect and pure. It is good indeed to see such Arahants.

Then the brahmin householders of Thullakoṭṭhita went to the Exalted One, and drawing near, some respectfully saluted him and sat on one side; some exchanged friendly greetings with the Exalted One and, after the customary words of friendship and civility, sat aside; some before taking their seats, extended their hands with palms together towards the Exalted One; some announced their names and families to him before sitting down; whilst others sat down in silence.

When they were seated, the Exalted One instructed, urged, roused, and encouraged them with talk on Dhamma.

Now, at that time a clansman called Raṭṭhapāla, the son of the leading clan in that same Thullakoṭṭhita, was sitting in the assembly. Then it occurred to him: As I understand Dhamma, given by the Exalted One, it is not possible, while living in a household, to lead the Holy Life as utterly perfect and pure as a polished shell. Suppose I were to shave off my hair and beard, put on the yellow cloth, and go forth from the home life into homelessness?

Then the brahmin householders of Thullakoṭṭhita, having, been instructed, urged, roused and encouraged by the Exalted One with talk on Dhamma, and delighting in his words and agreeing, rose from their seats and after paying homage to him, they departed, keeping their right sides towards him.

Soon after they had gone,[6] Raṭṭhapāla the clansman went to the Exalted One, and after paying homage to him, sat down at one side. Then he said to the Exalted One: Venerable Sir, as I understand the Dhamma given by the Exalted One, it is not possible while living in a household to lead the Holy Life as utterly perfect and pure as a polished shell. Venerable Sir, I want to cut off my hair and beard, put on the yellow cloth, and

---

6. Raṭṭhapāla waited until the others had left as he feared that relatives and friends of his family who were among the visitors, would disapprove of his wish for Acceptance and try to prevent it because he was the only son of his parents. (Commentary).

go forth from the home life into homelessness. May I receive the going forth under the Exalted One, may I receive the Full Acceptance?

Have you your parents' permission, Raṭṭhapāla, to go forth from the home life into homelessness?"

"No. Venerable Sir, I have not."

"Tathāgatas[7] do not give the Going-forth to a son without the parents' permission, Raṭṭhapāla."

"Venerable Sir, I shall see to it that my parents permit me to go forth from the home life into homelessness."

Then the clansman Raṭṭhapāla rose from his seat, and after paying homage to the Exalted One, he left keeping his right side towards, him. He went to his parents and said to them: "Mother and father, as I understand Dhamma given by the Exalted One, it is impossible, while living in a household, to lead the Holy Life as utterly perfect and pure as a polished shell. I want to shave off my hair and beard, put on the yellow cloth, and go forth from the home life into homelessness. Give me permission to go forth from the home life into homelessness."

When he had said this, his parents replied: "Dear Raṭṭhapāla, you are our only son, dear and beloved: you have been nurtured in comfort, brought up in comfort. You know nothing of suffering, dear Raṭṭhapāla. Even in case of your death, only unwillingly we should lose you, but while you are still living, how should we give you our permission to go forth from the home life into homelessness?"

A second and a third time the clansman Raṭṭhapāla said to his parents: "Mother and father ... Give me permission to go forth from the home life into homelessness."

For the third time his parents replied: "Dear Raṭṭhapāla... But while you are, still living, how should we give you our permission to go forth from the home life into homelessness?"

Then, not receiving his parents' permission for the Going-forth, the clansman Raṭṭhapāla lay down there on the bare

7. The Buddhas, (literally "gone to Thusness")—those who see things as they really are.

floor (and said) "Right here I shall either die or get the Going-forth."

Then the clansman Raṭṭhapāla's parents said to him: "Dear Raṭṭhapāla, you are our only son, dear and beloved: you have been nurtured in comfort, brought up in comfort. You know nothing of suffering, dear Raṭṭhapāla. Get up, dear Raṭṭhapāla eat, drink, and amuse yourself! While eating, drinking and amusing yourself you can enjoy sense-pleasures and do meritorious deeds. Even in case of your death, only unwillingly we should lose you. But while you are still living, how should we give you our permission to go forth from the home life into homelessness?"

When this was said that clansman Raṭṭhapāla was silent.

A second and a third time his parents said to him: "Dear Raṭṭhapāla, you are our only son ... how should we give you our permission to go forth ...?"

For the third time Raṭṭhapāla was silent.

Then the clansman Raṭṭhapāla's friends went to him and (repeated his parents' arguments) ... For the third time Raṭṭhapāla was silent.

Then Raṭṭhapāla's friends went to his parents and said to them: "Mother and father, this clansman Raṭṭhapāla has lain down there on the bare floor (thinking), "Right here I shall either die or get the Going-forth." Now if you do not give him your permission to go forth from the home life into homelessness, he will die there. But if you give him your permission, you will see him after he has gone forth. And if he does not enjoy the Going-forth, what else will he do than return here? So give him your permission to go forth from the home life into homelessness."

"Then we give the clansman Raṭṭhapāla our permission to go forth from the home life into homelessness. But when he has gone forth, he must visit his parents." [8]

So Raṭṭhapāla's friends went to him and told him: "Get up

8. It seems that they were so averse to his Going-forth that they could not tell him directly, only letting him know by way of his friends.

dear Raṭṭhapāla, your parents have given you their permission to go forth from the home life into homelessness. But when you have gone forth, you must visit your parents."

The clansman Raṭṭhapāla then got up, and when he had regained strength,[9] he went to the Exalted One, and after paying homage to him, sat down at one side. When he had done so, he said: Venerable Sir, I have my parents' permission to go forth from the home life into homelessness. May the Exalted One let me go forth." So the clansman Raṭṭhapāla received the going forth under the Exalted One, and he received the Full Acceptance.

Then soon after venerable Raṭṭhapāla's Full Acceptance when he had been accepted a fortnight, the Exalted One, having stayed at Thullakoṭṭhita as long as he chose, set out on tour to Sāvatthī. Wandering by stages, he arrived at Sāvatthī and stayed there in Jeta's Grove, in Anāthapiṇḍika's Park.

Meanwhile the venerable Raṭṭhapāla lived alone and secluded, diligent, ardent, and resolute. And the goal for the sake of which clansmen go forth from the home life into homelessness, that highest perfection of the Holy Life, before long[10] he came to know directly, in that very life, realizing it for himself, entering upon it and abiding in it: Birth has ceased, the Holy Life has been lived, completed the task and nothing further remains after this, thus he knew. And venerable Raṭṭhapāla was one of the Arahants.

Then venerable Raṭṭhapāla went to the Exalted One, and after paying homage to him, sat down at one side. Then he said: Venerable Sir, I wish to see my parents, if I have the Exalted One's permission."

Then the Exalted One, penetrating mentally the mind of venerable Raṭṭhapāla, knew thus: "The clansman Raṭṭhapāla is incapable of forsaking the training and reverting to what he

---

9. A fact emphasizing that he had fasted for sometime.

10. "Before long" is explained by the Commentary as twelve years. The fact that the servant-woman did not recognize him by his appearance and face but only from certain characteristics and his voice, seems to support the commentary's explanation.

has abandoned," and he told him, "Do now, Raṭṭhapāla, what you think fit at this time. Venerable Raṭṭhapāla rose from his seat, and after paying homage to the Exalted One, he departed keeping his right side towards him. Then he set his resting place in order, and taking his bowl and (outer) robe, he set out to go to Thullakoṭṭhita. Wandering by stages, he eventually arrived at Thullakoṭṭhita. There he lived in King Koravya's Migacira Garden.[11] Then when it was morning he dressed, and taking his bowl and (Outer) robe, went into Thullakohita for alms. As he was wandering from house to house he came to his own father's house.

Now on that occasion venerable Raṭṭhapāla's father was sitting in the hall of the central door having his hair dressed. He saw venerable Raṭṭhapāla coming in the distance, and seeing him, he said: "Our only son, so dear and precious to us, was made to go forth by these monkish shavelings."[12] Then venerable Raṭṭhapāla received neither alms nor polite refusal at his own father's house, and instead he got only abuse.

Now, at that time a slave woman belonging to one of venerable Raṭṭhapāla's relations, was about to throw away some stale porridge. (Seeing this,) venerable Raṭṭhapāla spoke to her: "Sister, if that is to be thrown away, then pour it in my bowl here."

While she was doing so, she recognized characteristic features of his hands and feet and of his voice. Thereupon she went to his mother and said: "If it pleases you, my lady, you should know that my lord's son Raṭṭhapāla is back."

"Oh, indeed? If you speak the truth, you are a slave woman no more!"

Then venerable Raṭṭhapāla's mother went to his father and said: "If it pleases you, householder, you should know that

---

11. This garden was given by the king for wandering monks of all kinds so that if they arrived too late to enter a monastery for the night, they would be able to stay there

12. The Commentary says he felt resentment against the bhikkhus because he wrongly believed that they had callously prevented his son from visiting his parents for so long.

they say the clansman Raṭṭhapāla is back!"

Just then venerable Raṭṭhapāla was eating the stale porridge by the wall of a certain (shelter). His father went to him and said "Raṭṭhapāla my dear, surely there is ...[13]and you will be eating stale porridge! Is there not your own home to go to?

Where, householder, is there a home for us who have gone forth from the home life into homelessness? We are homeless ones, householder. We did come to your home, householder, but we got neither alms nor polite refusal, only abuse we got.

Come, Raṭṭhapāla dear, let us go to the house.

Enough, householder, I have finished my meal for the day. Then, Raṭṭhapāla dear, accept tomorrow's meal." Venerable Raṭṭhapāla accepted in silence.

Knowing that his son had accepted, Raṭṭhapāla's father went back to his own house. There he had a large heap made of gold coins and bullion and had it hidden by screens. Then he told venerable Raṭṭhapāla's former wives: "Come, daughters-in-law, dress yourselves up in the way in which Raṭṭhapāla used to hold you most dear and beloved."

When the night was ended, venerable Raṭṭhapāla's father had good food of various kinds prepared in his own house, and he had the time announced to the venerable Raṭṭhapāla, "It is time, dear Raṭṭhapāla, the meal is ready."

Then, in the morning venerable Raṭṭhapāla dressed, and taking his bowl and (outer) robe, he went to his father's house, and sat down on the seat made ready.

Then his father had the pile of gold coins and bullion uncovered and said: "This, Raṭṭhapāla dear, is your mother's wealth, this other your father's, and that is your ancestral wealth. Raṭṭhapāla dear, you can use the wealth and make merit. Come then, renounce the training, return to what you have abandoned, use the wealth, and make merit!"

---

13. According to the Commentary, Raṭṭhapāla's father was so overcome by grief that he could not complete his sentence and only exclaimed, "Surely there is ..." He may have wished to say; Surely there is enough food and wealth in our house—"and you will be eating stale porridge."

"Householder, if you would do my bidding, then have this pile of gold coins and bullion loaded on carts and carried away to be dumped in the River Ganges in mid-stream. And why should you do so? Because, householder, it will be for you a source of sorrow and lamentation, pain, grief and despair."

Then venerable Raṭṭhapāla's former wives clasped both his feet, saying to him, "What are they like, young master, the nymphs for the sake of whom you lead the Holy Life?"

"We do not lead the Holy Life for the sake of nymphs, sisters."

"The young master Raṭṭhapāla calls us "Sisters," they cried, and they fell down fainting on the spot.

Then venerable Raṭṭhapāla told his father, "Householder, if there is a meal to be given, then give it. Do not harass us."

"Eat then dear Raṭṭhapāla, the meal is ready."

Then with his own hands venerable Raṭṭhapāla's father served and satisfied him with sumptuous food, solid and soft. When venerable Raṭṭhapāla had eaten and had withdrawn his hand from the bowl, he stood up and offered those stanzas:

Behold a puppet here pranked out;
A body built up out of sores,
Sick, and much object for concern,
Where no stability abides.

Behold a figure here pranked out,
With jewelry and earrings too,
A skeleton wrapped up in skin,
Made creditable in its clothes.

Its feet adorned with henna dye
And powder smeared upon its face
It may beguile a fool, but not
A seeker of the Further Shore.

Its hair dressed in octavo plaits,
And unguent smeared upon the eyes,
It might beguile a fool, but not
A seeker of the Further shore.

A filthy body, decked without,
Like a new-pained unguent pot;
It may beguile a fool, but not
A seeker of the Further Shore.

The deer-hunter sets well the snare,
But yet the doer springs not the trap;
We ate the bait, and we depart,
Leaving the hunters to lament.

When venerable Raṭṭhapāla had spoken these stanzas while standing, he then went to the King Koravya's Migacira Garden and sat down at the root of a tree to pass the day.

Then King Koravya addressed his gamekeeper: "Good gamekeeper, get the Migacira Garden tidied up, so that we may go to the pleasure garden to see a pleasing spot."

"Yes, sire" the game keeper replied.

Now, while he was having the Migacira Garden tidied up, he saw venerable Raṭṭhapāla seated at the root of a tree to pass the day. On seeing him he went to King Koravya and told him: "Sire, the Migacira Garden has been tidied up. But a clansman called Raṭṭhapāla is there, the son of the leading clan in this same Thullakohita, of whom you have always spoken highly, he is seated at the root of a tree to pass the day."

"Then, good gamekeeper, enough of the pleasure garden for today. We shall now pay respect to that Master Raṭṭhapāla."

And he further said, "Give away all the solid and soft root food that has been prepared!" Then King Koravya had a number of state carriages got ready and mounting one of them, he drove from Thullakoṭṭhita with the full pomp of royalty to see venerable Raṭṭhapāla. He drove thus as far as the road was passable for carriages, and then he got down from his carriage and with a following of the highest officials he went on foot to where venerable Raṭṭhapāla was. He exchanged greetings with venerable Raṭṭhapāla, and when the courteous and amiable talk was finished, he stood at one side. Then he said: "Here is an elephant rug. Let Master Raṭṭhapāla be seated on it."

"There is no need, great king. Sit down. I am sitting on my own mat."

King Koravya sat down on a seat made ready, and having done so, he said:

"Master Raṭṭhapāla, there are four kinds of loss. After undergoing these losses, some people here shave off hair and beard, put on the yellow cloth and go forth from the home life into homelessness. What are the four? They are loss through ageing, loss through sickness, loss of property, and loss of relatives."

"And what is loss through ageing? Here someone is old, aged, burdened with years, advanced in life, and come to the last stage. He considers thus, 'I am old, aged, burdened with years, advanced in life, and come to the last stage. It is no more possible for me to acquire unacquired possessions or to increase possessions already acquired. Suppose I were to shave off my hair and beard, put on the yellow cloth and go forth from the home life into homelessness?' So he who has undergone that loss through ageing, shaves off hair and beard, puts on the yellow cloth and goes forth from the home life into homelessness. This is called the loss through ageing. But Master Raṭṭhapāla is still young, black-haired, endowed with the blessing of youth, in the prime of life. There is none of this loss through ageing for Master Raṭṭhapāla. What has Master Raṭṭhapāla known or seen or heard that he has gone forth from the home life into homelessness?"

"And what is loss through sickness? Here someone is afflicted with sickness, is suffering and gravely ill. He considers thus, 'I am afflicted with sickness; I am suffering and gravely ill. It is no more possible for me to acquire ... Suppose ... I were to go forth from the home life into homelessness?' So he who has undergone this loss through sickness ... goes forth from the home life into homelessness. This is called the loss through sickness. But Master Raṭṭhapāla has now no affliction or ailment, having a good digestion that is neither too cool nor too warm but medium. There is none of this loss through sickness for Master Raṭṭhapāla. What has Master Raṭṭhapāla known or seen or heard, that he has gone forth from the home life into homelessness?"

"And what is loss of property? Here someone is rich, with great wealth and great property. Gradually these properties of his dwindle away. He considers thus, 'Formerly I was rich with great wealth and great property. It is no more possible for me to acquire unacquired possessions or to increase possessions already acquired. Suppose ... I were to go forth from the home life into homelessness?' So he who has undergone this loss of property ... goes forth from the home life into homelessness. This is called loss of property. But Master Raṭṭhapāla is the son of the leading clan in this same Thullakoṭṭhita. There is none of this loss of property for Master Raṭṭhapāla. What has Master Raṭṭhapāla known or seen or heard that, he has gone forth from the home life into homelessness?"

"And what is loss of relations? Here someone has many friends and companions, relatives and kin. Gradually these relatives of his dwindle away. He considers thus, 'Formerly I had many friends and companions, relatives and kin. Gradually those relatives of mine have dwindled away. It is no more possible for me to acquire unacquired possessions or to increase possessions already acquired. Suppose I were to cut off my hair and beard, put on the yellow cloth and go forth from the home life into homelessness?' So he who has undergone that loss of relatives, shaves off hair and beard, puts on the yellow cloth and goes forth from the home, life into homelessness. This is called loss of relatives. But Master Raṭṭhapāla has many friends and companions, relatives and kin in this same Thullakoṭṭhita. There is none of this loss of relatives for Master Raṭṭhapāla. What has Master Raṭṭhapāla known or seen or heard that he has gone forth from the home life into homelessness?"

"These, Master Raṭṭhapāla, are the four kinds of loss, undergoing which some people here shave off hair and beard, put on the yellow cloth and go forth from the home life into homelessness. Master Raṭṭhapāla has none of these. What has he known or seen or heard that he has gone forth from the home life into homelessness?"

"Great King, there are four Summaries of Dhamma which have been given by the Exalted One who knows and sees, who is Arahant and fully enlightened. Knowing and seeing and hearing them, I went forth from the home life into homelessness. What are the four?"

"'(Life in any) world is unstable, it is swept away': This is the first Summary of Dhamma given by the Exalted One who knows and sees, who is Arahant and fully enlightened. Knowing and seeing and hearing it, I went forth from the home life into homelessness."

"'(Life in any) world has no shelter and no protector': This is the second Summary of Dhamma given ...."

"'(Life in any) world has nothing of its own; it has to leave all and pass on': This is the third Summary of Dhamma given ...."

"'(Life in any) world is incomplete, is insatiate and the slave of craving': This is the fourth Summary of Dhamma given by the Exalted One who knows and sees, who is Arahant and fully enlightened. Knowing and seeing and hearing it, I went forth from the home life into homelessness." [14]

These, great King, are the four Summaries of Dhamma given by the Exalted One who knows and sees, who is Arahant and fully enlightened. Knowing and seeing and hearing them, I went forth from the home life into homelessness.

"'(Life in any) world is unstable, it is swept away' was what Master Raṭṭhapāla said; but how should the meaning of that statement be understood?"

"What do you think about this, great King: when you were twenty years old and twenty-five years old, were you an expert rider of elephants, an expert horseman, an expert charioteer, an expert bowman, an expert swordsman, strong in thigh and arm, sturdy and proficient in warfare?"

---

14. Summaries of the Teaching (*dhammuddesa*),—The Pali text of these four terse maxims is as follows:

1. Upanīyati loko addhuvo 'ti.

2. Attāno loko anabhissaro 'ti.

3. Assako loko, sabbaṃ pahāya gamanīyan 'ti.

4. Ūno loko atitto taṇhādāso 'ti.

"Certainly, Master Raṭṭhapāla, at the age of twenty and twenty-five years, I was an expert rider of elephants ... sturdy and proficient in warfare; sometimes I thought that I had superhuman strength. I saw none who could equal me in strength."

"And now, great King, what do you think: Are you still so strong; in thigh and arm, sturdy and proficient in warfare?"

"No, Master Raṭṭhapāla, now I am old, aged, burdened with years, advanced in life, and have come to the last stage; my years have turned eighty. Sometimes I moan to put my foot here and I put it elsewhere."

"It was on account of this, great King, that the Exalted One who knows and sees, who is Arahant and fully enlightened, said, '(Life in any) world is unstable, it is swept away,' and when I knew and saw and heard that, I went forth from the home life into homelessness."

"It is wonderful, Master Raṭṭhapāla, it is marvellous, how well that has been expressed by the Exalted One who knows and sees, who is Arahant and fully enlightened: '(Life in any) world is unstable, it is swept away,' for so it is indeed!"

"Master Raṭṭhapāla, there are in this court elephantry and cavalry and charioteers and infantry, which will serve to subdue any threat to it. Now Master Raṭṭhapāla has said that '(Life in any) world has no shelter and no protector.' How should the meaning of that statement be understood?"

"What do you think about this, great King: Have you any chronic illness?"

"I have a chronic wind sickness, Master Raṭṭhapāla. Sometimes my friends and companions, my relatives and kin, stand round me (thinking): "Now King Koravya is about to die, now King Koravya is about to die."

"Now, great King, what do you think: Can you have it thus with your friends and companions, your relatives and kin: "Come my good friends and companions, my relatives and kin! Let all of you present share out this pain, so that my feeling of pain should be less!" or do you have to experience that feeling of pain all by yourself alone?"

"No, Master Raṭṭhapāla, I cannot have it thus (that my

friends and companions, my relatives and kin, share out my feeling of pain), but I have to experience my pain all by myself alone."

"It was on account of this, great King, that the Exalted One who knows and sees, who is Arahant and fully enlightened, said, '(Life in any) world has no shelter and no protector,' and when I knew and saw and heard that, I went forth from the home life into homelessness."

"It is wonderful, Master Raṭṭhapāla, it is marvellous how well that has been expressed by the Exalted. One ...: '(Life in any) world has no shelter and no protector,' for so it is indeed!"

"Master Raṭṭhapāla, there is in this court ample gold coin and bullion stored away both in the ground and above it. Now Master Raṭṭhapāla has said that '(Life in any) world has nothing of its own, it has to leave all and pass on.' How should the meaning of this statement be understood?"

"What do you think about this, great King: You are now furnished and endowed with the five fields of sensual desires and enjoy them. But can you have it thus of the life to come: "May I be likewise furnished and endowed with these five fields of sensual desires and enjoy them!," or will others take over this property, while you will have to pass on according to your actions?"

"I cannot have it thus ... Master Raṭṭhapāla. On the contrary, others will take over this property while I shall have to pass on according to my actions."

"It was on account of this, great King, that the Exalted One ... said, '(Life in any) world has nothing of its own, it has to leave all and pass on,' and when I knew and saw and heard that, I went forth from the home life into homelessness."

"It is wonderful, Master Raṭṭhapāla, ... how well that has been expressed by the Exalted One...: '(Life in any) world has nothing of its own, it has to leave all and pass on,' for so it is indeed!"

"'(Life in any) world is incomplete, is insatiate and the slave of craving,' was what Master Raṭṭhapāla said; but how should the meaning of that statement be understood?"

"What do you think, great King: Do you live in this prosperous Kuru country as its ruler?"—"Yes Master Raṭṭhapāla, I do."—"What do you think about this, great King? If a trustworthy and reliable man came to you from the east and said, "Please to know, great King, that I come from the east and there I saw a large country, powerful and rich, very populous and crowded with men. There are plenty of elephantry there, plenty of cavalry, plenty of charioteers and plenty of infantry; there is plenty of ivory there, and plenty of gold and bullion both unworked and worked, and there are plenty of women for wives. With such and such a force you can conquer it. Conquer it then, great King!"" "What would you do?"—"We should conquer it and live there as its ruler, Master Raṭṭhapāla."—"What do you think about this, great King: if a trustworthy and reliable man came to you from the west.... from the north.... from the south, and there I saw a large country ... Conquer it, great King! What would you do?"—"We should conquer it, too, and live there as its ruler, Master Raṭṭhapāla."

"It was on account of this, great King, that the Exalted One who knows and sees, who is Arahant and fully enlightened, said, '(Life in any) world is incomplete, is insatiate and the slave of craving,' and when I knew and saw and heard that, I went forth from the home life into homelessness."

"It is wonderful, Master Raṭṭhapāla, it is marvellous how well that has been expressed by the Exalted One who knows and sees, who is Arahant and fully enlightened: "(Life in any) world is incomplete, insatiate and the slave of craving," for so it is indeed!"

That is what venerable Raṭṭhapāla said and having thus spoken, he said further:

> I see men wealthy in the world who yet
> Give not, from ignorance, their gathered riches
> But greedily will hoard away their wealth,
> Through longing for still further sensual pleasures.

A king who by his force conquered the earth
And even lords the land the ocean bounds
Is yet unsated with the sea's near shore And hungers
for its further shore as well.

Most other men as well, not just a king,
Encounter death with craving unabated;
With plans still incomplete they leave the corpse;
Desires remain unsated in the world.

His relatives lament him, rend their hair,
Crying Ah me! Alas! Our love is dead!
Then bear away the body wrapped in shrouds,
To place it on a pyre and burn it there.

Clad in a single shroud, he leaves behind
His property, impaled on stakes he burns,
And as he died, no relatives or kin
Or friends could offer refuge to him here.

The while his heirs annex his wealth, this being
Must now arise according to his deeds;
And as he dies nothing can follow him:
Not child nor wife not wealth nor royal estate.

Longevity is not acquired with wealth
Nor can prosperity banish old age;
Short is this life, as all the sages say;
Eternity it knows not, only change.

The rich man and the poor man both shall feel
(Death's) touch, as do the fool and sage alike;
But while the fool lies stricken by his folly
No sage will ever tremble at the touch.

Better than wealth is understanding, then.
By which the final goal can here be gained;
For, doing evil deeds in many lives,
Men fail, through ignorance, to reach the goal.

As one goes to the womb and to another world,
Renewing the successive round, so others
With no- more understanding, trusting him,
Go also to the womb and to another world.

Just as a robber caught in burglary,
An evil-doer suffers for his deed
So people after death, in the next world,
The evil-doers, suffer for their deeds.

Sense-pleasures, varied, sweet, delightful,
In many different ways disturb the mind.
Seeing the peril in these sensual joys,
O King! I chose to lead the homeless life.

As fruits fall from the tree, so also men,
Both young and old, fall when this body breaks
Seeing this, too, I have gone forth, O King!
Better by far is the monk's life assured."

(MN 82.
Based on the translation by Ñāṇamoli Thera,
see Wheel 110, BPS.)

Appendix II—
Ordination Procedure in Brief

Procedure of Acceptance as a Bhikkhu

The candidate, having already fixed the date of ordination or acceptance with his Teachers, and his supporters having purchased already his requisites and the gifts for the ordaining Sangha, on the day for Acceptance has his head and beard shaved completely. Afterwards, he changes into two white cloths, an upper one leaving the right shoulder bare, and a lower one like a sarong.

At the appointed time he goes barefoot to the temple bearing in his hands white lotus-buds and followed by his relatives and friends carrying gifts. When he comes to the temple he may circumambulate it three times while recollecting the virtues of the Buddha, Dhamma and Sangha. Entering the temple he offers the lotus-buds, a symbol of purity, in front of the Buddha-image and lights candles and incense. The precise details of his actions vary with different temples and their traditions.

After making the offering, he sits down on a mat facing the Buddha-image near the back of the temple with his relatives and friends sitting nearby. All wait now for the Preceptor and Teachers with the other witnessing bhikkhus to arrive. When they are seated, having made a triple prostration first, the candidate prostrates to the Preceptor and then approaching him on his knees, carrying his bundle of robes over his forearms, hands in *añjali*, says[15]:

"Venerable Sir, I go for refuge to that Lord, though long attained to Parinibbāna, together with the Dhamma and the Bhikkhu Saṅgha. May I obtain, Venerable Sir, the Going-forth in the Dhamma-Vinaya of the Lord, may I obtain the Acceptance.[16]"

This is repeated three times followed by another formula thrice repeated:

"Venerable Sir, I beg for the Going-forth. Having taken these yellow robes please give me the Going-forth, Venerable Sir, out of compassion for me."

The Preceptor receives the set of robes, and the candidate, hands in *añjali*, listens carefully to his explanation of the Triple Gem, Buddha, Dhamma, and Sangha, under the second of which he outlines moral conduct, meditation and wisdom and how the practice of these things brings great benefit. Following on from this the Preceptor teaches his pupil the five unattractive parts of the body as the meditation to use should his mind be upset by lust and the Holy Life made difficult for him. Those five are then repeated word by word after the Preceptor, in both normal and reverse order:

"Head-hair, body-hair, nails, teeth, skin; skin, teeth, nails, body-hair, head-hair."

When this is complete, the Preceptor extracts the yellow shoulder-cloth from the set of robes and places it over the white cloth of the candidate. From this moment the candidate is a sāmaṇera though he has not yet received his ten precepts. The Preceptor further points out the use of the different robes after which the new sāmaṇera retires and is helped to put on his robes correctly by one of the bhikkhus.

Having done this, he goes to his Teacher and after offering flowers, incense, and candles and prostrating, asks for the

---

15. The wording of the Going-forth varies in different Theravāda traditions. Here the version used in Dhammayut temples in Thailand is given. For this in detail see *Ordination Procedure,* Mahamakut Press, Bangkok. For another (Mahā-nikāya) version see *Ordination according to Thai Buddhist Tradition,* compiled by Piyasīlo Bhikkhu, Wat Sraket Rājavara Mahāvihāra, Bangkok. Both these accounts have the Pali words of Going-forth and Acceptance. The version issued by BPS, Kandy, according to the Sinhalese Siam-nikāya) method, (*Ordination in Theravāda Buddhism,* Wheel 56) is without the Pali. Hands in *añjali"* means having the hands held palms together at heart level in a respectful attitude.

16. The last clause is omitted in the case of a candidate requesting the Going-forth only, that is, just becoming a sāmaṇera novice).

Refuges and Precepts in these words:

"Venerable Sir, I beg for the Refuges and Precepts."

This is repeated three times after which the Teacher chants:

"Homage to the Exalted One, the Arahant, Perfectly Enlightened One!" by himself.

After the sāmaṇera has repeated this thrice, the Teacher says:

"What I say, you should say"

And the sāmaṇera replies:

"Yes, Venerable Sir."

Then the Teacher chants the Refuges, the sāmaṇera repeating his words:

To the Buddha I go for Refuge. To the Dhamma I go for Refuge. To the Sangha I go for Refuge. For the second time... For the third time...

When the Refuges are complete then the Teacher chants each of the Precepts with the sāmaṇera following him:

"Refraining from killing living creatures.[17]

Refraining from taking what is not given.

Refraining from unchaste conduct.

Refraining from speaking falsely.

Refraining from distilled and fermented intoxicants which are the occasion for carelessness.

Refraining from eating at the wrong time (noon till dawn).

Refraining from dancing, singing, music, and going to see entertainments.

Refraining from wearing garlands, smartening with perfumes, and beautifying with cosmetics.

Refraining from (using) a high or large bed.

Refraining from accepting gold and silver (-money).

I undertake these ten rules of training."

This completes the Going-forth of a sāmaṇera. If the sāmaṇera will not become a bhikkhu on this occasion, he then

---

17. When the Precepts (Five or Eight) are given, the formula is longer like this: I undertake the rule of training to refrain from killing living creatures, and so on with the rest. For the Eight Precepts, join together precepts seven and eight in the above list as the seventh, and add number nine as the eighth.

receives gifts first for the Preceptor and Teacher, respectfully offering them, then for the invited bhikkhus and finally receives his own requisites and other suitable gifts. If he will go on to the Acceptance, he prostrates three times to his Teacher, turns to his lay-supporters and receives the almsbowl from them which he then carries to the Preceptor to whom he prostrates again. He offers him also flowers, incense and candles and then chants as follows:

"Venerable Sir, I beg for dependence." (Three times)

"May you be my Preceptor, Venerable Sir."

The Preceptor will say:

"It is good. It is suitable. It is convenient. It is proper."

"Make a pleasing effort!"

To each of which phrases the sāmaṇera replies:

"It is good, Venerable Sir,"

and continues:

From this day onward the thera's burden will be mine. I shall be the burden of the thera."

and then prostrates three times. The Preceptor then instructs him briefly about the sāmaṇera's Pali name and his own and how they should be used when answering the questions.

The Teacher now puts the bowl in its sling on the sāmaṇera's back and questions him about that bowl and the robes he is wearing:

"This is your almsbowl."

"Yes, Venerable Sir," (replies the sāmaṇera).

"This is your outer robes."

"Yes, Venerable Sir."

"This is your upper robe."

"Yes, Venerable Sir."

"This is your under robe."

Having ascertained that they belong to him, the Teacher tells him to retire and stand at a place at the back of the temple behind a mat upon which his Teacher (or Teachers, as sometimes there are two) will stand. Meanwhile the Teacher, having prostrated, recites three times the "*Namo tassa* ..." and then informs the Sangha as follows:

"Let the Sangha listen to me, Venerable Sirs. This ... (Pali name of the sāmaṇera—we will say that it is 'Nāga') wishes for the Acceptance from the Venerable ... (Preceptor's name, say it is 'Padīpo'[18]). If there is the complete preparedness of the Sangha, I shall examine Nāga."

The Teacher(s) then rises and walks to the mat in front of Nāga and examines him as follows:

"Listen, Nāga, this is the time for truth, the time for what is factual. Whatever has occurred, that, in the midst of the Sangha, will be asked about. Whatever is so, that should be told. Whatever is not so, that should be told. Do not be embarrassed! Do not be confused! They will ask you as follows:[19] 'Do you have such diseases as these?' 'Leprosy?' (Nāga: 'No, Venerable Sir.'). 'Ulceration?' ('No, Venerable Sir.'). 'Ringworm?' ('No, Venerable Sir.'). 'Consumption?' ('No, Venerable, Sir). 'Epilepsy? ('No, Venerable Sir.'). 'Are you human being?[20]' ('Yes, Venerable Sir.'). 'Are you a man?' ('Yes, Venerable Sir.'). 'Are you a free man?' ('Yes, Venerable Sir.'). 'Are you without debt?' ('Yes, Venerable Sir.'). 'Are you exempt from government service?' ('Yes, Venerable Sir.'). 'Have you been permitted by your mother and father?' ('Yes, Venerable Sir.'). Are you fully twenty years of age? ('Yes, Venerable Sir.'). 'Have you the bowl and robes complete?' ('Yes, Venerable Sir.'). 'What is your name?' ('Venerable Sir, I am named Nāga.'). 'What is your Preceptor's name?' ('Sir, my Preceptor's name is Venerable Padīpo.')."

The Teacher returns to the Sangha, prostrates, and then respectfully informs the Sangha as follows:

"Let the Sangha listen to me, Venerable Sirs. Nāga wishes for the Acceptance from Venerable Padīpo. He has been

---

18. *Nāga* means an aspirant for ordination, a great being (snake, elephant) including a great man, while *padīpo* is Pali for a lamp. All bhikkhus have a Pali name given by their preceptors at the time of Acceptance.

19. See Chapter VIII, Section 4 of the booklet quoted.

20. This question is asked as non-human beings are said to have got the Acceptance in the Buddha's days.

examined by me. If there is complete preparedness of the Sangha, let Nāga come here."

The Teacher turns to Nāga saying "Come here!" Nāga approaches the Sangha, kneels and prostrates three times to his Preceptor and recites:

"Venerable Sir, I beg for the Acceptance. May the Sangha raise me up, out of compassion. For the second … third time …"

It is then the Preceptor's time to speak those words:

"Now, Reverend Sirs, this sāmaṇera named Nāga wishes for the Acceptance from me. Desiring Acceptance he begs it from the Sangha. I request all this from the Sangha. It is good, Reverend Sirs, if when all the Sangha has questioned this sāmaṇera named Nāga about the obstructing circumstances and acknowledged complete preparedness, that we shall accept him by the Act of Four (announcements) including the motion which is firm and proper to the occasion, bringing the Act to a conclusion."

The Teacher now chants the preliminaries and questions already asked the candidate, within the Sangha. They need not be repeated here. Immediately after the last answer made by Nāga, the Teacher chants the following motion followed by three announcements:[21]

"Let the Sangha listen to me, Venerable Sirs. This Nāga, wishes for the Acceptance from Venerable Padīpo. He is free of the obstructing circumstances. His bowl and robes are complete. Nāga begs for the Acceptance from the Sangha with Venerable Padīpo as Preceptor. ..... If there is the complete preparedness of the Sangha, let the Sangha accept Nāga with Venerable Padīpo as Preceptor. This is the motion."

"Let the Sangha listen to me, Venerable Sirs. This Nāga (repeat the above). The Sangha accepts Nāga with Venerable Padīpo as Preceptor. If Acceptance is agreeable to the Venerable Ones of Nāga, with Venerable Padīpo as Preceptor, let them be

21. This is the essential part of the Acceptance when the Sangha, by a motion and three announcements accepts the new bhikkhu. Any fault in these, or an objection from the assembled bhikkhus renders the Act null and void.

silent. He to whom it is not agreeable should speak."

"A second time I speak about this matter. Let the Sangha listen to me (as preceding paragraph)."

"A third time I speak about this matter. Let the Sangha listen to me (as above)."

"Nāga has been accepted by the Sangha with Venerable Padīpo as Preceptor. It is agreeable to the Sangha, therefore it is silent. So I record it."

Nāga is now a bhikkhu. The time of his Acceptance is recorded. The Preceptor now chants the passages on the Four Supports (almsfood, robes, lodging and medicines) and the Four Things never-to-be-done (sexual intercourse, taking what is not given, depriving of life, and laying claim to superior human states[22]). At the end, Nāga replies, "Yes, Venerable Sir" and prostrates three times, then receives from his supporters the gifts for his Preceptor and Teacher(s), which he presents to them respectfully. Afterwards, smaller gifts are given to the witnessing bhikkhus[23]. Bhikkhu Nāga then receives whatever suitable gifts his supporters wish to give him.

---

22. See the Four Defeats, Chapter III.
23. At least five bhikkhus are required for Acceptance of another. But usually more are invited. The Preceptor and Teacher must be senior bhikkhus competent in Dhamma and Vinaya, and they must know the Acceptance Procedure so that the Pali is without faults.

Glossary of Pali Words

Abhidhamma: the books of psychological and philosophical analysis and synthesis based on the Suttas (q.v.). See Ch. IV.

Arahant: one who has perfected himself by the practice of moral conduct, meditation, penetrative wisdom and so experienced Nibbāna (q.v.) Ch. II. Arahantship: the state of being an Arahant.

Ariya: one who is ennobled (including Arahants), having seen Nibbāna momentarily and by cutting off some fetters, become a Stream-winner, Once-returner and Non-returner. (For definitions, see *Buddhist Dictionary*, BPS).

Bhikkhu: a Buddhist monk ordained by at least five other monks in accordance with the Buddha's instructions and undertaking to practise the Dhamma and Vinaya (q.v.). Ch. VI.

Bhikkhunī: a Buddhist nun similarly ordained. Ch. VII.

Buddha: the title of Gotama Siddhattha after he discovered the way to attain Enlightenment (Bodhi). Any discoverer of the Path to Bodhi who then possesses the Three Wisdoms, etc.

Buddhahood: the state of being a Buddha. Ch. I.

Dhamma (in Sanskrit, *Dharma*): Truth, Law, Teaching, Path of Practice, the Buddha's Teachings.

Dukkha: all unsatisfactory experience, suffering, ill; may be mental or physical, gross or subtle.

Kamma (*karma*): intentional actions of mind, speech, body, all originating in the mind with decision or choice and having inherently a fruit or result for the doer in accordance with the action done.

Kuṭi: A bhikkhu's or nun's hut. Ch. V, VI.

Nibbāna (*Nirvāna*): the ultimate Buddhist goal—the cutting-off by wisdom—insight of greed, aversion and delusion, thus establishing the heart in a state of purity, compassion and wisdom, which goes beyond existence. Ch. I.

Pātimokkha: the code of 227 fundamental precepts for bhikkhus.

Ch. III.

Sālā: hall for listening to Dhamma, practising meditation etc., in a vihāra (q.v.). Ch. V, VI.

Samaṇa: one who makes himself peaceful, hence usually (but not always) a bhikkhu or nun. *Mahāsamaṇa*: an epithet of the Buddha—the Great one who is Peaceful.

Sāmaṇera: a "little *samaṇa,* a boy under 20, training to become a bhikkhu or one who becomes a *sāmaṇera* (novice) before Acceptance, irrespective of age. Ch. III.

Sangha: the Order of bhikkhus, or of bhikkhunīs; or the Community of all Buddhists, ordained or lay, who are ennobled with insight to Nibbāna—the Noble (*ariya,* q.v.) Sangha. Ch. II, III, IV, V.

Stupa (Sanskrit, Pali—*thūpa*): reliquary monuments also known as *cetiya* (*chedi, zedi*) or *cetiya, dagoba, pagoda,* etc. Ch. V.

Sutta: a discourse of the Buddha or an Arahant. Ch. IV.

Thera: a bhikkhu of more than ten rains (years) in the Sangha.

Theravāda: the Teachings of the senior disciples of the Buddha who were Arahants. The Buddhism practised in south and south-east Asia nearest to the form taught by the Buddha. Ch. IV.

Vihāra: monastery where bhikkhus live and temple with Buddha-images, stupas etc. for the devotions of both bhikkhus and lay people. Ch. V, VI.

Vinaya: the Disciplinary code of bhikkhus and bhikkhunīs (and laity in some contexts). Ch. III.

ABBREVIATIONS

Sutta references are to discourse number, except for Theragāthā, Dhammapada and Suttanipāta, for which reference is to the verse number.

Vin	Vinaya Piṭaka
DN	Dīgha Nikāya (Sutta number)
MN	Majjhima Nikāya (Sutta number)
SN	Saṃyutta Nikāya (Saṃyutta and sutta number)
AN	Aṅguttara Nikāya (Nipāta and sutta number)
Thī	Theragātha
Th	Therīgāthā
Dhp	Dhammapada
Sn	Suttanipāta
Ud	Udāna
J	Jātaka (Story)

Of Related Interest

THE LIFE OF THE BUDDHA
According to the Pali Canon
Bhikkhu Ñāṇamoli

Among the numerous lives of the Buddha, this volume may well claim a place of its own. Composed entirely from texts of the Pali Canon, the oldest authentic record, it portrays an image of the Buddha which is vivid, warm, and moving. Chapters on the Buddha's personality and doctrine are especially illuminating, and the translation is marked by lucidity and dignity throughout.

BP 101S, 379 pp.

THE DHAMMAPADA
The Buddha's Path of Wisdom
Translated by Acharya Buddharakkhita

The most beloved Buddhist classic of all time, the Dhammapada is an anthology of over 400 verses on the ethics, meditation, and wisdom of Buddhism. This translation by a long-term student of the work transmits the spirit and content as well as the style of the original. Includes the original Pali text. With introduction by Bhikkhu Bodhi.

BP 203S 158 pp.

BUDDHA, MY REFUGE
Contemplation of the Buddha based on the Pali Suttas
Bhikkhu Khantipalo

This book weaves together a rich variety of texts from the Pali Canon illustrating each of the Buddha's nine outstanding virtues. The result is a beautiful and inspiring anthology of suttas on the personality of the Blessed One.

BP 409, 134 pp.

Prices according to latest catalogue (http://www.bps.lk)

THE BUDDHIST PUBLICATION SOCIETY

The BPS is an approved charity dedicated to making known the Teaching of the Buddha, which has a vital message for all people.

Founded in 1958, the BPS has published a wide variety of books and booklets covering a great range of topics. Its publications include accurate annotated translations of the Buddha's discourses, standard reference works, as well as original contemporary expositions of Buddhist thought and practice. These works present Buddhism as it truly is—a dynamic force which has influenced receptive minds for the past 2500 years and is still as relevant today as it was when it first arose.

For more information about the BPS and our publications, please visit our website, or write an e-mail, or a letter to the:

Administrative Secretary
Buddhist Publication Society
P.O. Box 61
54 Sangharaja Mawatha
Kandy • Sri Lanka
E-mail: bps@bps.lk
Web site: http://www.bps.lk
Tel: 0094 81 223 7283 • Fax: 0094 81 222 3679